First World War
and Army of Occupation
War Diary
France, Belgium and Germany

14 DIVISION
Headquarters, Branches and Services
Royal Army Veterinary Corps
Assistant Director Veterinary Services
1 May 1915 - 28 February 1919

WO95/1885/2

The Naval & Military Press Ltd
www.nmarchive.com
Published in association with The National Archives

Published by

The Naval & Military Press Ltd

Unit 10 Ridgewood Industrial Park,

Uckfield, East Sussex,

TN22 5QE England

Tel: +44 (0) 1825 749494

www.naval-military-press.com

www.nmarchive.com

This diary has been reprinted in facsimile from the original. Any imperfections are inevitably reproduced and the quality may fall short of modern type and cartographic standards.

Contents

Document type	Place/Title	Date From	Date To
Heading	WO95/1885 1915 May-Feb 1919 Asst Dis Vetinay Services 4th Division		
Heading	14th Division Asst Dir. Vety Services May 1915-Feb 1919		
War Diary	Aldershot	01/05/1915	19/05/1915
War Diary	Boulogne	20/05/1915	20/05/1915
War Diary	Watten	21/05/1915	27/05/1915
War Diary	Steenvoorde	28/05/1915	30/05/1915
War Diary	Westoutre	01/06/1915	14/06/1915
War Diary	L. 13 C	14/06/1915	21/06/1915
War Diary	H 7. C 9.8	22/06/1915	31/10/1915
Heading	14th Division A.D.I.S Vol 2		
Heading	War Diary Of Major E. B. Bartlett. A.V.C. A.D.V.S. 14th (Light) Division. From November 1st 1915 To December 31st 1915		
War Diary		01/11/1915	31/12/1915
Miscellaneous	Nominal Roll Of Officers N.C.O And Men, Army Veterinary Corps. 14th (Light) Division.	20/12/1915	20/12/1915
Miscellaneous	Nominal Roll Of The 26th Mobile Veterinary Section, 14th (Lt) Division.	20/12/1915	20/12/1915
Miscellaneous	A.D.V.S 14th Div. Vol 3		
War Diary	H 7 C 7.7 Sheet 28	01/01/1916	01/01/1916
War Diary	A.D.V.S. 14th Div. Vol. 4 Feb. 1916		
War Diary		12/02/1916	29/02/1916
Miscellaneous	A.D.V.S. 14 Div Vol 5 Mar 1916		
War Diary		01/03/1916	31/05/1916
Miscellaneous	Warrant Officers,		
Miscellaneous	14th Div A.D.V.S. June 1916		
War Diary		02/06/1916	31/07/1916
Heading	War Diary Of A.D.V.S., 14th (Light) Division. August, 1916. Volume		
War Diary		01/08/1916	30/09/1916
Heading	War Diary Of A.D.V.S., 14th (Light) Divn. October 1st-October 31st '16		
War Diary		01/10/1916	31/10/1916
Heading	War Diary Of Major Dayliers A.V.C. A.D.V.S. 14th Division From 1st Nov 1916 To 30 Nov 1916 Volume X		
War Diary		01/11/1916	30/11/1916
War Diary		11/11/1916	24/11/1916
Heading	War Diary Of A.D.V.S. 14th Light Division From 1st December 1916 To 31st December 1916 (Volume No.-)		
War Diary	Lecauroy	01/12/1916	31/12/1916
Heading	War Diary Of A.D.V.S. 14th Division From 1st Jan 1917 To 31st Jan 1917 Volume No		
War Diary		01/01/1917	31/01/1917
Heading	War Diary Of A.D.V.S. 14th Division. From February 1st To February 28th 1917 Volume		
War Diary		11/02/1917	28/02/1917

Heading	War Diary Of A.D.V.S. 14th Div. Volume 46 (Mar. 1st To Mar 31st 1917)		
War Diary		01/03/1917	31/03/1917
Heading	War Diary Of A.D.V.S. 14th Division From April 1st To April 30th 1917 (Volume No. 47)		
War Diary		01/04/1917	30/04/1917
Heading	War Diary Of A.D.V.S. 14th Div. From 1st May To 31st May 1917 (Volume No. 48)		
War Diary		01/05/1917	31/05/1917
Heading	War Diary Of D.A.D.V.S. 14th Div. From June 1st To June 25th 1917 (Volume 49)		
War Diary		01/06/1917	25/06/1917
Heading	War Diary Of D.A.D.V.S. 14th Div. From July 1st To July 31st 1917 (Volume 50)		
War Diary		08/07/1917	31/07/1917
Heading	War Diary Of D.A.D.V.S. 14th Div. From Aug 1st To Aug 31st 1917 (Volume No 51)		
War Diary		01/08/1917	31/08/1917
Heading	War Diary Of D.A.D.V.S. 14th Division From September 1st To 30th September 1917 (Volume No 52)		
War Diary		01/09/1917	30/09/1917
Heading	War Diary Of D.A.D.V.S. 14th Div. From Oct 1st To Oct 31st 1917 (Volume No 53)		
Miscellaneous	Appendix I Copy Of Letter Sent To Q 14th Div On The Subject Of Clipping Of Artillery Corps		
Miscellaneous	Appendix II	26/09/1917	26/09/1917
War Diary		01/10/1917	19/10/1917
Heading	War Diary Of D.A.D.V.S. 14th Division. From November 3rd To November 30th 1917 (Volume No 54)		
War Diary	Berthen	03/11/1917	11/11/1917
War Diary	Wizernes	12/11/1917	30/11/1917
Heading	War Diary of D.A.D.V.S. 14th Div Dec 1st to Dec 31st 1917 (Volume No 55)		
War Diary	Mersey Camp 28. H.1.A.4.5	01/12/1917	06/12/1917
War Diary	Mersey Camp	06/12/1917	26/12/1917
War Diary	Wizernes	27/12/1917	31/12/1917
Heading	War Diary Of D.A.D.V.S. 14th Div. January 1st To January 31st 1918 (Volume No. 56)		
War Diary	Wizernes	01/01/1918	02/01/1918
War Diary	Mericourt Sur Somme.	03/01/1918	23/01/1918
War Diary	Guiscard	24/01/1918	27/01/1918
War Diary	Jussy	28/01/1918	31/01/1918
Miscellaneous	Contagions Animal Disease In Clastres Area	31/01/1918	31/01/1918
Heading	War Diary of D.A.D.V.S. 14th Div February 21st To 28th (Volume No. 57)		
War Diary	Jussy	01/02/1918	17/03/1918
War Diary	Petit Detroit	18/03/1918	21/03/1918
War Diary	Bussy	21/03/1918	23/03/1918
War Diary	C U Y	24/03/1918	24/03/1918
War Diary	Bourmont	25/04/1918	26/04/1918
War Diary	Estrees St Denis	27/04/1918	28/04/1918
War Diary	Rantigny	29/04/1918	29/04/1918
War Diary	Avrechy	30/04/1918	30/04/1918
War Diary	Boursines	31/04/1918	31/04/1918

Heading	War Diary of D.A.D.V.S. 14th Div. from April 4th to April 30th (Volume No.-)		
War Diary	Aubigny	04/04/1918	04/04/1918
War Diary	Amiens	04/04/1918	08/04/1918
War Diary	Fresnoy Au Val	09/04/1918	09/04/1918
War Diary	Frucourt	10/04/1918	10/04/1918
War Diary	Feuquieres	11/04/1918	11/04/1918
War Diary	Maresquel	12/04/1918	12/04/1918
War Diary	Heuqueliers	13/04/1918	15/04/1918
War Diary	Ecquedecques	16/04/1918	16/04/1918
War Diary	Ecquirre	17/04/1918	19/04/1918
War Diary	Ecquedecques	20/04/1918	21/04/1918
War Diary	Coyecque	22/04/1918	29/04/1918
War Diary	Torcy	30/04/1918	30/04/1918
Heading	War Diary of D.A.D.V.S. 14th Div. from 1st to 31st May 1918 Vol 31		
War Diary	Torcy	01/05/1918	17/05/1918
War Diary	St. Quentin	18/05/1918	13/06/1918
War Diary	Wierre Effroy	04/07/1918	11/07/1918
War Diary	Eperlecques	12/07/1918	19/08/1918
War Diary	Chateau Couthors	20/08/1918	31/08/1918
Heading	War Diary of D.A.D.V.S. 14th Div. September 1st to 30th 1918		
War Diary	Chateau Couthors	01/09/1918	19/09/1918
War Diary	Abeele	20/09/1918	28/09/1918
War Diary	28 G 19 d	29/09/1918	30/09/1918
Heading	War Diary of D.A.D.V.S. 14th Division 1st to 31st October 1918		
War Diary	Waratah Camp	01/10/1918	01/10/1918
War Diary	Caestre	07/10/1918	16/10/1918
War Diary	Neuve Eglise	17/10/1918	17/10/1918
War Diary	Kandahar Camp	18/10/1918	18/10/1918
War Diary	Blanc Four	19/10/1918	20/10/1918
War Diary	Mouscron	21/10/1918	31/10/1918
Heading	War Diary of D.A.D.V.S. 14th Div. for November 1918		
War Diary	Mouscron	01/11/1918	03/11/1918
War Diary	Turcoing	04/11/1918	30/11/1918
Heading	War Diary of D.A.D.V.S. 14th Div. (1st to 31st December 1918)		
War Diary	Rue Chanzy Turcoing	01/12/1918	21/12/1918
War Diary	Rue Chanzy Turcoing Hdq 14 Div	22/12/1918	31/12/1918
Heading	War Diary of D.A.D.V.S. 14 Div. (January 1st to 31st 1919).		
War Diary	Turcoing 14 Div H.Q. Rue Chanzy	01/01/1919	31/01/1919
Heading	War Diary of D.A.D.V.S. 14 Div. (1st to 28th February 1918).		
War Diary	Hdq. 14th Division Turcoing	01/02/1919	28/02/1919

WO95/1885 4th Division

1915 May - Feb 1919

Asst Dir Vetinary Services

14TH DIVISION

ASST DIR. VETY SERVICES

MAY 1915 - FEB 1919

4

WAR DIARY
or
INTELLIGENCE SUMMARY
(Erase heading not required.)

Army Form C. 2118

13

Instructions regarding War Diaries and Intelligence Summaries are contained in F. S. Regs., Part II. and the Staff Manual respectively. Title Pages will be prepared in manuscript.

Place	Date 1915	Hour	Summary of Events and Information	Remarks and references to Appendices
Aldershot	May 18th	1 am	The 14th (Light) Division, which had completed its training at Aldershot having been formed in October 1914, received orders to embark at once. The Division consists of:- Head Quarters (Divisional) 41st Infantry Brigade 7th K.R.R. 7th R.B. 8th K.R.R. 8th R.B. 43rd Infantry Brigade 6th Somerset L.I. 6th D.C.L.I. 6th K.O.Y.L.I. 10th Durham L.I. 42nd Infantry Brigade 5th Shropshire L.I. 5th Oxford & Bucks L.I. 9th K.R.R. 9th R.B. Artillery 46th Bde R.F.A. 47th Bde R.F.A. 48th Bde R.F.A. 49th Bde R.F.A. 14th Heavy Battery 14th Divl Ammunition Column.	WB

5

WAR DIARY
or
INTELLIGENCE SUMMARY
(Erase heading not required.)

Instructions regarding War Diaries and Intelligence Summaries are contained in F. S. Regs., Part II. and the Staff Manual respectively. Title Pages will be prepared in manuscript.

Army Form C. 2118

14

Place	Date	Hour	Summary of Events and Information	Remarks and references to Appendices
			Divisional Engineers — A.S.C	
			No 61 Field Coy — 14 Divl Train	
			" 62 " " — R.A.M.C	
			" 89 " " — No 42 Field Ambulance	
			No 1 Signal Coy — " 43 "	
			" 44 "	
			Cavalry — Pioneers	
			1 Squadron Duke Lancaster Own Yeomanry — 11th Kings L'pool Regiment	
			26th Mobile Vet Section — 25 Sanitary Section	
			The Divisional Staff consists of	
			G.O.C. - Maj Gen Couper — D.A.Q.M.G. Capt Vyvyan	WB
			G.S.O.(1) - Lt Col Isaack — A.D.M.S. Lt Col Pettie	
			G.S.O.(2) - Major Davey — D.A.D.M.S. Major Hartigan	
			G.S.O.(3) - Major Armitage — A.D.V.S. Major Bartlett	
			A.A.&Q.M.G. Lt Col Turner — D.A.D.O.S. Major Freeman	
			D.A.A.&Q.M.G. Capt Campn — A.P.M. Major Curt	

1875 Wt. W593/826 1,000,000 4/15 J.B.C. & A. A.D.S.S./Forms/C. 2118.

Instructions regarding War Diaries and Intelligence Summaries are contained in F. S. Regs., Part II. and the Staff Manual respectively. Title Pages will be prepared in manuscript.

6

WAR DIARY
or
INTELLIGENCE SUMMARY
(Erase heading not required.)

Army Form C. 2118

15

Place	Date	Hour	Summary of Events and Information	Remarks and references to Appendices
Aldershot	May 15		Veterinary Arrangements of Personnel:- Major E. B. Bartlett A.D.V.S. Lieut G. S. Tharnewill a/a to 41st Infantry Bde & in charge of the 41st Inf Bde, 46th Bde R.F.A., 61st Fd Coy R.E. 44th Fd Ambulance and No 1 Coy Divl Train comprising 41st Bde Area. Lieut J. H. Jamie, a/a 42nd Inf Bde & in charge of 42nd Inf Bde, 47th Bde R.F.A., 62nd Fd Coy R.E. - 42nd Fd Ambulance, No 2 Coy Divl Train Lieut A. V. Meeke a/a 43rd Inf Bde & in charge of 43rd Inf Bde, 48 Bde R.F.A. 89 Field Coy R.E. 43rd Fd Ambulance, No 3 Coy Divl Train. Lieut J O'Carroll, a/a 49th Bde R.F.A & in charge also of 14th Hy Battery Lieut L L Steele, a/a Divl Train & in charge also of Divl Ammunition Column & Divl Cavalry when they join the Division. Lieut L. J. Weir i/c Mobile Vet Section. Strength of Division in animals is 5530	EBB

1875 Wt. W593/826 1,000,000 4/15 J.B.C. & A. A.D.S.S./Forms/C. 2118.

Instructions regarding War Diaries and Intelligence Summaries are contained in F. S. Regs., Part II. and the Staff Manual respectively. Title Pages will be prepared in manuscript.

WAR DIARY
or
INTELLIGENCE SUMMARY
(Erase heading not required.)

Army Form C. 2118

7

16

Place	Date	Hour	Summary of Events and Information	Remarks and references to Appendices
	May 19	4.30pm	Moved off with Divl Hd Qrs from the G. Siding. A very fine clear day.	
		7.0pm	Arrived at Folkestone and embarked on the Mail boat.	
		9.0pm	Moved off from Folkestone	
		10.30pm	Arrived at Boulogne after a very smooth and uneventful passage.	
Boulogne	" 20	10.30am	Left Boulogne by car for Watten to await the arrival of the Division which is taking four days to embark and crossing by the two routes -- Troops - Folkestone to Boulogne. Animals Transport - Southampton to Havre.	
		12.30pm	Arrive St OMER - Head Quarters of 2 Branch of the Army. Met Capt Bright A.V.C. attached to the Head Quarters	
		2pm	Left for WATTEN by car.	
		4pm	Arrive WATTEN and take up billets.	
WATTEN	- 21		Units arrive during the day in fine weather.	
		10pm	News arrives that the last part of our Division due to leave today, will not leave at present. Reason not given.	
- do -	- 22		A hot day. Troops arrive all day. 46th Bde R.F.A arrive at WATTEN having left Aldershot on the first day of embarking - 19th. Considering the distance we are away from the front	SWB

1875 Wt. W593/826 1,000,000 4/15 J.B.C. & A. A.D.S.S./Forms/C. 2118.

8

WAR DIARY
or
INTELLIGENCE SUMMARY
(Erase heading not required.)

Army Form C. 2118

17

Instructions regarding War Diaries and Intelligence Summaries are contained in F. S. Regs., Part II. and the Staff Manual respectively. Title Pages will be prepared in manuscript.

Place	Date	Hour	Summary of Events and Information	Remarks and references to Appendices
	1915 May.		the ground room allotted for troops seems very small, and I pointed out the fact that the animals were too cramped after their travelling. A little more room was given by removing one Battery out of four.	
WATTEN	23rd		Whit Sunday. Troops continue to arrive all day.	
"	24th		Troops arrive during the day.	
	25th	5pm	All units of Division have arrived including a Motor Machine Gun Section which was last to arrive.	
			D.D.V.S. of II Army arrived and left copies of Routine Orders and instructions.	
			The horses of the Division now they are assembled are a very fine lot of animals. I doubt if there is a Division so well horsed in its classes. Mules are also of very high class. Argentine mules about 15·3.	
			The shoeing question during our preparation at Aldershot has been one of considerable importance, on account of lack of Farriers and shoeing smiths in England. Up to time of leaving England the Artillery Brigades were ten Farriers under strength. viz:	

Instructions regarding War Diaries and Intelligence Summaries are contained in F. S. Regs., Part II. and the Staff Manual respectively. Title Pages will be prepared in manuscript.

WAR DIARY
or
INTELLIGENCE SUMMARY
(Erase heading not required.)

Army Form C. 2118

9

18

Place	Date	Hour	Summary of Events and Information	Remarks and references to Appendices
			The 47th Bde being two short -	
			- 49th " " three "	
			- Ammun: Column " three "	
			14 Heavy Battery " one "	
			62nd Field Co of RE " one "	
			Infantry Battalions and Artillery were all short of shoeing smiths and these were not forthcoming so classes were formed to instruct likely men in cold shoeing. Five classes were formed, ranging from 4 men to 12 men in each, with chosen farriers as instructors, and as the men became efficient - - able to remove shoes prepare feet and fit and nail on shoes - - they were passed out by Veterinary Officers. By this method during the later half of March up to the time of embarking, the strength of the Division in Cold Shoers was brought up to its full strength, and with a reserve of about 50%.	
WATTEN	May 26th	10 am	41st Inf. Bde. 46th Bde R.F.A 61st Co of R.E No 2 Section Signal Co of RE and 44th Fd Ambulance move off to area immediately west & S.W. of YPRES. Remainder of Division remain in WATTEN area.	[initials]

1875 Wt. W593/826 1,000,000 4/15 J.B.C. & A. A.D.S.S./Forms/C. 2118.

Instructions regarding War Diaries and Intelligence Summaries are contained in F. S. Regs., Part II. and the Staff Manual respectively. Title Pages will be prepared in manuscript.

10

WAR DIARY
or
INTELLIGENCE SUMMARY
(Erase heading not required.)

Army Form C. 2118

19

Place	Date	Hour	Summary of Events and Information	Remarks and references to Appendices
WATTEN	May 27	6am	Head Quarters move from WATTEN to STEENVOORDE via CASSELL.	
		2 P.m.	Arrive STEENVOORDE and find DDVS had called to see me before my arrival	
			The first party of horses were sent back to Railhead from WATTEN to ST OMER today by 26th Mobile Veterinary Section	
			Weather turned suddenly cold	
			The Division is billetted in area triangle STEENVOORDE – HAZEBOUCK – BAILLEUL, with M.V.S at LA BREARDE. Railhead EBBLINGHAM.	
STEENVOORDE	– 28		Remain at STEENVOORDE area. Other Divisional troops pass through during the day on the way to the front	
			Weather very dry. Roads all paved with cobbles in the centre, with about 4 feet on each side of very rough dusty going	
– do –	– 29		Remain.	
– do –	30th	5. am.	Left for WESTOUTRE to join up with the 2nd Corps of the 2nd Army	
		8. am	Arrive WESTOUTRE. Mobile Veterinary Section occupies farm at point about one kilometre east of WESTOUTRE on HECKSCHEN – OUDERDOM road	GBB
			The Division is replacing the 3rd Division in this area and (for)	

1875 Wt. W593/826 1,000,000 4/15 J.B.C. & A. A.D.S.S./Forms/C. 2118.

Instructions regarding War Diaries and Intelligence Summaries are contained in F. S. Regs., Part II. and the Staff Manual respectively. Title Pages will be prepared in manuscript.

11

WAR DIARY
or
INTELLIGENCE SUMMARY
(Erase heading not required.)

Army Form C. 2118

20

Place	Date	Hour	Summary of Events and Information	Remarks and references to Appendices
			for the next few days will be under instruction for trench work etc along the front.	
			The only returns called for up to the present by DDVS are A.F. A 2000 weekly and a return of horses left at farms etc on the march up. This is very satisfactory. I find great difficulty in getting a return out of anybody. Horses have been left about the country now on the march up, without any word having been given to me.	
WESTOUTRE	June 1		Received letter from D.D.V.S. asking opinion about the shoeing arrangements for Infantry Battalions.	
			Replied that I failed to find any arrangements made in this Division when I came to it, and suggested what has already been suggested no doubt – the training of shoeing smiths at the Base as in England under A.V.C management.	
			Spent most part of the day riding around this area trying to find Divisional units. They are so tucked away to avoid being seen that it is difficult to find them. Any information on the position is unobtainable locally, and almost unobtainable from the Staffs at present. The weather remains very dry, and I notice a tendency for wounds not to heal	EMB

12

WAR DIARY
or
INTELLIGENCE SUMMARY
(Erase heading not required.)

Army Form C. 2118

21

Instructions regarding War Diaries and Intelligence Summaries are contained in F. S. Regs., Part II. and the Staff Manual respectively. Title Pages will be prepared in manuscript.

Place	Date	Hour	Summary of Events and Information	Remarks and references to Appendices
			heal. This may be due in part also to the fact that the water for dressing purposes + all purposes is out of these stagnant pools.	
			I cannot see how this force can be kept here unless we get rain regularly to fill up the water holes.	
WESTOUTRE	June 2		Met Major Edwards and Conder but had not time to discuss the situation with them.	
			The guns and Battalions are now getting into positions and all the animals are picketted in rear about 4 miles from the trenches. Owing to our units being intermixed with other Divisions (3rd and 25th) it will take V.Os a few days to find whereabouts of everybody, so I am leaving them alone.	
			I find there is a great tendency to avoid giving V.Os servants that are shared with one or two other officers.	
			I have suggested drawing two horses for the Bde Area V.Os one for the Inf Bde, and one for the Artillery Bde, + keeping them both with a batman from one or the other unit.	WB
-do-	June 3		Still dry and hot. Bombardment going on all day and (night)	

Instructions regarding War Diaries and Intelligence Summaries are contained in F. S. Regs., Part II. and the Staff Manual respectively. Title Pages will be prepared in manuscript.

13

WAR DIARY
or
INTELLIGENCE SUMMARY
(Erase heading not required.)

Army Form C. 2118

22

Place	Date	Hour	Summary of Events and Information	Remarks and references to Appendices
WESTOUTRE	June 3rd		but no result perceptible.	
			41st Infantry Bde detached for instruction with the 5th Division	
			61st, 62nd and 89th Fd Coy R.E. detached at VLAMERTINGHE outside our area.	
- do -	June 4th		One Battery of the 49th Bde of Howitzers detached from Division (A Battery). No 110 Battery R.G.A. & 116 Battery R.G.A. attached to this area.	
			Railhead for 14 Division is at CAESTRE.	
- do -	June 9th		Very hot thunder weather with very little rain.	
			The Divl Squadron Cavalry (Duke Lancaster Own Yeomanry) moved from BOESCHEPE to farm 3/4 mile due East of WESTOUTRE.	
			Owing to shortage of bran supply, had Divisional Order published that all units get green grass in lieu of 2lbs of corn. The grass to be obtained by units locally and payment to be made by Supply Officer of district.	
			Started system of draining & filtering water through ashes and tins wherever there is any running water near horse lines.	SBB
- do -	June 10th		I find great tendency towards planting Remount work (Capt. ...)	

1875 Wt. W593/826 1,000,000 4/15 J.B.C. & A. A.D.S.S./Forms/C. 2118.

Instructions regarding War Diaries and Intelligence Summaries are contained in F. S. Regs., Part II. and the Staff Manual respectively. Title Pages will be prepared in manuscript.

14 WAR DIARY
or
INTELLIGENCE SUMMARY
(Erase heading not required.)

Army Form C. 2118

23

Place	Date	Hour	Summary of Events and Information	Remarks and references to Appendices
WESTOUTRE	Jun 13th		upon A.D.V.S. of Division. This is natural of course because A.D.V.S of a Division is the only one of the Staff, in most cases probably, who has any dealing with the Officers i/c of horses, & they naturally turn to him. Our horses are just recovering from injuries of the neck, done on the journey over from England. In many cases these wounds are caused by the nosebag full of corn being slung around the horses necks, & left there for hours in the trucks and ships. Inspected the Divl Cavalry horses today, and find them a poor lot indeed. I cast six of them aged about 20, poor & small & worn out. Lt Col McDougal came to see me, he was acting for Lt Col Wilson DDVS 2nd Army.	
- do -	June 13		Lt Col Wilson D.D.V.S visited us on return from leave to England.	
- do -	June 14		Head Quarters, 41st, 42nd Infantry Bdes, Signal Coy, Hd Quarters Divl Train and Divl Cavalry received orders at midnight to move at 8 am. Mobile Vety Section to move at noon. Marched via BOESCHEPE and ABEELE to position on Map 27 "Belgium (and	WBB

1875 Wt. W593/826 1,000,000 4/15 J.B.C. & A. A.D.S.S./Forms/C. 2118.

Instructions regarding War Diaries and Intelligence Summaries are contained in F. S. Regs., Part II. and the Staff Manual respectively. Title Pages will be prepared in manuscript.

WAR 15 DIARY
or
INTELLIGENCE SUMMARY
(Erase heading not required.)

Army Form C. 2118

24

Place	Date	Hour	Summary of Events and Information	Remarks and references to Appendices
WESTOUTRE	June 14th		Part of France" L13.c. where we took up position in the open about 3 kilometres west of POPERINGHE.	
			All Artillery + 43rd Bde. Inf. left in LA CLYTTE area	
L13C	June 14th		Mobile Vet. Section placed in farm K24 B 64. just off the main road ABEELE - WATOU.	
	16th		Two of our Brigades were in action for the first time during the night. There were 2000 casualties during the night. Visited 41st + 42nd Brigades just outside VLAMERTINGHE, and the guns back at LA CLYTTE area.	
	17		Batch of 60 Remounts arrived from HAVRE. Good horses but 50% of them sick.	
	19th		Medicines indented for last week brought up from Base today. Divisional Order inserted that Remounts should be isolated as much as possible for three weeks after arrival.	
	21st		Saw the best pattern of dipping hole for drawing water out of standing pools at which all our horses have to be watered. A square hole about 3ft square + 3ft deep is dug about 5 yards from the pond, + is connected to the pond by a connecting (trench)	WB

1875 Wt. W593/826 1,000,000 4/15 J.B.C. & A. A.D.S.S./Forms/C. 2118.

Instructions regarding War Diaries and Intelligence Summaries are contained in F. S. Regs., Part II. and the Staff Manual respectively. Title Pages will be prepared in manuscript.

WAR 16 DIARY
or
INTELLIGENCE SUMMARY
(Erase heading not required.)

Army Form C. 2118

25

Place	Date	Hour	Summary of Events and Information	Remarks and references to Appendices
L.13c	June 21st		trench about 1 foot wide into which are sunk two boxes with their ends knocked out, & covered in with filtering cloth. Between the two boxes can be placed, cinders or sand or stones. The receiving hole which must be boarded around the sides has a hole left to receive the water from the connecting trench the hole also being covered with sacking or other filtering substance. This makes a clean place to dip the water from without fouling the pond & does ~~not~~ a certain amount of filtering.	
			The four Artillery Bdes 46th, 47th, 48th & 49th with Divisional Ammunition Column move from LA CLYTTE area into billets Map 27 K 9, 10, 11, 12 - 13, 16, 17, 18, 21, 22, 23 & 24 into good farms. This area is the best we have been in, it has not been used by any troops for some considerable time, it is clean and the water supply is good.	
H7C 9.8	June 22		Head Quarters of Division move forward to Map 28 H7C 9.8 in open area close to VLAMERTINGHE without billetting. Some tents supplied. Area under shell fire daily.	
			41st & 42nd Infantry Bdes moved to same area. 43rd Bde remains with the Artillery, Divl Amm Column, Divl Train etc.	WB

1875 Wt. W593/826 1,000,000 4/15 J.B.C. & A. A.D.S.S./Forms/C. 2118.

Instructions regarding War Diaries and Intelligence Summaries are contained in F. S. Regs., Part II. and the Staff Manual respectively. Title Pages will be prepared in manuscript.

17

WAR DIARY
or
INTELLIGENCE SUMMARY
(Erase heading not required.)

Army Form C. 2118

26

Place	Date	Hour	Summary of Events and Information	Remarks and references to Appendices
H7C 9.8	June 24th		49th Bde RFA moves up to Map 28 H5b into cramped camping ground close to main road. Drinking water in this area is much limited, owing to number of troops in the area.	
			Neighbouring Divisions, 3rd & 5th, are close up on us and in many cases share ponds with our Units for watering animals.	
	25th		46th Bde RFA move up to Map 28 H 20/21 also into very cramped areas. Very heavy rain fell today & saved the water supply in the water pools. Shelling around the area continues daily & necessitates moves of units. 41st Inf Bde Transport shift camp from H14a to H4a today.	
			It is noticed that units do not comply with order to isolate Remounts. Reminder issued.	
			After the rain special attention to be paid to choice of pools, to see that those connected with drainage of farm yards etc. are not used.	
			Weekly conference of V.Os. at Head Quarters. Lt Lewis unable to attend. Sick.	SBB

1875 Wt. W593/826 1,000,000 4/15 J.B.C. & A. A.D.S.S./Forms/C. 2118.

Instructions regarding War Diaries and Intelligence Summaries are contained in F. S. Regs., Part II. and the Staff Manual respectively. Title Pages will be prepared in manuscript.

18

WAR DIARY
or
INTELLIGENCE SUMMARY
(Erase heading not required.)

Army Form C. 2118

27

Place	Date	Hour	Summary of Events and Information	Remarks and references to Appendices
	June 26		More rain fell today, but not heavy	
	28th		48th Bde R.F.A moved up to area Map 28 G17 c+d. The guns of these Brigades, 46th, 48th, 49th are all in action in this small area. Owing to the daily changes of positions of units of the Division it is very difficult to locate units. The whereabouts of units cannot be got definitely from Q Branch.	
	29th		There is a great tendency for the Transport Officers to allow feeding of animals off the ground. Strong orders issued to ensure the use of nosebags. The rations issued in forage are – Riders: Corn 10 lbs Hay 10 lbs – Light Draught Corn 12 lbs Hay 10 lbs. including mules. Heavy Draught Corn 19 lbs Hay 10 lbs. The hay ration is to be made up to 12 + 15 respectively by local purchase of green grass.	
	30th		Railhead moved from ~~[illegible]~~ CAESTRE to GODEWAERSVELDE.	
	July 1st		A system of keeping one Inf Bde and one Bde R.F.A in the trenches and two of each in reserve is in vogue. The rest reserve being.	

(in)

1875 Wt. W593/826 1,000,000 4/15 J.B.C. & A. A.D.S.S./Forms/C. 2118.

Army Form C. 2118

28

19

Instructions regarding War Diaries and Intelligence Summaries are contained in F. S. Regs., Part II. and the Staff Manual respectively. Title Pages will be prepared in manuscript.

WAR DIARY
or
INTELLIGENCE SUMMARY
(Erase heading not required.)

Place	Date	Hour	Summary of Events and Information	Remarks and references to Appendices
			in the neighbourhood of Head Quarters, and the second Reserve about six miles in rear, behind POPERINGHE.	
			Recommended the use of Reims instead of head ropes as much as possible during the dry weather.	
	July 3rd		The crops are beginning to ripen and the hay is being cut. The supply of green grass or green oats is therefore shortening and getting scarce in some districts. The oat supply & Hay (10 lbs) continues very good and the health and condition of animals is very good.	
	5th		Now that the Division has taken over its area & units only move about in the area inspections can be arranged daily & V.Os find very little difficulty in locating their units.	
	9th		Want of rain is again making itself felt - ponds are getting very low.	
			W.O. letter received re Reduction of V.Os to six per Division including Mobile Veterinary Section; excluding A.D.V.S. V.O's to be given two horses & a batman. A.D.V.S a car.	[illegible]

1875 Wt. W593/826 1,000,000 4/15 J.B.C. & A. A.D.S.S./Forms/C. 2118.

Instructions regarding War Diaries and Intelligence Summaries are contained in F. S. Regs., Part II. and the Staff Manual respectively. Title Pages will be prepared in manuscript.

WAR DIARY 20
or
INTELLIGENCE SUMMARY
(Erase heading not required.)

Army Form C. 2118

29

Place	Date	Hour	Summary of Events and Information	Remarks and references to Appendices
	July 10th		There has been no difficulty in this Division which has been mobilized on this basis of officers & horses, up to the present, because so many officers of all units have no use for their horses and V.Os have had plenty of horses to ride for the asking.	
	- 11th		Recommended three men for the rank of Sergeant, to replace three Lance Corporals at present with Infantry Bdes. Three Horsefall Destructors received in the Division for use in Transport Camps in this Area to dispose of horse manure. On my inspection of units, both Artillery & Infantry, I am always being asked if forges cannot be produced. I am strongly recommending that 3 forges be sanctioned for use of Divl Ammun: Column where the question of Transport can be easily dealt with. I am of opinion that it would be economical.	
	- 14th		D.D.V.S. 2nd Army inspected 26th Mobile Vety Section with me in attendance	
	- 15th		On inspecting 43rd Inf Bde this morning - the shoeing was not good. The excuse given was that casualties in Shoeing Smiths are not being filled up by O.C. units.	SBB

Instructions regarding War Diaries and Intelligence Summaries are contained in F. S. Regs., Part II. and the Staff Manual respectively. Title Pages will be prepared in manuscript.

21

WAR DIARY
or
INTELLIGENCE SUMMARY
(Erase heading not required.)

Army Form C. 2118

30

Place	Date	Hour	Summary of Events and Information	Remarks and references to Appendices
	July 15		Divisional Order inserted that Infantry Bdes render a return on 20th of each month showing Shoers employed and under instruction.	
			I have strongly recommended the issue of 3 forges to Divl Amm. Column. In case of a movement these could & would be carried by the unit.	
			Heavy rain fall today - this should ensure water for the rest of the summer.	
	16th		On inspecting one of the Battalion Transport Camps today I discovered a method of feeding horses that will appeal to horsemasters. The Transport Officer had been taught to give hay always after feeding Oats. So his Heavy Draught received at 7 am. 9 lbs Oats - at noon half the days ration of hay (probably 6 lbs) - at 5.30 pm 10 lbs Oats & at 7 pm the remainder of the days ration of hay.	
				RB

1875 Wt. W593/826 1,000,000 4/15 J.B.C. & A. A.D.S.S./Forms/C. 2118.

22

WAR DIARY
or
INTELLIGENCE SUMMARY
(Erase heading not required.)

Army Form C. 2118

31

Instructions regarding War Diaries and Intelligence Summaries are contained in F. S. Regs., Part II. and the Staff Manual respectively. Title Pages will be prepared in manuscript.

Place	Date	Hour	Summary of Events and Information	Remarks and references to Appendices
	July 16th	3.30pm	The usual weekly meeting of V.O's of the Division at which I tried to impress upon them the importance of trying to advise officers on matters of general routine and horse-mastership and avoid confining their attention to the few animals shown up as sick by units. I fear some of the V.O's knowledge of horsemastership is not much & their advice to some of the Gunners' Majors would not count for much, but they could help many of the other units.	
	17th		Inspected 41st Inf Bde Transport Lines west of POPERINGHE. 9th K.R.R. Transport Officer has very little experience of animals and his Sergeants none, so they are not well done. No other officer can be spared for the work. This battalion brought a private forge from England, & have it in use but their shoeing is the worst in the Division. Other units of the Brigade were good in condition of animals. They all complain of difficulty of shoeing the H.D. horses with cold shoes because they break the shoes in altering.	EB

1875 Wt. W593/826 1,000,000 4/15 J.B.C. & A. A.D.S.S./Forms/C. 2118.

23

Army Form C. 2118

32

Instructions regarding War Diaries and Intelligence Summaries are contained in F. S. Regs., Part II. and the Staff Manual respectively. Title Pages will be prepared in manuscript.

WAR DIARY
or
INTELLIGENCE SUMMARY
(Erase heading not required.)

Place	Date	Hour	Summary of Events and Information	Remarks and references to Appendices
	July 19th		Arrangements have already been made with O.C. Divisional Train who frequently accompanies me on my rounds to his own unit and to Infantry Bdes Transport, to do shoeing of their H.D. horses in the Train Companies of the Brigade to which the Infantry belong. Any other horses or mules that may be difficult to shoe may also be sent	
				WB

1875 Wt. W593/826 1,000,000 4/15 J.B.C. & A. A.D.S.S./Forms/C. 2118.

Instructions regarding War Diaries and Intelligence Summaries are contained in F. S. Regs., Part II. and the Staff Manual respectively. Title Pages will be prepared in manuscript.

24

WAR DIARY
or
INTELLIGENCE SUMMARY
(Erase heading not required.)

Army Form C. 2118

33

Place	Date	Hour	Summary of Events and Information	Remarks and references to Appendices
	July 18.		Inspected 42nd Inf: Bde Transport Camp and find them all well looked after. Every unit under charge of Lt Laurie is always well looked after from the Veterinary point of view. Rode over to 46th Div: Hd Quarters to see Col McDougal ADVS. The climate is quite cool & there is too much rain for a good corn harvest - not enough sun.	
	" 19th		Inspected 46th Bde R.F.A. animals. Condition & general management good. Visited Mobile Vety Section	
	" 20		Inspected 47th Bde R.F.A. animals. Condition good except C Battery which I reported to O.C. of the Brigade.	
	" 21		Inspected 48th Brigade R.F.A. Condition of animals good.	

25

WAR DIARY
or
INTELLIGENCE SUMMARY
(Erase heading not required.)

Army Form C. 2118

34

Instructions regarding War Diaries and Intelligence Summaries are contained in F. S. Regs., Part II. and the Staff Manual respectively. Title Pages will be prepared in manuscript.

Place	Date	Hour	Summary of Events and Information	Remarks and references to Appendices
	22nd		Inspected 49th Bde R.F.A animals. Condition and general management good. C Battery which is detached was not seen.	
	23rd		Inspected 44th Fd Ambulance. Animals well done.	
			Visited Mob: Vety Section	
		3.30 pm	Usual meeting of V.O's.	
	24th		Inspected 42nd Fd Ambulance. Condition good. Shoeing very good. All three of the Fd Ambulances have good shoeing smiths, & they also have forges, allowed by War Establishment.	
	25th		Inspected 43rd Fd Ambulance. Condition bad & the whole routine bad. Strongly recommended a Transport Officer (there is none at present) & a new Sergeant.	
				SBB

1875 Wt. W593/826 1,000,000 4/15 J.B.C. & A. A.D.S.S./Forms/C. 2118.

26

Army Form C. 2118

35

Instructions regarding War Diaries and Intelligence Summaries are contained in F. S. Regs., Part II. and the Staff Manual respectively. Title Pages will be prepared in manuscript.

WAR DIARY
or
INTELLIGENCE SUMMARY
(Erase heading not required.)

Place	Date	Hour	Summary of Events and Information	Remarks and references to Appendices
	July 26th		Inspected 61st Fd Coy R.E. Condition Fair. These animals are doing hard work drawing material to & from YPRES & up to the trenches daily. They are the hardest worked animals in the Division & they are well looked after.	
	27th		Inspected 62nd Fd Coy R.E. Animals on the whole not looking well - Officer not being very interested.	
	28th		Inspected 90th Fd Coy R.E. Animals very good. A good farrier who is interested in horse management. Officers of these units naturally have not time to personally look after their horses. They are continually at the trenches	SBB

1875 Wt. W593/826 1,000,000 4/15 J.B.C. & A. A.D.S.S./Forms/C. 2118.

Instructions regarding War Diaries and Intelligence Summaries are contained in F. S. Regs., Part II. and the Staff Manual respectively. Title Pages will be prepared in manuscript.

27

WAR DIARY
or
INTELLIGENCE SUMMARY
(Erase heading not required.)

Army Form C. 2118

36

Place	Date	Hour	Summary of Events and Information	Remarks and references to Appendices
	July 29		Inspected Signal Coy R.E. Animals good and well done. Excellent Transport Sergeant.	
	30th		Inspected Divl Cavalry. Animals good. Usual meeting of V.Os at Hd Quarters	
				WB

1875 Wt. W593/826 1,000,000 4/15 J.B.C. & A. A.D.S.S./Forms/C. 2118.

28.

WAR DIARY
or
INTELLIGENCE SUMMARY
(Erase heading not required.)

Army Form C. 2118

37

Instructions regarding War Diaries and Intelligence Summaries are contained in F. S. Regs., Part II. and the Staff Manual respectively. Title Pages will be prepared in manuscript.

Place	Date	Hour	Summary of Events and Information	Remarks and references to Appendices
	August 1st	7.0am	Visited 41st Inf Bde Transport Lines.	
		8.30.	Office.	
		11.0.	Inspected No 2 Coy Divl Train – Condition & general management good, very good.	
			O.C. Divl Train has awarded prizes for men with the best turn out. I judged the Parade for O.C.	
		2.0	Spent two hours going round Incinerators for destruction of manure from Horse Lines.	
			They are very slow to work without fuel of some kind.	
			I suggest to Sanitary Section that other refuse such as old papers, old clothing etc should be sent to Incinerators.	
		5.30	Rode to visit Signal Coy Lines.	
			Cast one horse to be returned to M.V.S for Base.	
				SBB

1875 Wt. W593/826 1,000,000 4/15 J.B.C. & A. A.D.S.S./Forms/C. 2118.

29

Army Form C. 2118

38

Instructions regarding War Diaries and Intelligence Summaries are contained in F. S. Regs., Part II. and the Staff Manual respectively. Title Pages will be prepared in manuscript.

WAR DIARY
or
INTELLIGENCE SUMMARY
(Erase heading not required.)

Place	Date	Hour	Summary of Events and Information	Remarks and references to Appendices
	Aug 2nd	7.0a	Visited 42nd Inf: Bde Transport Lines.	
		8.30a	Office	
		11.0a	Inspected No 1 Coy Divl Train. On reorganizing Train there are about 30 H.D horses returned to this Company from the others - these are not a good lot & will require special care & probably in many cases casting because they are horses that have shewn lameness on occasions, & some are old horses etc, sweepings of other companies.	
		2.0pm	Office	
		3.0pm	Went to YPRES to see Police horses etc. Considerable bombardment going on, also bombarding VLAMERTINGHE. Only a few horses are at YPRES under cover during the day. At night the regimental transport of units in the trenches goes to YPRES by the side roads as much as possible. Wheels of carts wrapped in sacking & old motor tyres in sections.	WBB

1875 Wt. W593/826 1,000,000 4/15 J.B.C. & A. A.D.S.S./Forms/C. 2118.

30

Army Form C. 2118

39

WAR DIARY
or
INTELLIGENCE SUMMARY
(Erase heading not required.)

Instructions regarding War Diaries and Intelligence Summaries are contained in F. S. Regs., Part II. and the Staff Manual respectively. Title Pages will be prepared in manuscript.

Place	Date	Hour	Summary of Events and Information	Remarks and references to Appendices
	Aug 3rd	7.0am	Visited 43rd Inf Bde Transport Lines.	
		8.30.	Office.	
		11.0	Inspected 41st Bde R F A with Lt Laurie. Lines cramped, but exigencies do not allow of anything else. Conditions of animals good, except C Battery. The DDR 2nd Army accompanied me + thought the animals looking very well indeed except the above.	
		2.0pm	Office.	
		4.30pm	Visited Mob. Vety Section at WATOU in new camp. All in good order. Good kitchen arrangements, and good horse lines for the summer. ~~Good~~ An excellent farm with good barn accomodation for the men. Lieut Weir is very good at general management of a Mobile Section. Takes care of his men + horses, + makes the most of the resources of the locality.	SBB

31

Instructions regarding War Diaries and Intelligence Summaries are contained in F. S. Regs., Part II. and the Staff Manual respectively. Title Pages will be prepared in manuscript.

WAR DIARY
or
INTELLIGENCE SUMMARY
(Erase heading not required.)

Army Form C. 2118

40

Place	Date	Hour	Summary of Events and Information	Remarks and references to Appendices
	Aug 4th	7 0am	Rode around Kings L'pool Battalion Transport. Find them short of Hay-nets & nose bags due to not indenting for them. Animals condition fair.	
		8 30am	Office.	
		9 30am	Motored to CAESTRE to visit Remount Field Section with DDR & DDVS 2nd Army.	
			Obtained 8 mules to replace 8 killed last night by shell fire at VLAMERTINGHE on the road to YPRES.	
			Remount Fd Section was being inspected with a view to being declared clear of Mange - after quarantine.	
		2 0pm	Office.	
		2 30pm	Inspected 3 Coy Divl Train & awarded prizes for the best turn out.	
		5 30pm	Visited Maj. Conyngham at 6 Div Hd Qrs. Discussed reduction of his establishment of V.O's.	
		7 0pm	Office.	EBB

Army Form C. 2118

32

41

WAR DIARY
or
INTELLIGENCE SUMMARY

(Erase heading not required.)

Instructions regarding War Diaries and Intelligence Summaries are contained in F. S. Regs., Part II. and the Staff Manual respectively. Title Pages will be prepared in manuscript.

Place	Date	Hour	Summary of Events and Information	Remarks and references to Appendices
	Aug 5	7.0am	Visited 61 & 62 Coy R.E.	
		8.30am	Office.	
		10.30am	Inspected Divl Ammun: Column on WATOU ROAD. Recommended through AQMG that a forge be supplied to each of the three Sections	
		2.0pm	Office	
		3.0"	Visited 47th Bde Ammun: Column. Discussed & settled with O.C. the situation as to whose duty it is to be responsible for sick animals.	
		5.30pm	Visited Major Conder at RENINGHELST	
		7.0pm	Office	
				[initials]

1875 Wt. W593/826 1,000,000 4/15 J.B.C. & A. A.D.S.S./Forms/C. 2118.

33

Army Form C. 2118

42

Instructions regarding War Diaries and Intelligence Summaries are contained in F. S. Regs., Part II. and the Staff Manual respectively. Title Pages will be prepared in manuscript.

WAR DIARY
or
INTELLIGENCE SUMMARY
(Erase heading not required.)

Place	Date	Hour	Summary of Events and Information	Remarks and references to Appendices
	Aug 6	7.0am	Visited 49th Bde R.F.A	
		8.30am	Office.	
		9.30am	Visited Mob: Vety Section to decide casting of horses.	
		2.0pm	Office	
		3.30pm	Weekly meeting of V.O's.	
			Shewed Mr Meeke letter written by me to DDVS asking that he be taken away from the Division on account of my continually having to reprimand him for not doing his work	
		5.30pm	Rode up the YPRES road to see the Transport going up with rations to the trenches.	
		7.0pm	Office.	
				RB

1875 Wt. W593/826 1,000,000 4/15 J.B.C. & A. A.D.S.S./Forms/C. 2118.

34

WAR DIARY
or
INTELLIGENCE SUMMARY
(Erase heading not required.)

Army Form C. 2118

43

Instructions regarding War Diaries and Intelligence Summaries are contained in F. S. Regs., Part II. and the Staff Manual respectively. Title Pages will be prepared in manuscript.

Place	Date	Hour	Summary of Events and Information	Remarks and references to Appendices
	Aug 7th	7.0am	Visited 46th Bde R.F.A two batteries.	
		9.0am	Office. Strongly recommended that forges (field) be supplied to Batteries & Ammun: Column of the new Army on account of the inexperience of farriers & shoeing smiths	
		11.0	Inspected No 4 Coy Div Train	
		2.0pm	Motored to Ordnance Stores with D.A.D.O.S to see what stores are on hand, that might be useful to me for the Section	
		6.0	Office.	
	8th	7.0am	Visited 47th Bde R.F.A four batteries	
		9.0am	Office. Received notice of Foot & Mouth disease outbreak at ABEELE	
		11.0am	Motored to ABEELE - verified outbreak reported to 5th Corps Hd Quarters in whose area it is, also to DDVS 2nd Army	
		3.0pm	Motored to M.V.S.	
		6.30pm	Office.	GBB

1875 Wt. W593/826 1,000,000 4/15 J.B.C. & A. A.D.S.S./Forms/C. 2118.

35

Army Form C. 2118

44

WAR DIARY
or
INTELLIGENCE SUMMARY
(Erase heading not required.)

Instructions regarding War Diaries and Intelligence Summaries are contained in F. S. Regs., Part II. and the Staff Manual respectively. Title Pages will be prepared in manuscript.

Place	Date	Hour	Summary of Events and Information	Remarks and references to Appendices
	Aug 9th	7.0am	Visited 41st Inf Bde Transport	
		8.30	Office	
		11-0	Inspected 44th Fd Ambulance	
		4.0pm	Rode to RENINGHELST to see Major Conder 3rd Div Hd Qrs	
		7.0am	Office.	
			Letter received to put in for Smoke Helmets for horses	
	Aug 10th	7.0am	Visited 43rd Inf Bde Transport.	
		8.30am	Office	
		10.30am	Inspected 42nd Field Ambulance	
		2.0pm	Office	
		4.0	Visit Major Conyngham 6th Div H Qrs	
		6.30	Office.	
				WB

36

Army Form C. 2118

45

Instructions regarding War Diaries and Intelligence Summaries are contained in F. S. Regs., Part II. and the Staff Manual respectively. Title Pages will be prepared in manuscript.

WAR DIARY
or
INTELLIGENCE SUMMARY
(Erase heading not required.)

Place	Date	Hour	Summary of Events and Information	Remarks and references to Appendices
	Aug 11th	7.0 am	Visit party saving corn for local inhabitants in the prohibited area near the front lines. Using our Divisional Transport	
		9.0	Office	
		11.0 am	Inspected 4 Ord Fd Ambulance	
		3.0 pm	Motored to Railhead & returned via ABEELE to see Foot and Mouth disease	
		6.0 pm	Office	
	Aug 12	8.30	Office	
		11.0 am	Inspected 11th Liverpools Transport & C Battery 46th Bde (R.F.A	
		4.0 pm	Visited YPRES	
		7.0 pm	Office	WB

1875 Wt. W593/826 1,000,000 4/15 J.B.C. & A. A.D.S.S./Forms/C. 2118.

34

Army Form C. 2118

46

WAR DIARY
or
INTELLIGENCE SUMMARY
(Erase heading not required.)

Instructions regarding War Diaries and Intelligence Summaries are contained in F. S. Regs., Part II. and the Staff Manual respectively. Title Pages will be prepared in manuscript.

Place	Date	Hour	Summary of Events and Information	Remarks and references to Appendices
	Aug 15th	6.45	Rode around lines of D Battery 49th Bde	
		8.30	Office	
		10.30	Inspect Transport of 42nd Inf Bde, with Bde Transport Officer. Condition of animals good. Many hay-nets lost in continual moving.	
			Shoeing backward owing to continual moves	
			Manes not kept well clipped	
			Green forage not regularly bought.	
			Find certain resentment against sending Heavy Draught animals to the Divl Train for shoeing, on account of the distance to the Train away from Units.	
		2.0	Office	
		3.30	Weekly meeting of VOs of Division. Lieut Steele absent. Impress upon VOs importance of helping unexperienced Shoeing smiths in the care of animals feet	
		6.0	Visit 1st Fd Coy R.E. Corps Troops.	SBB

1875 Wt. W593/826 1,000,000 4/15 J.B.C. & A. A.D.S.S./Forms/C. 2118.

34

Army Form C. 2118

Instructions regarding War Diaries and Intelligence Summaries are contained in F. S. Regs., Part II. and the Staff Manual respectively. Title Pages will be prepared in manuscript.

WAR DIARY
or
INTELLIGENCE SUMMARY
(Erase heading not required.)

47

Place	Date	Hour	Summary of Events and Information	Remarks and references to Appendices
H.Q. 9.8	Aug 14th	7.am	Rode around lines of Transport of 43rd Inf Bde who moved into present camp yesterday. Some heavy rain fell during the night making ground very muddy & slippery	
		8.45am	Office.	
		10.0	Rode back to inspect Nos 1 & 2 Coy Divl Train in the Rest Area. Saw V.O. i/c Lt Steele who was sick yesterday from vomitting - probably caused by dirty food judging by the billett used as a Mess.	
		2.0	Returned to Hd Qrs	
		3.0	By car to inspect 42nd Fd Ambulance. Found Army Commander there with D.M.S. Surg. Gen. Porter inspecting the unit. Animals good. Changed one Heavy L.D. horse from them with a light L.D. in the 89th Fd Coy R.E.	
		6.30	Return to Hd Qrs	
		7.0	Office.	WB

1875 Wt. W593/826 1,000,000 4/15 J.B.C. & A. A.D.S.S./Forms/C. 2118.

39.

Army Form C. 2118

WAR DIARY
or
INTELLIGENCE SUMMARY
(Erase heading not required.)

Instructions regarding War Diaries and Intelligence Summaries are contained in F. S. Regs., Part II. and the Staff Manual respectively. Title Pages will be prepared in manuscript.

48

Place	Date	Hour	Summary of Events and Information	Remarks and references to Appendices
	Aug 15	7.0	Rode to 46th Bde R.F.A. two batteries.	
		8.30	Office.	
		10.0a	~~Went to~~ Inspected 89th Field Coy R.E. & R.A. Head Quarters.	
		12.0a	Went to refilling point to see the Transport animals that come there daily.	
			Exchanged light horses R.E. for heavier horses of 43rd Fd Amb: The R.E. have now very heavy draught work to do & the heavier the horse the better.	
		2.0	Office.	
		4.0	Rode to Div Signal Coy & Head Quarters Divl Train.	
		6.30	Inspect Divl Hd Qtrs animals.	
		7.0	Office.	
				[initials]

1875 Wt. W593/826 1,000,000 4/15 J.B.C. & A. A.D.S.S./Forms/C. 2118.

40.

Instructions regarding War Diaries and Intelligence Summaries are contained in F. S. Regs., Part II. and the Staff Manual respectively. Title Pages will be prepared in manuscript.

WAR DIARY
or
INTELLIGENCE SUMMARY
(Erase heading not required.)

Army Form C. 2118

49

Place	Date	Hour	Summary of Events and Information	Remarks and references to Appendices
	Aug 16	7.0	Visited 7th K.R.R. & 41st Inf Bde & D.C.L.I. of 43rd Bde	
		8.30	Office	
		9.30	Rode to 46th Div Head Quarters & handed over papers & explained what had been done with reference to Foot & Mouth disease at ABEELE. (REBBE RENE)	
		11.30	Inspected new pack saddles at Somerset L.I. who are trying experiment of carrying rations to the trenches on pack ponies instead of cart	
		2.0	Office	
		5.0	Visited Somerset L.I. to see the loads put on the pack animals 50 lbs each side as advised by me, to avoid galling before the animals get used to the work. These animals go right up to the trenches in order to relieve the men in the trenches of the work of fetching rations from the dump. The men in fetching rations pass up and down the communication (trenches)	

41

Instructions regarding War Diaries and Intelligence Summaries are contained in F. S. Regs., Part II. and the Staff Manual respectively. Title Pages will be prepared in manuscript.

WAR DIARY
or
INTELLIGENCE SUMMARY
(Erase heading not required.)

Army Form C. 2118

50

Place	Date	Hour	Summary of Events and Information	Remarks and references to Appendices
			trenches, but the pack animals have to go up in the open. Some night when they are discovered there will be a stampede of any that are left alive.	
	Aug 17	7.0am	Visited 49th Bde, B & D Batteries & Ammunition Column.	
		8.30am	Office.	
		10.30	Inspected 41st Inf: Bde. Transport lines, 4 Battalions, a very great improvement in condition of animals of 7 K.R.R. since last inspection. Fortunately there is a change of Transport Officer of this unit.	
		2.0	Office.	
		4.0	Rode into VLAMERTINGHE on way to see the Transport going towards the trenches. Got caught in very heavy shell fire & came away. All transport in great confusion.	
		7.0	Office.	
			Very heavy bombardment all around us till 9 pm & heavy firing up at the trenches throughout the whole night.	RBB

1875 Wt. W593/826 1,000,000 4/15 J.B.C. & A. A.D.S.S./Forms/C. 2118.

42

Instructions regarding War Diaries and Intelligence Summaries are contained in F. S. Regs., Part II. and the Staff Manual respectively. Title Pages will be prepared in manuscript.

WAR DIARY
or
INTELLIGENCE SUMMARY
(Erase heading not required.)

Army Form C. 2118

51

Place	Date	Hour	Summary of Events and Information	Remarks and references to Appendices
	Aug 18th	9.0	Rode to VLAMERTINGHE to see damage done last night by shells.	
			Aeroplane came down with Engine trouble, landed on the plough land, and turned over on its back. Pilot unhurt.	
		8.30	Office. Received notice that ADVS. can retain two chargers	
		10.0	Rode back to Mob Vety Section, visited Divl Amm. Colum en route, & also 5th Mountain Battery - Return to Head-Quarters at 4.30 pm	
		5.0	Office. The corn is now cut all over the country & it makes a great improvement in riding facilities. The cobbled roads are impossible, & now one need never get on them except to cross them.	
			Received printed bills in French & Belgian regarding Foot & Mouth disease.	[illegible]

1875 Wt. W593/826 1,000,000 4/15 J.B.C. & A. A.D.S.S./Forms/C. 2118.

43

Army Form C. 2118

WAR DIARY
or
INTELLIGENCE SUMMARY
(Erase heading not required.)

Instructions regarding War Diaries and Intelligence Summaries are contained in F. S. Regs., Part II. and the Staff Manual respectively. Title Pages will be prepared in manuscript.

52

Place	Date	Hour	Summary of Events and Information	Remarks and references to Appendices
	Aug 19th	4.0	Visited 12th Fd Troop R.E. Corps Troops at VLAMERTINGHE Horses not looking well. Haynets not in use. Nose bags short of about twelve. Pointed out to O.C. that his horses were not being well done	
		9.0	Office	
		10.30	Visited 62nd & 89th Fd Co R.E.	
		12.0	- do - 11th Co R.G.A. Horses not being well fed & not looking well enough. Their custom has been to hay-up about 1/2 hour before feeding with corn. They cut no chaff & their supply of green food has been irregular.	
		2.0	Office	
		4.30	Rode to 10th D.L.I. to see pack animals start for the trenches.	WB

Instructions regarding War Diaries and Intelligence Summaries are contained in F. S. Regs., Part II. and the Staff Manual respectively. Title Pages will be prepared in manuscript.

44

WAR DIARY
or
INTELLIGENCE SUMMARY
(Erase heading not required.)

Army Form C. 2118

53

Place	Date	Hour	Summary of Events and Information	Remarks and references to Appendices
	Aug 20	7.0am	Visited Somerset L I & Durham L I.	
		8.30am	Office.	
		9.30	Inspected Head Quarter (Divl) horses	
		10.0am	Inspected 46th Bde R F A A. B & C Batteries & Ammn Colum.	
			B Battery not as good as the remainder - this is attributed to Bad water	
			The remainder were very good.	
		3.15pm	Office	
		3.30	Usual weekly meeting of VOs	
		5.30	Office	
			Weather dry & hot. Heavy bombardment most of the day & night.	
				SBB

45

WAR DIARY
or
INTELLIGENCE SUMMARY
(Erase heading not required.)

Army Form C. 2118

54

Instructions regarding War Diaries and Intelligence Summaries are contained in F. S. Regs., Part II. and the Staff Manual respectively. Title Pages will be prepared in manuscript.

Place	Date	Hour	Summary of Events and Information	Remarks and references to Appendices
	Aug 21	5.45	Motored to CAESTRE to receive batch of 32 Remounts. A fair lot of horses & mules. Met Major Pallin of the Blues ADVS of 3rd Division with their Hd Qrs at CAESTRE	
		9.0	Heavy rain & cold set in.	
		11.0	Inspected 41st Bde RFA. Condition & general management good & to a great extent due to the care & attention of Lt Laurie (AVC)	
		2.0	Office Most of the units of the Division are starting to make paved lines for use in the winter. At present the only place open to obtain stone & bricks from is YPRES which is so much bombarded that Divisions are limited to one day a week each, so the supply is very limited. I have asked for authority to start on VLAMERTINGHE which is practically a ruin. 1st leave has been opened for officers of the Division	SBB

1875 Wt. W593/826 1,000,000 4/15 J.B.C. & A. A.D.S.S./Forms/C. 2118.

46.

Instructions regarding War Diaries and Intelligence Summaries are contained in F. S. Regs., Part II. and the Staff Manual respectively. Title Pages will be prepared in manuscript.

WAR DIARY or INTELLIGENCE SUMMARY

(Erase heading not required.)

Army Form C. 2118

55

Place	Date	Hour	Summary of Events and Information	Remarks and references to Appendices
Aug 21		4.30	Rode with A.D.M.S to 44th Field Ambulance at POPERINGHE.	
		7.15	Office	
Sunday Aug 22		7.0	Rode to Kings L'pool Transport Lines, and to VLAMERTINGHE.	
		8.30	Office	
		9.30	Church	
		10.30	Motored to Mob Vety Section. Inspected Smoke Helmets for horses & think them unpractical. Inspected horses for Base tomorrow etc. Called at D.A.C. Head Quarters to ask what percentage of shoes they could <u>make</u> with forges & tools.	
		2.30	Office	
		4.0	Rode to SHERPENBERG HILL.	
		7.0	Office. A second crop of clover is now at its best and is being used fresh-cut by units of the Division.	RB

1875 Wt. W593/826 1,000,000 4/15 J.B.C. & A. A.D.S.S./Forms/C. 2118.

Instructions regarding War Diaries and Intelligence Summaries are contained in F. S. Regs., Part II. and the Staff Manual respectively. Title Pages will be prepared in manuscript.

47

WAR DIARY
or
INTELLIGENCE SUMMARY
(Erase heading not required.)

Army Form C. 2118

56

Place	Date	Hour	Summary of Events and Information	Remarks and references to Appendices
	Aug 23rd	6.45 am	Visited Ox & Bucks & Somerset L.I. Lines, also lines of 1st Cavalry Bde Fd Coy R.E. who have H II horses belonging to 49th Divl Train. Found them very badly done, & reported matter to O.C. Coy & to O.C. Train.	
		8.30	Office	
		10.0	Inspected 48th Bde R.F.A.	
		2.30	Office.	
		3.30	Major Conyngham called to see me.	
		5.30	Rode back through the M.M.P lines & Hd Qtrs of Divl Train	
		7.0	Office.	
			Rumours of German warships & Transport having been sunk in Riga Bay.	
				WB

1875 Wt. W593/826 1,000,000 4/15 J.B.C. & A. A.D.S.S./Forms/C. 2118.

48

Army Form C. 2118

57

Instructions regarding War Diaries and Intelligence Summaries are contained in F. S. Regs., Part II. and the Staff Manual respectively. Title Pages will be prepared in manuscript.

WAR DIARY
or
INTELLIGENCE SUMMARY
(Erase heading not required.)

Place	Date	Hour	Summary of Events and Information	Remarks and references to Appendices
	Aug 24th	7.0	Rode to Transport Lines of 9th R.B. + 9th K.R.R.	
		8 30	Removed office from Farm building into tent for the sake of improved sanitation.	
		10.0	Inspected 48th Bde Amm: Column. R.F.A.	
		11.0	- do - 49th Bde R.F.A. A.B.C Batteries + Ammun: Column	
			Report bad condition of C Battery horses to O.C. 49th Bde	
			Report pond out of which 48th Bde A.C. are watering unfit for watering. Sanitary officer marks it "out of bounds for all purposes"	
		2.0	Office.	
		5.0	Visited Signal Coy R.E.	
			Heavy bombardment continues all round the camp particularly along the VLAMERTINGHE – YPRES road	
			Marked absence of enemy aircraft.	WB

1875 Wt. W593/826 1,000,000 4/15 J.B.C. & A. A.D.S.S./Forms/C. 2118.

49

Instructions regarding War Diaries and Intelligence Summaries are contained in F. S. Regs., Part II. and the Staff Manual respectively. Title Pages will be prepared in manuscript.

WAR DIARY
or
INTELLIGENCE SUMMARY
(Erase heading not required.)

Army Form C. 2118

58

Place	Date	Hour	Summary of Events and Information	Remarks and references to Appendices
	Aug 25	7.0.	Visited Transport Lines of 9th R.B. - 9th K R R - Hd Qtrs 42nd Inf Bde & 6th Siege Battery R.G.A.	
		8.30	Office.	
		10.0	Visited 48th Bde R.F.A to enquire about need of A.V.C Sergeants in units as laid down G 1098.	
		12.0	Called at 6th Corps Hd Qtrs.	
		2.0	Office.	
		2.30	Rode to 47th Bde R.F.A. units to enquire as for 48th Bde above.	
			New A.D.M.S Col Guise Moores C.B. R.A.M.C. arrived vice Col Lavie. The corn harvest in this neighbourhood may be said to be finished, & it is wonderful how the inhabitants have cut it & saved it with so little labour available. Our soldier labour has been used in a very small way. A very hot day.	WB

1875 Wt. W593/826 1,000,000 4/15 J.B.C. & A. A.D.S.S./Forms/C. 2118.

50

Instructions regarding War Diaries and Intelligence Summaries are contained in F. S. Regs., Part II. and the Staff Manual respectively. Title Pages will be prepared in manuscript.

WAR DIARY
or
INTELLIGENCE SUMMARY
(Erase heading not required.)

Army Form C. 2118

59

Place	Date	Hour	Summary of Events and Information	Remarks and references to Appendices
	Aug 26	8.30	Office	
		9.0	Motored to Railhead, & to Advance Remount Section.	
		2.0	Office.	
			Special activity of aeroplanes in the district.	
			Very hot day, bright sun & no wind.	
	27th	4.0	Rode & visited 5th Shrops L.I. & Ox & Bucks Transport, also Transport of 9th K R R.	
		8.30	Office.	
		9.15	Rode to inspect Divisional Cavalry. Cast three horses for Veterinary reasons. Am not struck with the horsemastership of the unit.	
		2.15	Office.	
		3.30	Weekly meeting of VO's at Hd Quarters.	
			The hottest day of the summer up to the present.	SRB

1875 Wt. W593/826 1,000,000 4/15 J.B.C. & A. A.D.S.S./Forms/C. 2118.

51

Army Form C. 2118

60

Instructions regarding War Diaries and Intelligence Summaries are contained in F. S. Regs., Part II. and the Staff Manual respectively. Title Pages will be prepared in manuscript.

WAR DIARY
or
INTELLIGENCE SUMMARY
(Erase heading not required.)

Place	Date	Hour	Summary of Events and Information	Remarks and references to Appendices
	Aug 28	7.0	Rode to 61st + 62nd Fd Coy R.E.	
		8.30	Office.	
		10.0	Motored to Sects 1-2-3 Divl Ammun: Column specially with reference to subject of proposed Sergeants of A.V.C being attached.	
			Also to D Battery 46th Bde R.F.A.	
		11.30	Visited Mob: Vety Section.	
			Noted that broken axles of limber wagons, Travelling Kitchens, Water Carts etc would make good anvils.	
		2.0	Office.	
		4.0	Major Conder came to see me.	
		5.30	Rode to 7th R.B. 41st Inf Bde to see Transport Officer about inspection.	
		7.0	Office.	
			Some of the water pools are beginning to run very low.	
			Very hot dry day.	WB

1875 Wt. W593/826 1,000,000 4/15 J.B.C. & A. A.D.S.S./Forms/C. 2118.

52

Army Form C. 2118

WAR DIARY
or
INTELLIGENCE SUMMARY
(Erase heading not required.)

Instructions regarding War Diaries and Intelligence Summaries are contained in F. S. Regs., Part II. and the Staff Manual respectively. Title Pages will be prepared in manuscript.

61

Place	Date	Hour	Summary of Events and Information	Remarks and references to Appendices
	Aug 29th	7.0	Rode to 1st Fd Troop R.E., 49th Bde A.C. & 47th Bde Amn Column.	
		8.30	Office.	
		9.30	Motored to Corps Head Quarters & on to Mobile Vety Sect.	
		5.0	Went to position East of VLAMERTINGHE to see animals damaged in stampede from Digging Party of previous night due to being shelled.	
	Aug 30	7.15	Rode to VLAMERTINGHE.	
		8.30	Office.	
		9.15	Motored to POPERINGHE.	
		11.0	Inspected 41st Inf Bde Transport.	
		2.30	Met D.D.V.S. 2nd Army.	
		6.0	Visited Head Quarters Divl Train.	
		7.0	Office.	
			Rain set in today with marked fall of temperature.	SBB

1875 Wt. W593/826 1,000,000 4/15 J.B.C. & A. A.D.S.S./Forms/C. 2118.

53 54 missed

WAR DIARY
or
INTELLIGENCE SUMMARY
(Erase heading not required.)

Army Form C. 2118

62

Instructions regarding War Diaries and Intelligence Summaries are contained in F. S. Regs., Part II. and the Staff Manual respectively. Title Pages will be prepared in manuscript.

Place	Date	Hour	Summary of Events and Information	Remarks and references to Appendices
	Aug 31	830	Office	
		1030	Inspected 42nd Inf Bde Transport. Condition good & very well turned out altogether.	
		2:30	Visited Mob. Vet. Sect: to see men proposed by O.C. for promotion to rank of Sergeant.	
		630	Office.	
			A dull cold day with high wind from S.W	
			Practically no bombardment today for the first time	
			Applied for leave to England.	
			The corn ration for horses (L.D.) is Oats 8 lbs Crushed Maize 4 lbs, Hay 10 lbs & the equivalent of two pounds of hay to be bought locally.	
				GBB

1875 Wt. W593/826 1,000,000 4/15 J.B.C. & A. A.D.S.S./Forms/C. 2118.

Instructions regarding War Diaries and Intelligence Summaries are contained in F. S. Regs., Part II. and the Staff Manual respectively. Title pages will be prepared in manuscript.

WAR DIARY 55.
or
INTELLIGENCE SUMMARY.
(Erase heading not required.)

Army Form C. 2118.

September 1915

Place	Date	Hour	Summary of Events and Information	Remarks and references to Appendices
Sept	1st	–	Rain & cold wind Inspected 43rd Inf. Bde Transport. With reference to the pack pony transport to the trenches there is a great tendency to overload the animals – putting up 250 to 300 lbs on the saddle. As the animals are not yet hardened to the saddles this is bound to lead to galls especially as the men are not very careful in dressing the loads. Special attention was drawn to this.	
Sept	2		Inspected C Battery 49th Bde R.F.A. reported badly upon on the 24th August. A very great improvement noticeable in the routine of the stables & horsemastership generally.	
Sept	3rd		Went on leave to England. Duty to be done by Lt Laurie.	WBB

56.

Army Form C. 2118.

Instructions regarding War Diaries and Intelligence Summaries are contained in F. S. Regs., Part II. and the Staff Manual respectively. Title pages will be prepared in manuscript.

WAR DIARY
or
INTELLIGENCE SUMMARY.
(Erase heading not required.)

September 1915

Place	Date	Hour	Summary of Events and Information	Remarks and references to Appendices
	Sept 10		Returned from leave. Weekly meeting of V.O.s. Sergeants of AVC posted to units of the Division according to my list forwarded to DDVS 3rd Army	
	Sept 11th Sept		Lt Thornewill goes on leave — duties split up amongst nearest V.O.s & myself. Visited Mob. Vety Sect. by Car — also C/46 R.F.A. at Watou. Wrote to Col Hobson No 1 Remount Depot Rouen asking for a good horse as a charger.	
	Sept 12th		Visited 9th R.B. & 5 Shrops L.I. D Battery 46 Bde R.F.A. A Battery 46 Bde R F A & 46 Bde Ammn Col.	

54

Army Form C. 2118.

WAR DIARY
or
INTELLIGENCE SUMMARY.
(Erase heading not required.)

Instructions regarding War Diaries and Intelligence Summaries are contained in F. S. Regs., Part II. and the Staff Manual respectively. Title pages will be prepared in manuscript.

September 1915

Place	Date	Hour	Summary of Events and Information	Remarks and references to Appendices
	Sept 13	11-0	Inspected Div. Amm. Column. Nos. 1 & 3 Sections WATOU. Animals well done & in good condition	
	"	10-0	Inspected Div. Cavalry. Animals not well done. Informed C.O. that I do not think his animals looking well. My suggestion of a couple of months ago about preparing Reins with either creasote or Alum mixed with the grease in preparation was not considered of any use by the Ordnance Department — the number of reins eaten by animals is a big item. The perfect summer weather of the last 10 days is breaking up. Cloudy sky & colder but practically no rain.	

WBB

1577 Wt. W10791/1773 500,000 1/15 D. D. & L. A.D.S.S./Forms/C. 2118.

58

Army Form C. 2118.

WAR DIARY
or
INTELLIGENCE SUMMARY.
(Erase heading not required.)

Instructions regarding War Diaries and Intelligence Summaries are contained in F. S. Regs., Part II. and the Staff Manual respectively. Title pages will be prepared in manuscript.

September 1915

Place	Date	Hour	Summary of Events and Information	Remarks and references to Appendices
	Sept 14		Inspected No 2 Section D.A.C. near Poppringhe Mules looking fair in condition. Horses on the whole bad. Report sent to C.O.	
		3.30	Visited horse show of 6th Division well run by Major Conder an excellent show in every way.	
			Corps letter ~~stopping~~ proposes ~~stopping~~ increase supply of heelropes for horses. I recommend that 10% of the strength of animals should be available & that this is sufficient. Animals are changing their coats.	Q. 820 12-9-15
			Visited 46/A.C. & RA Head Quarters	

SBB

59.

Army Form C. 2118.

WAR DIARY
or
INTELLIGENCE SUMMARY.
(*Erase heading not required.*)

Instructions regarding War Diaries and Intelligence Summaries are contained in F. S. Regs., Part II. and the Staff Manual respectively. Title pages will be prepared in manuscript.

September 1915

Place	Date	Hour	Summary of Events and Information	Remarks and references to Appendices
	Sept 15	7-0	Visited Transport Lines of 9th KRR & 5th Ox & Bucks.	
		10-0	Visited lines of C/49 R.F.A. & B/49 R.F.A.	
		11-0	Visited 46th Bde Amm Col.	
		3-0	Visited Mob. Vety Section	
		5-0	Visited 89 Coy R.E. to interview C.O. who applied for an extra ration for his animals. I think his animals have a good ration & look well.	
			Smoke helmets for horses issued to units.	
			The weather is perfect autumn weather like a good English September.	
			In answer to our application for forges & tools for making horse shoes throughout the Division, a letter from H.Q. states that forges & tools cannot be supplied on account of the transport not being available to carry them in case of a move but it is hoped that shoes will be made.	WB

60

Army Form C. 2118

WAR DIARY
or
INTELLIGENCE SUMMARY.
(Erase heading not required.)

Instructions regarding War Diaries and Intelligence Summaries are contained in F. S. Regs., Part II. and the Staff Manual respectively. Title pages will be prepared in manuscript.

September 1915

Place	Date	Hour	Summary of Events and Information	Remarks and references to Appendices
	Sept. 16th	7-0	Visited 49th Bde R.F.A.	
		10.0	Inspection by Corps Commander of all the Infantry Transport of the Division. This inspection was very much appreciated by me & by all the Transport officers. In these positions the Transport has very hard work to perform. Units are always changing position & every night in all weather there is the journey up to the trenches along the roads. The traffic & confusion & danger of these journeys when the enemy are shelling the roads has to be seen to be understood. The General did not fail to impress upon the men the fact that though he did not often come to see them, he thoroughly appreciated their good work.	
			Lt Meake applied for leave which I did not approve of ~~[illegible]~~.	WB

61.

Instructions regarding War Diaries and Intelligence Summaries are contained in F. S. Regs., Part II. and the Staff Manual respectively. Title pages will be prepared in manuscript.

WAR DIARY
or
INTELLIGENCE SUMMARY.
(Erase heading not required.)

Army Form C. 2118.

September 1915

Place	Date	Hour	Summary of Events and Information	Remarks and references to Appendices
	Sept 19.		Inspected 61 Fd Coy R.E. Animals very good.	
		11-0	Attend Court Martial to give evidence.	
			Visited 46th Bde Amm Col.	
		3.30	Usual meeting of V.O.s except Lt Hornswill.	
			A very hot day. The dry weather continues & the water holes are beginning to show the want of rain in many cases. We keep so many horses up in this advanced area that it is wonderful how the water has lasted out. Practically every farmstead is occupied ~~continually~~ continuously either by a Battery of horses or an Ammunition Column or by Infantry Regt Transport etc. In the rest area the difficulty naturally does not arise so much because farms can be given a rest.	
				EBB

1577 Wt. W10791/1773 500,000 1/15 D. D. & L. A.D.S.S./Forms/C. 2118.

62

Army Form C. 2118.

WAR DIARY
or
INTELLIGENCE SUMMARY.
(*Erase heading not required.*)

Instructions regarding War Diaries and Intelligence Summaries are contained in F. S. Regs., Part II. and the Staff Manual respectively. Title pages will be prepared in manuscript.

September 1915

Place	Date	Hour	Summary of Events and Information	Remarks and references to Appendices
	Sept 18		Lt Honeywill returns from leave, one day overdue on account of the boat not running.	
		10.30	Visited 46th & 48th Bde Ammn. Cols. 9th RB & 9th KRRR Transports	
		4.0	Visited 49th Bde R.F.A.	
	19th		It is quite extraordinary to find how few officers in charge of horses know what rations they are entitled to draw. With the Infantry 95% do not know. I continually try to impress upon officers the advisability of getting hold of a chaff cutter from any farm but it is difficult to get them to attach much importance to it, and chaff cutters of course cannot be drawn from Ordnance.	
		2.0	Motored to Remount Section Cassel to choose some horses for the Division.	
			Another perfect autumn day. Very severe bombardment all day & all night.	WB

1577 Wt. W10791/1773 500,000 1/15 D. D. & L. A.D.S.S./Forms/C. 2118.

63

Instructions regarding War Diaries and Intelligence Summaries are contained in F. S. Regs., Part II. and the Staff Manual respectively. Title pages will be prepared in manuscript.

WAR DIARY
or
INTELLIGENCE SUMMARY.
(Erase heading not required.)

Army Form C. 2118.

September 1915

Place	Date	Hour	Summary of Events and Information	Remarks and references to Appendices
	Sept 2		Inspected 49th Bde of Artillery Horse Lines. Reported bad condition of C. Battery due in my opinion wholely to neglect of ordinary stable routine. Units of the Division are on the whole getting on well with making standings of brick, stone flags, sleepers etc for the winter. The great difficulty is to get any material. For many units Ypres is a great distance to take wagons to gather material and in any case units are only allowed one day per week in Ypres. Other places around here are not allowed to be drawn on for materials. Heavy bombardment of Ypres & Vlamertinghe to day – the heaviest for a month.	WB

1577 Wt. W10791/1773 500,000 1/15 D. D. & L. A.D.S.S./Forms/C. 2118.

64

Army Form C. 2118

WAR DIARY
or
INTELLIGENCE SUMMARY.
(Erase heading not required.)

Instructions regarding War Diaries and Intelligence Summaries are contained in F. S. Regs., Part II. and the Staff Manual respectively. Title pages will be prepared in manuscript.

September 1915

Place	Date	Hour	Summary of Events and Information	Remarks and references to Appendices
	Sep 21st		Inspected four batteries & Amm-Col. of 46th Bde R.F.A. Found them all well turned out & in good condition.	
			Sent in recommendation for special mention asked for by D.D.V.S. few days ago & on which I have since received a wire asking me to expedite reply. I think this a matter that should be discussed by D.D.V.S. with A.D.V.S.' of Division to give A.D.V.S. an idea of uniformity of recommendation. Ideas might differ so much as to the officer or man that should be specially mentioned.	
			I find in my rounds that with the present state of warfare when horses seldom do hard days of work & are picketted on lines in the open, Collar Chains are the most desirable form of head gear for tying horses up. Ropes & Reins are eaten & pulled about so much & very difficult to handle in wet weather.	WB

1577 Wt. W10791/1773 500,000 1/15 D. D. & L. A.D.S.S./Forms/C. 2118.

65

Army Form C. 2118.

Instructions regarding War Diaries and Intelligence Summaries are contained in F. S. Regs., Part II. and the Staff Manual respectively. Title pages will be prepared in manuscript.

WAR DIARY
or
INTELLIGENCE SUMMARY.
(Erase heading not required.)

September 1915

Place	Date	Hour	Summary of Events and Information	Remarks and references to Appendices
	Sept 22		Inspected horse lines of 47th Bde R.F.A. & Ammn Col. Most of these animals have fallen off in condition during the last month — except D Battery. This is in my opinion due to the Sergeant Majors being taken away to the gun positions & leaving the horses to men who are not up to the work. D Battery has never allowed the Sergt Major to leave the horse lines for more than a few days.	
			Visited Somerset Light Inf. Transport.	
			Received ~~orders~~ Circular Memo from D.V.S. (V 925) that V.O's must certify that they have examined personally every horse in their charge. It always appears to me to be a pity to issue an order that you know cannot be carried out.	EBB

66

Instructions regarding War Diaries and Intelligence Summaries are contained in F. S. Regs., Part II. and the Staff Manual respectively. Title pages will be prepared in manuscript.

WAR DIARY
or
INTELLIGENCE SUMMARY.
(Erase heading not required.)

Army Form C. 2118

September 1915

Place	Date	Hour	Summary of Events and Information	Remarks and references to Appendices
	Sept 23rd	7.0	Visited Lines of Shrop. L. I. Transport.	
		9.30	Inspected 46th Bde R.F.A. horse lines & Bde Amm. Col. which took till 4 p.m.	
		4.30	Visited Mob. Vety. Sect. to see man under arrest.	
		9.0	Office.	
			Owing to shortage of green fodder — am advising local purchase of oat straw for chaff to make up the missing portion of hay ration.	
			The subject of clipping for the winter is now being considered, & a letter from the Corps has come round saying that as a general rule clipping will be forbidden — Divisional Commanders to give permission for clipping in special cases.	
			My remarks were — that Trace-high clipping will depend upon the amount of work horses are required to do, & it is the only form of clipping that should be allowed apart from Mange & Veterinary Reasons. I advise very strict orders being issued against clipping of any horses legs below the elbow or stifle.	WB

1577 Wt. W10791/1773 500,000 1/15 D. D. & L. A.D.S.S./Forms/C. 2118.

67

Instructions regarding War Diaries and Intelligence Summaries are contained in F. S. Regs., Part II. and the Staff Manual respectively. Title pages will be prepared in manuscript.

WAR DIARY
or
INTELLIGENCE SUMMARY.
(Erase heading not required.)

Army Form C. 2118.

September 1915

Place	Date	Hour	Summary of Events and Information	Remarks and references to Appendices
	Sept 24th		Motored to advance Remount Section to choose horses	
		3.30	Usual meeting of C.O.s	
			Rain fell during last night & during to day. All arrangements appear ready for an attack on a big scale	
	25th	9-0	Visited Mob. Vety Section	
			Rain fell all day.	
			Attack which started at 4 a m continued through the day and is in conjunction with the attack all along the front which is to be the effort for advance on the western front.	
				[illegible initials]

68

Army Form C. 2118

WAR DIARY
or
INTELLIGENCE SUMMARY.

(Erase heading not required.)

Instructions regarding War Diaries and Intelligence Summaries are contained in F. S. Regs., Part II. and the Staff Manual respectively. Title pages will be prepared in manuscript.

September 1915

Place	Date	Hour	Summary of Events and Information	Remarks and references to Appendices
	Sept 26	a.m.	Visited 41st 42 + 43rd Head Quarters of Brigade Transports. All second line Transport drawn ready in case of a move.	
		3 p.m.	D.D.V.S. 2nd Army came to see me. A clear bright day with strong sun.	
	" 27		Inspected 44th + 42nd Fd Ambulances. Animals in good condition.	
	" 28		Inspected 43rd Fd Ambulance. Animals in fair condition. Weather suddenly turned cold with North wind.	
	" 29		Rain all day + cold wind. All the standings for horses flooded 2 inches deep in mud, like winter.	WBB

1577 Wt. W10791/1773 500,000 1/15 D. D. & L. A.D.S.S./Forms/C. 2118.

69.

Instructions regarding War Diaries and Intelligence Summaries are contained in F. S. Regs., Part II. and the Staff Manual respectively. Title pages will be prepared in manuscript.

WAR DIARY

or

INTELLIGENCE SUMMARY.

(Erase heading not required.)

Army Form C. 2118.

September 1915

Place	Date	Hour	Summary of Events and Information	Remarks and references to Appendices
	Sept 30th		Visited V.O.s except Lt Steele.	
			I notice in War Establishment New Army (2) other Ranks laid down with V.O.s in R.F.A. Brigades & Div. Train.	
			Application sent to D.D.V.S. to ask if these are supplied by A.V.C.	
		2.30	Attack made by 3rd Division on our right.	
		8-0	not successful.	
				FBB

70

Army Form C. 2118

WAR DIARY
or
INTELLIGENCE SUMMARY.
(Erase heading not required.)

Instructions regarding War Diaries and Intelligence Summaries are contained in F. S. Regs., Part II. and the Staff Manual respectively. Title pages will be prepared in manuscript.

October 1915

Place	Date	Hour	Summary of Events and Information	Remarks and references to Appendices
	October 1st		Inspected 61 - 62 & 89th Companies R.E. Animals in good condition. Good winter standings made. The usual meeting of V.O.	
	2nd		Inspected No 1 Divisional Signal Company. Animals well done & winter standings made. An excellent Sergeant in charge of animals. Very cold nights with frost. Clear fine days with hot sun	
	3rd		Sunday Heavy rain fell	
	8th		Nights are beginning to get ~~wintry~~ like winter nights. It is dark at 5.30 & the nights are cold. Units are asking for rugs for animals ~~&~~ men. Usual meeting of V.O.s at which D.D.V.S. Col Wilson arrived.	WB

1577 Wt. W10791/1773 500,000 1/15 D. D. & L. A.D.S.S./Forms/C. 2118.

71

Army Form C. 21[illegible]

Instructions regarding War Diaries and Intelligence Summaries are contained in F. S. Regs., Part II. and the Staff Manual respectively. Title Pages will be prepared in manuscript.

WAR DIARY
or
INTELLIGENCE SUMMARY
(Erase heading not required.)

October 1915

Place	Date	Hour	Summary of Events and Information	Remarks and references to Appendices
	Oct 9th		Inspected 41st Inf. Bde Transport Lines & furnished report to Brigade Commander. Called for a Return ~~[illegible]~~ of units in possession of Chaff Cutters – units having the use of chaff cutters belonging to neighbouring units & those have no use of chaff cutters.	
	" 11th		Inspected 42nd Inf Bde Transport & reported. This Transport is in perfect condition & very well run indeed. Horse Lines & huts for men are being made vigorously by the units of the Division. Fine dry weather.	
	12th		Inspected 43rd Inf Bde Transport & reported animals on the whole in good condition. Not enough interest taken in producing bulk of food for Heavy draught horses. This can	GMB

1875 Wt. W593/826 1,000,000 4/15 J.B.C. & A. A.D.S.S./Forms/C. 2118.

72

Instructions regarding War Diaries and Intelligence Summaries are contained in F. S. Regs., Part II. and the Staff Manual respectively. Title Pages will be prepared in manuscript.

WAR DIARY
or
INTELLIGENCE SUMMARY
(Erase heading not required.)

Army Form C. 21[illegible]

October 1915

Place	Date	Hour	Summary of Events and Information	Remarks and references to Appendices
			can be done.	
-	15th		Inspected with DDVS 2nd Army, 47th Bde RFA & 48th Bde R.F.A.	
	16th		Visited Mob Vety Sect with reference to hutments of men for the winter. Decided that with the Barn of the Farm which is at their disposal no huts are required. Applied for 5 tents for the men to sleep in when the weather is dry. This is the wish of the men themselves. Shoes (horse) pierced for Cogs are arriving from the Base preparatory to frosty weather. Shortage of Veterinary medicines being felt slightly. No perchloride of Mercury in stores!	
				WB

1875 Wt. W593/826 1,000,000 4/15 J.B.C. & A. A.D.S.S./Forms/C. 2118.

73

Army Form C. 2118.

WAR DIARY
or
INTELLIGENCE SUMMARY
(Erase heading not required.)

Instructions regarding War Diaries and Intelligence Summaries are contained in F. S. Regs., Part II. and the Staff Manual respectively. Title Pages will be prepared in manuscript.

October 1915.

Place	Date	Hour	Summary of Events and Information	Remarks and references to Appendices
	Oct 17th		Up to quite lately, the difficulty of obtaining wood for building purposes was well marked. Now there is a plentiful supply & units are all erecting stabling and huts for the men but it is late in the season! Weather remains dry but is getting cold.	
	22nd		Usual meeting of V.O.s. Discussed the use & abuse of Mob. Vety Section with Division. Recommended Lt Laurie for Command of a Section, in answer to offer of appointment from D.D.V.S. 2nd Army.	
	23rd		Inspected 48th Bde R.F.A. forges which the farriers have done so well in constructing. They have erected good workable forges suitable for making shoes in, with powerful bellows & cleverly arranged blast. They also have produced full size anvils from somewhere.	WBB

74

Army Form C. 21[illegible]

WAR DIARY
or
INTELLIGENCE SUMMARY
(Erase heading not required.)

Instructions regarding War Diaries and Intelligence Summaries are contained in F. S. Regs., Part II. and the Staff Manual respectively. Title Pages will be prepared in manuscript.

October 1915

Place	Date	Hour	Summary of Events and Information	Remarks and references to Appendices
RH	24th		The question of a Float for the use of Mob. Vety Sect. still presents some difficulty, in that when it is wanted, the owner himself has it in use or has lent it to somebody else. An old Float has lately been found at Ypres and with the aid of the Corps workshop who are putting a new wheel & new floor, will become a useful addition to the Section as long as we continue under this form of warfare in which a Mobile Section really becomes an advanced Veterinary Section in its functions.	Y 736 DDVS 2nd Army
	25th		Visited 49th Bde R.F.A. whose horse lines are the most advanced of the Division. It was not thought that they would remain in their present position for the winter, until within the last three days so they had not done anything towards laying down lines & overhead coverings etc. Now the rain	WB

1875 Wt. W593/826 1,000,000 4/15 J.B.C. & A. A.D.S.S./Forms/C. 2118.

75

Instructions regarding War Diaries and Intelligence Summaries are contained in F. S. Regs., Part II. and the Staff Manual respectively. Title Pages will be prepared in manuscript.

WAR DIARY
or
INTELLIGENCE SUMMARY
(Erase heading not required.)

Army Form C. 21[illegible]

October 1915

Place	Date	Hour	Summary of Events and Information	Remarks and references to Appendices
			has begun to fall daily and material in the form of bricks etc is very difficult to get. The result is that horses are standing up to their hocks in mud & it will be a very difficult matter to get them made at all unless a further dry period sets in.	
			All the officers & personnel of Divisional Head Quarters have been in tents up to now. During the last fortnight we have built mud huts or wood huts individually.	
	Oct 30th		Rain has continued to fall daily, but the thermometer keeps moderately high. There has been no frost up to the present.	
			Orders received for Lt Cowan to join this Division to take over Lt Laurie's duties, the latter to report to 24th Division to take over Mob Vety Section. 24th Division is at RENNINGHELST. only four miles from here.	[initials]

1875 Wt. W593/826 1,000,000 4/15 J.B.C. & A. A.D.S.S./Forms/C. 2118.

Instructions regarding War Diaries and Intelligence Summaries are contained in F. S. Regs., Part II. and the Staff Manual respectively. Title Pages will be prepared in manuscript.

76.

WAR DIARY
or
INTELLIGENCE SUMMARY
(Erase heading not required.)

Army Form C. 2118.

October 1915.

Place	Date	Hour	Summary of Events and Information	Remarks and references to Appendices
	Oct 31st		Horse rugs for the Division have arrived from the Base. Artillery bombardment of these back areas goes on daily & nightly & it is noticeable that a big percentage of the percussion shells do not burst in the soft ground. Slight loss of animals however continues from shell fire amongst transport.	WB

1875 Wt. W593/826 1,000,000 4/15 J.B.C. & A. A.D.S.S./Forms/C. 2118.

Instructions regarding War Diaries and Intelligence Summaries are contained in F. S. Regs., Part II. and the Staff Manual respectively. Title pages will be prepared in manuscript.

WAR DIARY 55
or
INTELLIGENCE SUMMARY.
(Erase heading not required.)

Army Form C. 2118.

63

Place	Date	Hour	Summary of Events and Information	Remarks and references to Appendices
	Sept 1st		Rain & cold wind. Inspected 45th Inf Bde Transport. With reference to the pack pony transport to the trenches there is a great tendency to overload the animals putting up 250 to 300 lb. on the saddle. As the animals are not yet hardened to the saddle there is bound to be sore backs especially as the men are not very careful in adjusting the loads. Special attention was drawn to this.	
	Sept 2		Inspected C Batty 49th Bde RFA reported badly upon on the 24th August. A very great improvement noticeable in the condition of the stables & horsemastership generally.	
	Sept 3		Went on leave to England. Duty to be done by Lt Laurie.	EBB

1577 Wt. W10791/1773 500,000 1/15 D. D. & L. A.D.S.S./Forms/C. 2118.

56.

Instructions regarding War Diaries and Intelligence Summaries are contained in F. S. Regs., Part II. and the Staff Manual respectively. Title pages will be prepared in manuscript.

WAR DIARY
or
INTELLIGENCE SUMMARY.
(Erase heading not required.)

Army Form C. 2118.

64

Place	Date	Hour	Summary of Events and Information	Remarks and references to Appendices
	Sept 10		Returned from leave. Weekly meeting of V.O.: Sergeants of AVC posted to units of the Division according to my list provided to DDVS 3rd Army	
	Sept 11		Lt Thorowgood goes on leave – duties split up amongst nearest VOs (myself) Visited Mob Vety Sect. by Car also C/46 R.F.A. at Watou Wrote to Lt A. Gibson i/c Remount Depot Rouen asking for a good horse as a charger.	
	Sept 12		Visited 9th R.B. [illegible] D Battery 46 Bde R.F.A. A Battery 46 Bde R.F.A. & 46 Bde Ammn Col	
				WB

Instructions regarding War Diaries and Intelligence Summaries are contained in F. S. Regs., Part II. and the Staff Manual respectively. Title pages will be prepared in manuscript.

57

WAR DIARY
or
INTELLIGENCE SUMMARY.
(Erase heading not required.)

Army Form C. 2118.

65

Place	Date	Hour	Summary of Events and Information	Remarks and references to Appendices
	Sept 13	11.0	Inspected Div Ammn Column Nos 1 & 3 Sections WATOU. Animals well done & in good condition	
		10.0	Inspected Div Cavalry. Animals not well done. Informed C.O. that I do not think his animals looking well.	
			My suggestion of a couple of months ago about preparing Reins with either Creosote or Alum mixed with the grease in preparation was not considered of any use by the Ordnance Department — the number of Reins eaten by animals is a big item.	
			The perfect summer weather of the last 10 days is breaking up. Cloudy sky & colder but practically no rain.	

1577 Wt. W10791/1773 500,000 1/15 D. D. & L. A.D.S.S./Forms/C. 2118.

58

WAR DIARY
or
INTELLIGENCE SUMMARY.
(Erase heading not required.)

Army Form C. 2118.

66

Instructions regarding War Diaries and Intelligence Summaries are contained in F. S. Regs., Part II. and the Staff Manual respectively. Title pages will be prepared in manuscript.

Place	Date	Hour	Summary of Events and Information	Remarks and references to Appendices
	Sept 14		Inspected No 2 Section D.A.C. near Poperinghe. Mules looking fair in condition. Horses on the whole bad. Report sent to C.O.	
		3 30	Visited horse show of 6 Division well run by Maj Conder an excellent show in every way.	
			VI Copy Letter ~~[illegible]~~ proposes ~~[illegible]~~ increase supply of headropes for horses. I recommend that 10% of the strength of animal should be available & that this is sufficient. Animals are changing their coats	2. 820 12-9-15
			Visited 46/A & R.A. Head Quarters	

WBB

1577 Wt. W10791/1773 500,000 1/15 D. D. & L. A.D.S.S./Forms/C. 2118.

59.

WAR DIARY
or
INTELLIGENCE SUMMARY.
(Erase heading not required.)

Army Form C. 2118.

Instructions regarding War Diaries and Intelligence Summaries are contained in F. S. Regs., Part II. and the Staff Manual respectively. Title pages will be prepared in manuscript.

67

Place	Date	Hour	Summary of Events and Information	Remarks and references to Appendices
	Sept 15	1.0	Visited Transport Lines of 9th KRR & 5th Ox & Bucks.	
		10.0	Visited lines of C/49 RFA & B/49 RFA.	
		11.0	Visited 46 Bde Ammn Col.	
		2.0	Visited Mob. Vety Section	
		3.0	Visited 89 Coy RE to interview C.O. who applied for an extra ration for his animals. I think his animals have a good ration & look well.	
			Smoke helmets for horses issued to units.	
			The weather is perfect autumn weather like a good English September.	
			In answer to our application for forges & tools for making horse shoes throughout the Division, a letter from H.Q. states that forges & tools cannot be supplied on account of the transport not being available to carry them in case of a move but it is hoped that shoes will be made.	EBB

1577 Wt. W10791/1773 500,000 1/15 D. D. & L. A.D.S.S./Forms/C. 2118.

60

Instructions regarding War Diaries and Intelligence Summaries are contained in F. S. Regs., Part II. and the Staff Manual respectively. Title pages will be prepared in manuscript.

WAR DIARY
or
INTELLIGENCE SUMMARY.
(Erase heading not required.)

Army Form C. 2118.

68

Place	Date	Hour	Summary of Events and Information	Remarks and references to Appendices
	Sept 16th	7 0	Visited 49th Bde R J G.	
		10 0	Inspection by Corps Commander of all the Infantry Transport of the Division. This inspection was very much appreciated by me & by all the Transport officers. In these positions the Transport has very hard work to perform. Units are always changing position & every night in all weather there is the journey up to the trenches along the roads. The traffic & confusion & danger of these journeys when the enemy are shelling the roads has to be seen to be understood. The General did not fail to impress upon the men the fact that though he did not often come to see them, he thoroughly appreciated their good work.	
			Lt Drake applied for leave which I did not approve of because he does not work well enough.	EBB

1577. Wt. W10791/1773 500,000 1/15 D. D. & L. A.D.S.S./Forms/C. 2118.

61

WAR DIARY
or
INTELLIGENCE SUMMARY.
(Erase heading not required.)

Army Form C. 2118.

69

Instructions regarding War Diaries and Intelligence Summaries are contained in F. S. Regs., Part II. and the Staff Manual respectively. Title pages will be prepared in manuscript.

Place	Date	Hour	Summary of Events and Information	Remarks and references to Appendices
	6 Sept 17.		Inspected 61 Fd Coy R.E. Animals very good.	
		11 0	Attended Court Martial to give evidence	
			Visited 46° Div Amm Col	
		3 30	Usual meeting of V.O's except 1 Horsework.	
			A very hot day. The dry weather continues & the water holes are beginning to show the want of rain in many cases. To keep so many horses up in this advanced area that it is wonderful how the water has lasted out. Particularly every farmstead is occupied ~~continuously~~ continuously either by a Battery of horses or an Ammunition Column or by Infantry Regt Transport etc. In the rest area the difficulty naturally does not arise so much because farms can be given a rest.	

62

Army Form C. 2118.

WAR DIARY
or
INTELLIGENCE SUMMARY.
(Erase heading not required.)

Instructions regarding War Diaries and Intelligence Summaries are contained in F. S. Regs., Part II. and the Staff Manual respectively. Title pages will be prepared in manuscript.

70

Place	Date	Hour	Summary of Events and Information	Remarks and references to Appendices
	Sept 16		Lt Honeywill returns from leave, one day overdue on account of the boat not running.	
		10 30	Visited 46th & 48th Bde Amm Col. 9th RB & 9th KRR Transport	
		4 0	Visited 49th Bde RFA	
	19th		It is quite extraordinary to find how few officers in charge of horses know what rations they are entitled to draw with the Infantry 9/10 do not know. I continually try to impress upon them the advisability of getting hold of a Chaff Cutter from any farm but it is difficult to get them to attach much importance to it and chaff cutters of course cannot be drawn from ordnance.	
		2-0	Motored to Remount Section Cassel to choose some horses for the Division.	
			[illegible] day.	
			Very heavy bombardment all day & all night.	WBB

63

WAR DIARY
or
INTELLIGENCE SUMMARY.
(*Erase heading not required.*)

Army Form C. 2118.

71

Instructions regarding War Diaries and Intelligence Summaries are contained in F. S. Regs., Part II. and the Staff Manual respectively. Title pages will be prepared in manuscript.

Place	Date	Hour	Summary of Events and Information	Remarks and references to Appendices
	Jan 2		Inspected 49th Bde of Artillery horse lines Reported bad condition of C Battery due in my opinion wholely to neglect of ordinary stable routine. Units of the Division are on the whole getting on well with making standings of brick, stone flags, sleepers etc for the winter. The great difficulty is to get any material — for many units Ypres is a great distance to take wagons to collect material and in any case units are only allowed one day per week in Ypres. Other places around there are not allowed to be drawn on for materials Heavy bombardment of Ypres & Vlamertinghe to-day — the heaviest for a month.	RB

1577 Wt. W10791/1773 500,000 1/15 D. D. & L. A.D.S.S./Forms/C. 2118.

64

Army Form C. 2118.

Instructions regarding War Diaries and Intelligence Summaries are contained in F. S. Regs., Part II. and the Staff Manual respectively. Title pages will be prepared in manuscript.

WAR DIARY
or
INTELLIGENCE SUMMARY.
(Erase heading not required.)

72

Place	Date	Hour	Summary of Events and Information	Remarks and references to Appendices
	Sep. 21		Inspected four batteries & Ammn Col of 48th Bde R.F.A. Found them all well turned out & in good Condition.	
			Sent in recommendation for special mention asked for by D.D.V.S. few days ago & on which I have since received a wire asking me to expedite reply. I think this a matter that should be discussed by D.D.V.S. with A.D.V.S.' of Division to give A.D.V.S. an idea of uniformity of recommendation. Ideas might differ so much as to the officer or man that should be specially mentioned.	
			I find in my rounds that with the present state of warfare where horses seldom do hard days of work & are picketed in lines in the open, Collar Chains are the most desirable form of head gear for tying horses up. Ropes & Reins are eaten & pulled about so much & very difficult to handle in wet weather.	[illegible]

1577 Wt. W10791/1773 500,000 1/15 D. D. & L. A.D.S.S./Forms/C. 2118.

65

Army Form C. 2118.

Instructions regarding War Diaries and Intelligence Summaries are contained in F. S. Regs., Part II. and the Staff Manual respectively. Title pages will be prepared in manuscript.

WAR DIARY
or
INTELLIGENCE SUMMARY.
(Erase heading not required.)

93

Place	Date	Hour	Summary of Events and Information	Remarks and references to Appendices
	Sept 2nd		Inspected Horse Lines of 47th Bde RFA + Amm Col. Most of these animals have fallen off in condition during the last month – except D Battery. This is in my opinion due to the Sergeant Majors being taken away to the Gun positions + leaving the horses to men who are not up to the work. D Battery has never allowed the Sergt Major to leave the horse lines for more than a few days. Visited Somerset Light Inf Transport. Received Circular Memo from DVS (V 925) that VO must certify that they have examined personally every horse in their charge. It always appears to me to be a pity to issue an order that you know cannot be carried out.	RB

66

WAR DIARY
or
INTELLIGENCE SUMMARY.
(*Erase heading not required.*)

Instructions regarding War Diaries and Intelligence Summaries are contained in F. S. Regs., Part II. and the Staff Manual respectively. Title pages will be prepared in manuscript.

Army Form C. 2118.

74

Place	Date	Hour	Summary of Events and Information	Remarks and references to Appendices
	Sept 23rd	7 0	Visited Lines of Shrop L I Transport	
		9 30	Inspected 76th Bde R F A horse lines & Bde Ammn Col. which took till 4 p m	
		4 30	Visited Mob Vety Sect to see man under arrest	
		9 0	Office	
			Owing to shortage of Green fodder — am advising local purchase of oat Straw for Chaff to make up the increased portion of hay ration.	
			The subject of clipping for the winter is now being considered, & a letter from the Corps has come round saying that as a general rule clipping will be forbidden — Divisional Commanders to give permission for ~~the~~ clipping in special cases	
			My recommendation — that Trace high clipping will depend upon the amount of work horses are required to do, & it is the only form of clipping that should be allowed apart from Mange & Veterinary reasons. I advise very strict orders being issued against clipping of any horses leg below the elbow or stifle.	WB

1577 Wt. W10791/1773 500,000 1/15 D. D. & L. A.D.S.S./Forms/C. 2118.

67

WAR DIARY
or
INTELLIGENCE SUMMARY.
(Erase heading not required.)

Army Form C. 2118.

75

Instructions regarding War Diaries and Intelligence Summaries are contained in F. S. Regs., Part II. and the Staff Manual respectively. Title pages will be prepared in manuscript.

Place	Date	Hour	Summary of Events and Information	Remarks and references to Appendices
	Sept 24th		Motored to advance Remount Section to choose horses	
		3 30	Usual meeting of A.D.s	
			Rain fell during last night & during to day. All arrangements appear ready for an attack on a big scale	
	25th	9 a	Visited Mob Vety Section Rain fell all day Attack which started at 4 a m continued through the day and is in conjunction with the attack all along the front which is to be the [illegible] effort for advance on the western front	
				[illegible initials]

Instructions regarding War Diaries and Intelligence Summaries are contained in F. S. Regs., Part II. and the Staff Manual respectively. Title pages will be prepared in manuscript.

68

WAR DIARY
or
INTELLIGENCE SUMMARY.
(Erase heading not required.)

Army Form C. 2118.

76

Place	Date	Hour	Summary of Events and Information	Remarks and references to Appendices
	Sept 26	a.m.	Visited 41st 42 & 43rd Head Quarters of Brigade Transports. All second line Transport drawn ready in case of a move.	
		3 p.m.	D.D.V.S. 3rd Army came to see me. A clear bright day with strong sun.	
	27th		Inspected 41st & 42nd Fd Ambulances. Animals in good condition.	
	28		Inspected 43rd Fd Ambulance. Animals in fair condition. Weather suddenly turned cold with North wind.	
	29		Rain all day & cold wind. All the standings for horses flooded 4 inches deep in mud like water.	WB

69

Instructions regarding War Diaries and Intelligence Summaries are contained in F. S. Regs., Part II. and the Staff Manual respectively. Title pages will be prepared in manuscript.

WAR DIARY
or
INTELLIGENCE SUMMARY.
(Erase heading not required.)

Army Form C. 2118.

77

Place	Date	Hour	Summary of Events and Information	Remarks and references to Appendices
	Sept 30th		Visited V.O's except Lt Steele.	
			I notice in War Establishments New Army (2) other Ranks laid down with V.O's in R F A Brigades & Div Train.	
			Application sent to D.D.V.S. to ask if these are supplied by A.V.C.	
		2 30	Attack made by 3rd Division on our right.	
		8 0	not successful	
				GBB

Instructions regarding War Diaries and Intelligence Summaries are contained in F. S. Regs., Part II. and the Staff Manual respectively. Title pages will be prepared in manuscript.

70

WAR DIARY
or
INTELLIGENCE SUMMARY.

(Erase heading not required.)

Army Form C. 2118.

78

Place	Date	Hour	Summary of Events and Information	Remarks and references to Appendices
	October 1st		Inspected 61 62 & 89th Companies RE. Animals in good condition. Good winter standings made. The usual meeting of V.O.	
	2nd		Inspected No 1 Divisional Signal Company. Animals well done, winter standings made. An excellent Sergeant in charge of animals. Very cold night with frost. Clear fine day with hot sun	
	3rd		Sunday. Heavy rain fell	
	4th		Nights are becoming ~~[illegible]~~ more like winter nights. It is dark at 5.30 & the nights are cold. Units are asking for rugs for animals & for men. Usual meeting of V.O. at which DDVS Col Wilson arrived.	

SBB

1577 Wt. W10791/1773 500,000 1/15 D. D. & L. A.D.S.S./Forms/C. 2118.

Instructions regarding War Diaries and Intelligence Summaries are contained in F. S. Regs., Part II. and the Staff Manual respectively. Title Pages will be prepared in manuscript.

71

WAR DIARY
or
INTELLIGENCE SUMMARY
(Erase heading not required.)

Army Form C. 2118

79

Place	Date	Hour	Summary of Events and Information	Remarks and references to Appendices
	Octr 9th		Inspected 41st Inf Bde Transport Lines & furnished report to Brigade Commander.	
			Called for a Return ~~from~~ of units in possession of Chaff Cutters – units having the use of Chaff cutters belonging to neighbouring units & those have no use of Chaff cutters.	
	11th		Inspected 42nd Inf Bde Transport & reported. This Transport is in perfect condition & very well run indeed. Horse Lines & Huts for men are being made vigourously by the units of the Division.	
			Fine dry weather.	
	12th		Inspected 43rd Inf Bde Transport & reported animals on the whole in good condition. Not enough interest taken in producing bulk of food for Heavy draught horses. Im..an	EBP

1875 Wt. W593/826 1,000,000 4/15 J.B.C. & A. A.D.S.S./Forms/C. 2118.

72

Instructions regarding War Diaries and Intelligence Summaries are contained in F. S. Regs., Part II. and the Staff Manual respectively. Title Pages will be prepared in manuscript.

WAR DIARY
or
INTELLIGENCE SUMMARY
(Erase heading not required.)

Army Form C. 2118

80

Place	Date	Hour	Summary of Events and Information	Remarks and references to Appendices
			Cont to done.	
-	15th		Inspected with DDVS 2nd Army, 47th Bde RFA & 48th Bde R.F.A.	
	16th		Visited Mob Vety Sect with reference to treatment of men for the winter. Decided that with the Barn of the farm which is at their disposal no huts are required. Applied for 5 tents for the men to sleep in when the weather is dry. This is the wish of the men themselves. Shoes (horse) frost for Coy are arriving from the Base preparatory to frosty weather. Shortage of Veterinary medicines being felt slightly. No perchloride of Mercury in store!	WRB

1875 Wt. W593/826 1,000,000 4/15 J.B.C. & A. A.D.S.S./Forms/C. 2118.

73

Army Form C. 2118

81

WAR DIARY
or
INTELLIGENCE SUMMARY
(Erase heading not required.)

Instructions regarding War Diaries and Intelligence Summaries are contained in F. S. Regs., Part II. and the Staff Manual respectively. Title Pages will be prepared in manuscript.

Place	Date	Hour	Summary of Events and Information	Remarks and references to Appendices
	Oct 17th		Up to quite lately, the difficulty of obtaining wood for building purposes was well marked. Now there is a plentiful supply & units are all erecting stabling and huts for the men but it is late in the season. Weather remains dry but is getting cold.	
	22nd		Usual meeting of V.O.s. Discussed the use & abuse of Mob Vety Section with Division. Recommended Lt Laurie for Command of a Section in answer to offer of appointment from D.D.V.S. 2nd Army	
	23rd		Inspected 48 Bde R.F.A. forge which the farriers have done so well in constructing. They have erected good workable forges suitable for making shoes in, with powerful bellows & clearly arranged a blast. They also have produced fuel e.g. [illegible] from somewhere.	[illegible]

1875 Wt. W593/826 1,000,000 4/15 J.B.C. & A. A.D.S.S./Forms/C. 2118.

Army Form C. 2118

82

WAR DIARY
or
INTELLIGENCE SUMMARY

74

(Erase heading not required.)

Instructions regarding War Diaries and Intelligence Summaries are contained in F. S. Regs., Part II. and the Staff Manual respectively. Title Pages will be prepared in manuscript.

Place	Date	Hour	Summary of Events and Information	Remarks and references to Appendices
Rt	24th		The question of a Float for the use of Mob Vety Sect. still present[s] some difficulty in that when it is wanted the owner himself has it in use or has lent it to somebody else. An old Float has lately been found at Ypres and with the aid of the Corps workshop who are putting a new wheel & new floor, will become a useful addition to the Section as long as we continue under this form of warfare in which a Mobile Section really becomes an advanced Veterinary Section in its function.	Y 736 DDVS 2nd Army
	25th		Visited 49th Bde RFA whose horse lines are the most advanced of the Division. It was not thought that they would remain in their present position for the winter until within the last few days so they had not done anything towards laying down lines & overhead covering etc. Now they [are]	WBB

1875 Wt. W593/826 1,000,000 4/15 J.B.C. & A. A.D.S.S./Forms/C. 2118.

75

WAR DIARY
or
INTELLIGENCE SUMMARY
(Erase heading not required.)

Army Form C. 2118

83

Instructions regarding War Diaries and Intelligence Summaries are contained in F. S. Regs., Part II. and the Staff Manual respectively. Title Pages will be prepared in manuscript.

Place	Date	Hour	Summary of Events and Information	Remarks and references to Appendices
			has begun to fall daily and material in the form of bricks etc is very difficult to get. The result is that Horses are standing up to their hocks in mud. It will be a very difficult matter to get these made at all unless a further dry period sets in.	
			All the officers & personnel of Divisional Head Quarters have been in billets up to now. During the last fortnight we have built mud huts or wood huts individually.	
	Oct 30th		Rain has continued to fall daily but the thermometer keeps moderately high. There has been no frost up to the present.	
			Orders received for Lt Cowan to join the Division to take over Lt Lawne's duties, the latter to report to 24th Division to take over Mob Vety Section. 24th Division is at RENINGHELST only [illegible] miles from here.	WB

1875 Wt. W593/826 1,000,000 4/15 J.B.C. & A. A.D.S.S./Forms/C. 2118.

76

Army Form C. 2118

Instructions regarding War Diaries and Intelligence Summaries are contained in F. S. Regs., Part II. and the Staff Manual respectively. Title Pages will be prepared in manuscript.

WAR DIARY
or
INTELLIGENCE SUMMARY
(Erase heading not required.)

84

Place	Date	Hour	Summary of Events and Information	Remarks and references to Appendices
	Oct 31st		Horse rugs for the Division have arrived from the Base. Artillery bombardment of these back areas goes on daily & nightly & it is noticeable that a big percentage of the percussion shells do not burst in the soft ground. Slight loss of animals however continues from shell fire amongst transport. a	[illegible]

1875 Wt. W593/826 1,000,000 4/15 J.B.C. & A. A.D.S.S./Forms/C. 2118.

A.D.M.S. 14th Division

Vol: 2

121
7931

a.w.d.

Original

<u>CONFIDENTIAL</u>.

WAR DIARY

OF

MAJOR E. B. BARTLETT, A. V. C.

A.D.V.S. 14TH (LIGHT) DIVISION.

from November 1st 1915 to December 31st 1915.

==========

Original

Instructions regarding War Diaries and Intelligence Summaries are contained in F. S. Regs., Part II. and the Staff Manual respectively. Title Pages will be prepared in manuscript.

WAR DIARY
or
~~INTELLIGENCE SUMMARY~~
(Erase heading not required.)

Army Form C. 2118

Place	Date	Hour	Summary of Events and Information	Remarks and references to Appendices
	Nov 1st		Lieut. A. Cowan reports arrival from No 12 Vety Hospital to replace Lieut Laurie proceeding to 24th Division to take over charge of Mob. Vety Section. Rain fell most of the day & night	BB
	2nd		Lieut Laurie reports departure. Rain fell most of the day & night. All camps thoroughly sodden & roads in bad order. Collection of 4 animals to be cast for vice, inspected & cast by D D R 2nd Army.	BB

1875 Wt. W593/826 1,000,000 4/15 J.B.C. & A. A.D.S.S./Forms/C. 2118.

Original

Instructions regarding War Diaries and Intelligence Summaries are contained in F. S. Regs., Part II. and the Staff Manual respectively. Title Pages will be prepared in manuscript.

WAR DIARY

or

~~INTELLIGENCE SUMMARY~~

(Erase heading not required.)

Army Form C. 2118.

Place	Date	Hour	Summary of Events and Information	Remarks and references to Appendices
	Nov 3rd		Wrote to DDR to ask if there is any ruling as to what may be classed as "Horses heavy" in the Army, outside Shires & Clydesdales. There are many horses in our R.F.A. Brigades & Ammn Cols that though shown in establishments as L.D. are in reality Heavy horses & should be granted the allowance of 15 lbs Corn & 15 lbs Hay as shown in orders.	BB G.R.O. 1235
			The Division is now out of the Trenches, ~~the Guns being~~ and out of the firing line, for a period of rest after continually holding the Salient since the middle of June.	
			The Infantry Brigades in the Support Camps remain where they are & ~~the~~ ~~up~~ while the Brigade from the Trenches moves back to area west of WATOU.	
			Guns of the RFA Brigades come back to the wagon lines.	
			From the point of view of horses this move makes very little difference. When an Infantry Battalion is in the Trenches – its	

Original

Instructions regarding War Diaries and Intelligence Summaries are contained in F. S. Regs., Part II. and the Staff Manual respectively. Title Pages will be prepared in manuscript.

WAR DIARY

~~or~~

~~INTELLIGENCE~~ SUMMARY

(Erase heading not required.)

Army Form C. 2118.

Place	Date	Hour	Summary of Events and Information	Remarks and references to Appendices
			Transport is kept back about 4 miles in the vicinity of the Support Battalions & when those battalions come back from the trenches – the transport (1st Line) joins it wherever it may go. Now during the winter the leading consideration is to have a ~~set~~ settled position for every unit to return to, & settled wagon-lines for every Battery of Artillery horses so that every unit may reap the benefit of its own labour in shelters etc for men & horses. The Corps Commander has given great consideration to this matter.	
			Excellent work has been done by many units of the Division in making shelters for horses.	
			Shelters are made chiefly with Hoppoles as the main supports. Roofs are either straw covered with tarred sacks or Sheets of Iron taken from Ypres or other ruined villages, or Corrugated iron supplied by R.E., or	WB

1875 Wt. W593/826 1,000,000 4/15 J.B.C. & A. A.D.S.S./Forms/C. 2118.

Original

Instructions regarding War Diaries and Intelligence Summaries are contained in F. S. Regs., Part II. and the Staff Manual respectively. Title Pages will be prepared in manuscript.

WAR DIARY
or
~~INTELLIGENCE SUMMARY~~
(Erase heading not required.)

Army Form C. 2118.

Place	Date	Hour	Summary of Events and Information	Remarks and references to Appendices
			wire netting with a covering of canvas or tarred felt; in some cases tiles have been taken from ruined houses & set up & in others biscuit tins have been flattened out & nailed to form a roof. Every support pole within reach of horses has to be well surrounded by wire, taken from trusses of hay etc to protect the poles from being eaten. Shelters are only allowed to be put up near the hedges or against permanent buildings such as farm buildings. The back & sides of shelters are made of the same materials as the roofs & in some cases ingenious screens have been made of wooden frames about 10 ft long & 6 ft high with wire netting nailed both sides of the frame, the space being filled with good straw. These screens with cross pieces at the foot can be moved to whichever side the wind blows from.	WB

1875 Wt. W593/826 1,000,000 4/15 J.B.C. & A. A.D.S.S./Forms/C. 2118.

Original

Instructions regarding War Diaries and Intelligence Summaries are contained in F. S. Regs., Part II. and the Staff Manual respectively. Title Pages will be prepared in manuscript.

WAR DIARY
or
INTELLIGENCE SUMMARY
(Erase heading not required.)

Army Form C. 2118

Place	Date	Hour	Summary of Events and Information	Remarks and references to Appendices
			The floors or standings vary to a great extent according to the material obtainable. Some of the best are made of regular stone sets from Ypres as used on the pavé roads. but in most cases the bricks from the principal part. Bricks are either laid regularly (whole bricks) or more commonly put down as brick rubble, beaten in to the ground with or without cement. Slag from coal mines, as used on the railways has been used as a foundation in some of the best shelters, but the difficulty in obtaining building materials has been colossal & has depended upon individual energy, foresight and opportunity.	

HBB

1875 Wt. W593/826 1,000,000 4/15 J.B.C. & A. A.D.S.S./Forms/C. 2118.

Original

Instructions regarding War Diaries and Intelligence Summaries are contained in F. S. Regs., Part II. and the Staff Manual respectively. Title Pages will be prepared in manuscript.

WAR DIARY
or
~~INTELLIGENCE SUMMARY~~
(Erase heading not required.)

Army Form C. 2118.

Place	Date	Hour	Summary of Events and Information	Remarks and references to Appendices
	Nov 13		Inspected 62 Coy RE. Horses & mules in good Condition	
	" 14		Inspected 89 Fd Coy RE Animals in good Condition & well done. These units have excellent standings & shelters for their animals & have been in the same position for 4 months. Their opportunities for making good standings etc have been much better than the Infantry Transport & some of the Brigade Amm Column which have been continually moved from one ground to another.	GBB

1875 Wt. W593/826 1,000,000 4/15 J.B.C. & A. A.D.S.S./Forms/C. 2118.

Original

Instructions regarding War Diaries and Intelligence Summaries are contained in F. S. Regs., Part II. and the Staff Manual respectively. Title Pages will be prepared in manuscript.

WAR DIARY
or
~~INTELLIGENCE SUMMARY~~
(Erase heading not required.)

Army Form C. 2118.

Place	Date	Hour	Summary of Events and Information	Remarks and references to Appendices
	Nov. 15		Inspected Div Signal Company on parade. Horses well done. Rumours of the Division being for Servia are current.	
	16		Inspected 61 Coy RE. Horses in good condition & well done.	
				WB

1875 Wt. W593/826 1,000,000 4/15 J.B.C. & A. A.D.S.S./Forms/C. 2118.

Original

Instructions regarding War Diaries and Intelligence Summaries are contained in F. S. Regs., Part II. and the Staff Manual respectively. Title Pages will be prepared in manuscript.

WAR DIARY
or
INTELLIGENCE SUMMARY
(Erase heading not required.)

Army Form C. 2118.

Place	Date	Hour	Summary of Events and Information	Remarks and references to Appendices
	Nov 17th		Inspected 46th Bde R.F.A. four batteries near WATOU. Condition of animals good. No clipping has been done. Oat straw is being obtained locally & in lieu of the 2 lbs of hay under-drawn from Supplies.	
	Nov 18th		Inspected 26 Mob Vety Sect in marching order. DDVS 2nd Army was present, (not by appointment) & complimented Lt Weir on the turn out which was very good.	
	19th		The Division returns to the Trenches.	
				RB

1875 Wt. W593/826 1,000,000 4/15 J.B.C. & A. A.D.S.S./Forms/C. 2118.

Original

Instructions regarding War Diaries and Intelligence Summaries are contained in F. S. Regs., Part II. and the Staff Manual respectively. Title Pages will be prepared in manuscript.

WAR DIARY

or

~~INTELLIGENCE SUMMARY~~

(Erase heading not required.)

Army Form C. 2118.

Place	Date	Hour	Summary of Events and Information	Remarks and references to Appendices
	Nov 30th		I have carried out during the month the usual inspection of units & drawn attention to all deficiencies or improvements that may be made to the best of my ability. The conditions under which the work has to be carried out are about the limit & are too well known to be worth trying to describe. All the units of the Division entitled to A.V.C. Sergeants have been supplied with them up to date, i.e. all units which have not the old style F.Q.M.S. or Farrier Sergeant.	

SBB

1875 Wt. W593/826 1,000,000 4/15 J.B.C. & A. A.D.S.S./Forms/C. 2118.

Original

Instructions regarding War Diaries and Intelligence Summaries are contained in F. S. Regs., Part II. and the Staff Manual respectively. Title Pages will be prepared in manuscript.

WAR DIARY
or
INTELLIGENCE SUMMARY

(Erase heading not required.)

Army Form C. 2118

Place	Date	Hour	Summary of Events and Information	Remarks and references to Appendices
December	30th		At the beginning of the month there were rumours that the 14th Division would shortly be moving out of Belgium. From 3rd to 10th all the horses of the Division were tested with mallein by the intradermal palpebral method. The conditions for carrying out any such test are not ideal. Mud up to ones knees, hard rain, cold, & daylight only lasting from 8.30 till 4 pm. Some little assistance was given by order of D.D.V.S. 2nd Army with two officers from neighbouring Divisions and 5000 animals were tested & four reactors destroyed; nodules being found in the lungs of each animal destroyed. From 12th to 18th All Heavy Draught animals of the Div. were exchanged with 49th Division for double the number of Light Draught. Warm clothing Smoke Helmets etc	WB

1875 Wt. W593/826 1,000,000 4/15 J.B.C. & A. A.D.S.S./Forms/C. 2118.

Original

Instructions regarding War Diaries and Intelligence Summaries are contained in F. S. Regs., Part II. and the Staff Manual respectively. Title Pages will be prepared in manuscript.

WAR DIARY
or
INTELLIGENCE SUMMARY
(Erase heading not required.)

Army Form C. 2118.

Place	Date	Hour	Summary of Events and Information	Remarks and references to Appendices
			were handed back through Ordnance Stores & precedence given to 14th Div with all equipment required from the Base up to Dec 25th when orders of March by rail & road were all issued & the Division was to move on morning of 26th. On the night of 25th orders were received from 2nd Army to cancel the whole move.	
	Dec 23rd		Sergeants of A.V.C. posted to the Division to complete every Battery of Artillery, B.A.C.s & Sections of D.A.C. and Infantry Brigades	
	31st		The usual inspections have been carried out as opportunity has arrived.	WB

1875 Wt. W593/826 1,000,000 4/15 J.B.C. & A. A.D.S.S./Forms/C. 2118.

NOMINAL ROLL OF OFFICERS N.C.Os AND MEN, ARMY VETERINARY CORPS.

14TH (LIGHT) DIVISION.

Major E.B.Bartlett.,	A.D.V.S.
Lieut G.S.Thornewill.,	V.O. i/c 41st Brigade Group.
Liwut A.Cowan.,	V.O. i/c 42nd do do
Lieut A.V.Meeke.,	V.O. i/c 43rd do do
Lieut J.O'Carroll.,	V.O. i/c 49th Brigade R.F.A.
Lieut L.L.Steele.,	V.O. i/c 14th Divisional Train.

No S4/061158 Private Titchener.A.G., (A.S.C.) Clerk to A.D.V.S.

S.E. No 6202	Sergeant	Hall.W.,	attached	41st Infantry Brigade.
S.E. No 6533	do	Routley.A.W.H.,	attached	42nd Infantry Bde.
S.E. No 9376	do	Eden.H.	do	43rd Infantry Bde.
S.E. No 7390	do	Cox.H	do	D/46th Brigade R.F.A.
S.E. No ~~xxxx~~ 6432	do	Bones.H.C.	do	C/47th do do
S.E. No 6368	do	Carter.R.	do	D/47th do do
S.E. No 8028	do	Knott.S.	do	47th Bde Ammunition Clmn
S.E. No 3343	do	White.A.C.	do	A/48th Brigade R.F.A.
S.E. No 7560	do	Comer.E.W.	do	D/48th do do
S.E. No 7018	do	Threlkeld.W.A.J	do	48th Bde Ammunition Clmn
S.E. No 8096	do	Webb.E,	do	C/49th Brigade R.F.A.
S.E. No 8353	do	Smith.W.G.	do	D/49th do do
S.E. No 6489	do	Walford.O.L.	do	No 1 Sect: 14th D.A.C.
S.E. No 2407	do	Maddams.H.S.	do	No 2 do do
S.E. No 2278	do	Maddams.C.	do	No 3 do do

[signature] Major,
fa A.D.V.S.,
14 Div

NOMINAL ROLL OF THE 26TH MOBILE VETERINARY SECTION, 14TH (Lt) DIVISION.

Lieut: F.J.Weir., Officer Commanding.

	No 179	Sergeant	Campbell.A.
S.E.	No 3216	do	Roberts.R.L.
	No 699	Corporal	Lucas.R.
S.E.	No 4373	Farr: Sgt	Judd.J.F.
S.E.	No 4555	Private	Adams.W.
S.E.	No 4655	do	Ashworth.J.
	No 696	do	Bushby.W.
S.E.	No 1232	do	Barnes.W.
	No 674	do	Chantler.W.
S.E.	No 4622	do	Chilver.J.M.
S.E.	No 4595	do	Cureton.T.E.
	No 619	do	Franklin.H.
S.E.	No 6740	do	Haynes.H.R.
S.E.	No 5148	do	Hobbs.J.
S.E.	No 3047	do	Isgate.C.
S.E.	No 4593	do	Jackson.G.A.
	No 896	do	Kelly.P.
S.E.	No 4559	do	Lawson.D.
S.E.	No 7008	do	Lloyd.G.H.
S.E.	No 4558	do	Mitchell.W.B.
	No 691	do	Neal.F.
S.E.	No 4512	do	Raiker.W.
S.E.	No 2809	do	Smart.R.R.
S.E.	No 4808	do	Thompson.G.A.

No I/35168 Driver Noyes.G.)
No S.T./753 Driver Marshall.A.) A.S.C. Transport Drivers.

[signature] Major,
for A.D.V.S., 14 Div.

Instructions regarding War Diaries and Intelligence Summaries are contained in F. S. Regs., Part II. and the Staff Manual respectively. Title Pages will be prepared in manuscript.

WAR DIARY
or
INTELLIGENCE SUMMARY
(Erase heading not required.)

Army Form C. 2118

ADVS. 14th Div.

Place	Date	Hour	Summary of Events and Information	Remarks and references to Appendices
H 7 C 7.7 Sheet 28	January 1916		Last month the Division was prepared for a move to the East probably Egypt. Within 24 hours of the time fixed to begin the move, an order was issued Cancelling it. The Division has remained in the old area occupied since June 1915 up to the latter end of January. The Light Draught Horses taken over from 49th & 6th Divisions for the move have been re-exchanged & the Division is back on its old Establishment.	
			The difference in the Condition of the animals we have received, from the condition of those we handed over is remarkable & is the natural result of such an exchange. Such exchanges are very much to be avoided if possible.	RBB
			During the latter end of January the Division has taken over the area occupied formerly by the 49th Division	

1875 Wt. W593/826 1,000,000 4/15 J.B.C. & A. A.D.S.S./Forms/C. 2118.

Instructions regarding War Diaries and Intelligence Summaries are contained in F. S. Regs., Part II. and the Staff Manual respectively. Title Pages will be prepared in manuscript.

WAR DIARY
or
INTELLIGENCE SUMMARY
(Erase heading not required.)

Army Form C. 2118

ADVS 14th Div.

Place	Date	Hour	Summary of Events and Information	Remarks and references to Appendices
H.40.7.7 Sheet 28			This has meant moving into camps in many cases in worse condition than our old ones in which we had towards the end, erected stabling etc The weather has been mild on the whole — the wastage of animals has become abnormally large due to evacuation of debilitated animals after exchange. The roads over which the transport animals have to work are extremely bad — the wastage of animals being almost entirely confined to H.D. transport animals of the Train & Infantry transport. The supply of Veterinary stores from the Base has been well kept up on indents. The shoeing of animals has been moderately well done The supply of shoes, nosebags, hay nets etc has been good. The Hay Ration has been reduced from 10 lbs to 6 lbs	GBB

1875 Wt. W593/826 1,000,000 4/15 J.B.C. & A. A.D.S.S./Forms/C. 2118.

Instructions regarding War Diaries and Intelligence Summaries are contained in F. S. Regs., Part II. and the Staff Manual respectively. Title Pages will be prepared in manuscript.

WAR DIARY
or
INTELLIGENCE SUMMARY
(Erase heading not required.)

Army Form C. 2118

ADVS. 14th Div.

Place	Date	Hour	Summary of Events and Information	Remarks and references to Appendices
H4C4.4 Sheet 28			This is a great treat to the Heavy Draught horses and every endeavour has been made to add to the bulk of forage by purchase of oat straw & carrots from local farmers. The use of chaff cutters has been urged for all units.	
			G.B. Barton Major ADVS XIV Div.	GBB

1875 Wt. W593/826 1,000,000 4/15 J.B.C. & A. A.D.S.S./Forms/C. 2118.

A. D. V. S.
14th Div
Vol. 4.
Feb 1916

1916

Army Form C. 2118

WAR DIARY
or
INTELLIGENCE SUMMARY
(Erase heading not required.)

Instructions regarding War Diaries and Intelligence Summaries are contained in F. S. Regs., Part II. and the Staff Manual respectively. Title Pages will be prepared in manuscript.

A.D.V.S. 14 Division

Place	Date	Hour	Summary of Events and Information	Remarks and references to Appendices
	Feby 10th		The Division started to move from the YPRES Salient after nearly nine months of it, back one stage to district surrounding ESQUELLEBEC; the move was completed on the 15th by road.	
	14th		No 26 Mob. Vety Sect. moved from billet at WATOU to farm 2 kilometres due south of ESQUELLEBEC.	
	18th		The Division started to entrain from CASSELL and ESQELLEBEC stations for AMIENS. to take up billets N.W. of AMIENS around FLESSELLES as Div. Hd Quarters	
	22nd	10 a.m.	No 26 Mob. Vety Sect. entrained at CASSELL	
	23	4 a.m.	— do — took up billets at St. VAAST. in the village with the D.A.C. & moving under direct orders of C.R.A. The Division was to go into rest for three weeks in this area.	[signature]

1875 Wt. W593/826 1,000,000 4/15 J.B.C. & A. A.D.S.S./Forms/C. 2118.

Instructions regarding War Diaries and Intelligence Summaries are contained in F. S. Regs., Part II. and the Staff Manual respectively. Title Pages will be prepared in manuscript.

WAR DIARY
or
INTELLIGENCE SUMMARY
(Erase heading not required.)

Army Form C. 2118

A.D.V.S. 14 Division

Place	Date	Hour	Summary of Events and Information	Remarks and references to Appendices
	Feby 24th	11 pm	Orders received to move at once to area of DOULENS.	
	25		The Division moved to above area — snow having fallen through the night — but the roads easily workable.	
	26		No 26 Mob Vety Sect moved from St VAAST & billetted in DOULENS for the night.	
	26th		The Division moved from area of DOULENS to area Sus-St-LEGER. Hard frost through the night followed by heavy snowfall during the entire day made travelling very difficult & in many places on tops of hills impossible.	
	27th		Transport both horse & motor spent the day in getting to positions allotted for the previous day — snow still falling & in places where drifts have occurred it is as	[illegible signature]

Instructions regarding War Diaries and Intelligence Summaries are contained in F. S. Regs., Part II. and the Staff Manual respectively. Title Pages will be prepared in manuscript.

WAR DIARY
or
INTELLIGENCE SUMMARY
(Erase heading not required.)

Army Form C. 2118

A.D.V.S. 14 Division

Place	Date	Hour	Summary of Events and Information	Remarks and references to Appendices
			as much as six feet deep	
Feby	28th		Last night was again hard frost & during to day units have again spent the day in getting to positions allotted to them on the 26th.	
			The 26th Mob Vety Sect moved to BAYENCOURT.	
			Towards the latter end of today all roads have become workable	
	29th		Div H.Q. moved from Sus St LEGER to BARLY.	
			The thaw has set in & the roads have become very heavy & with the motor traffic have become very much broken up.	
			The soil is chalky in this district.	
			The XIV Division is part of the 6th Corps as it was at Ypres. but since arriving at AMIENS has come under 3rd Army.	W. Bartlett

1875 Wt. W593/826 1,000,000 4/15 J.B.C. & A. A.D.S.S./Forms/C. 2118.

Instructions regarding War Diaries and Intelligence Summaries are contained in F. S. Regs., Part II. and the Staff Manual respectively. Title Pages will be prepared in manuscript.

1916

WAR DIARY
or
~~INTELLIGENCE SUMMARY~~
(Erase heading not required.)

ADVS 14th Div.

Army Form C. 2118

Place	Date	Hour	Summary of Events and Information	Remarks and references to Appendices
March 1st			The Division is taking over a sector of the line from the French. The Villages handed over to the Division are — Part of ARRAS, DAINVILLE, BERNEVILLE, SIMONCOURT, WARLUS, WANQUETIN, FOSSEAUX, and HAUTVILLE, with ~~refilling~~ Railhead at SAULTY.	
			Owing to recent snowstorms and frost, the roads have become very much broken up & are only workable by horse transport. This entails very hard work upon draught horses. Refilling Point being Railhead — nine miles from many units.	
	2nd		26 M.V.S. moved from LIGNEREUIL to BARLY, temporarily allotted to us	
			B. Bartlett	

1875 Wt. W593/826 1,000,000 4/15 J.B.C. & A. A.D.S.S./Forms/C. 2118.

Instructions regarding War Diaries and Intelligence Summaries are contained in F. S. Regs., Part II. and the Staff Manual respectively. Title Pages will be prepared in manuscript.

WAR DIARY
or
~~INTELLIGENCE~~ SUMMARY
(Erase heading not required.)

Army Form C. 2118

Place	Date	Hour	Summary of Events and Information	Remarks and references to Appendices
March	3rd		Straw as an extra ration of forage is almost unobtainable in this district. but the full 10 lbs of hay is forthcoming from Supplies.	
			Mob Vety Sect. moved from BARLY to ~~H~~OSSEAUX.	
	15th		During march from Amiens some horses were left on line of march with inhabitants. The reporting of these cases by units was not satisfactory in spite of order issued on day previous to moving from Ypres district on the subject. Detachment of units, whose officers have not read Divisional orders, fail to give notice to Headquarters. We do so little moving about as a Division that no experience is gained at this.	

GB Bartlett

Instructions regarding War Diaries and Intelligence Summaries are contained in F. S. Regs., Part II. and the Staff Manual respectively. Title Pages will be prepared in manuscript.

WAR DIARY
or
INTELLIGENCE SUMMARY
(Erase heading not required.)

Army Form C. 2118

Place	Date	Hour	Summary of Events and Information	Remarks and references to Appendices
March	20th		Lieut COWAN resigned on completion of one years service & returned to ENGLAND to report to War Office.	
"	26th		Lieut CROWE joined to replace Lieut COWAN.	
"	30th		As far as possible, Veterinary officers are billetted in the different villages in which the Division is situated. There are seven villages and there is a V.O. in six of these, arranged as conveniently as possible according to units.	

G B Bartlett

Instructions regarding War Diaries and Intelligence Summaries are contained in F. S. Regs., Part II. and the Staff Manual respectively. Title Pages will be prepared in manuscript.

WAR DIARY
or
INTELLIGENCE SUMMARY
(Erase heading not required.)

Army Form C. 2118

Place	Date	Hour	Summary of Events and Information	Remarks and references to Appendices
March	30th		Special care has been taken to avoid putting animals into billets that have been occupied by French units affected with Contagious Diseases; by enquiries from the Local Maires. The water supply appears to be good. Each village has many good wells to the depth of about 40 feet and the animals from HAUTVILLE water at a good stream about 1 mile to the North of the Village.	
	31st		The usual inspections have been carried out daily by me when the weather has not been too bad & all the units have been seen once at least, but the month has been extremely rough & snow has fallen about 10 days during the month.	

G B Bartlett

1875 Wt. W593/826 1,000,000 4/15 J.B.C. & A. A.D.S.S./Forms/C. 2118.

Instructions regarding War Diaries and Intelligence Summaries are contained in F. S. Regs., Part II. and the Staff Manual respectively. Title Pages will be prepared in manuscript.

WAR DIARY
or
~~INTELLIGENCE SUMMARY~~
(Erase heading not required.)

Army Form C. 2118

Vol 6

A D V. S. 14th Division April.

Place	Date	Hour	Summary of Events and Information	Remarks and references to Appendices
	April		The usual inspections of animals have been carried out during the month & every unit has been inspected. The sick returns of Vety Officers are normal & contain as usual a great number of picked up nails. Special care is taken at Refilling point to have nails collected & buried but except in localised areas such as Refilling point there is not much to be done. The forage during the month has been on the whole good. Occasional bags of oats are mouldy but these are in most instances ~~no~~ replaced by good oats & the quantity made up at Refilling point on application being made. Two units were badly reported on for the condition of their	RB

1875 Wt. W593/826 1,000,000 4/15 J.B.C. & A. A.D.S.S./Forms/C. 2118.

Instructions regarding War Diaries and Intelligence Summaries are contained in F. S. Regs., Part II. and the Staff Manual respectively. Title pages will be prepared in manuscript.

WAR DIARY
or
INTELLIGENCE SUMMARY.
(Erase heading not required.)

April

Army Form C. 2118.

Place	Date	Hour	Summary of Events and Information	Remarks and references to Appendices
	April		their animals No 1 Section D.A.C and 7th KRR first line transport. These two units have been consistently bad for some time.	
			Remounts received from the Base (106) were good.	
			During the month there has been a great change for the better in the weather. The ground has dried up & animals can be picketted in the open & do well. Officers & men both take more interest in their animals when it is possible to get them clean. For months past the animals have been standing up to their hocks in mud & caked with mud in their winter coats. Unless O.C. units are good horsemasters they lose interest in their animals under such conditions.	
			Strict orders are issued as to the pace at which animals are to be ridden & driven ~~under~~ except under urgent conditions but there is still too much fast riding & driving	BB

T2134. Wt. W708—776. 500000. 4/15. Sir J. C. & S.

Instructions regarding War Diaries and Intelligence Summaries are contained in F. S. Regs., Part II. and the Staff Manual respectively. Title pages will be prepared in manuscript.

WAR DIARY
or
INTELLIGENCE SUMMARY.
(Erase heading not required.)

Army Form C. 2118.

April

Place	Date	Hour	Summary of Events and Information	Remarks and references to Appendices
	April		~~driving~~ going on. Officers are perhaps the biggest offenders & generally from ignorance. The supply of medicine & instruments indented for has been good except in the case of a Microscope. To me – the most impressive fact of the month is – how well animals when well done, can be kept on 12 lbs of oats & 10 lbs of hay. I refer particularly to big light draught gun horses. Mules received during the month as remounts have been particularly good. For the first time Calcium Sulphide for the Division has been made at the Mob Vety Section & a continual supply is kept up to units freshly made. A. G.S. limbered wagon was returned from the Mob Vety Section to Abbeville & a two-wheeled RSPCA float drawn to replace it – the float should do well in this	BB

Instructions regarding War Diaries and Intelligence Summaries are contained in F. S. Regs., Part II. and the Staff Manual respectively. Title pages will be prepared in manuscript.

WAR DIARY
or
INTELLIGENCE SUMMARY.
(Erase heading not required.)

April

Army Form C. 2118.

Place	Date	Hour	Summary of Events and Information	Remarks and references to Appendices
			His part of the line where roads are good.	
	25th		Orders have come from D.G. A.V.S. that all units of artillery are to have A.V.C. Sergeants whether they have old style of farriers or not.	
	28th		Letter from D.V.S. lays down the limit of Veterinary equipment allowed to units	D.V.S. 6/261/16 27.4.16
			Officers Vety Chests are to be brought on the account of A.D.V.S of Divisions & removed from the accounts of units.	
			Correspondence appears to be on the increase in this branch as well as in most others of the Army. It has increased since joining the 3rd Army with no advantage to the running of the work.	

[illegible signature]

T2134. Wt. W708—776. 500000. 4/15. Sir J. C. & S.

ADVS. 14.D.

Army Form C. 2118.

Vol 7

Instructions regarding War Diaries and Intelligence Summaries are contained in F. S. Regs., Part II. and the Staff Manual respectively. Title pages will be prepared in manuscript.

WAR DIARY
or
~~INTELLIGENCE SUMMARY.~~
(Erase heading not required.)

A D V S   14th Division   MAY.

Place	Date	Hour	Summary of Events and Information	Remarks and references to Appendices
MAY	1st		Inspected 42nd 43 & 44th Fd Ambulances. Reported badly on 43rd section at WANQUETIN. Bad A.S.C. Sergeant in charge.	
"	2nd		Inspected Liverpool Transport DAINVILLE. – Not well enough done considering the time there is spent in camp. Reported.	
"	3rd		Inspected 46 B.A.C. Not cooking sufficiently well done. Reported & taken out of stables into the open.	
			B/46 Also showing neglect. Reported to O.C. Brigade.	
	4th		Two Sarcoptic Mange found in No 3 Section D.A.C. – the V.O. is on leave	
			Nine others sent to Base with the two affected animals.	
	5th		Capt Steele V.O. to D.A.C & Train returns from leave.	
			Capt O Carroll goes on leave.	
			Mange found in C/49 Battery R.F.A. also No 1 Coy Train.	
			Nine animals from the Train & Six from C/49 evacuated.	
	8th		Inspected Div Cavalry D.L.O.Y. on their departure from the Division for good. Their condition was good for the first time.	[signature]

T2134. Wt. W708–776. 500000. 4/15. Sir J. C. & S.

Instructions regarding War Diaries and Intelligence Summaries are contained in F. S. Regs., Part II. and the Staff Manual respectively. Title pages will be prepared in manuscript.

WAR DIARY
or
INTELLIGENCE SUMMARY.
(Erase heading not required.)

Army Form C. 2118.

ADVS 14th Div — MAY

Place	Date	Hour	Summary of Events and Information	Remarks and references to Appendices
MAY.	8th		Inspect 7 KRR Transport. Cannot report well on them yet. Am trying to get Transport Officer and Sergeant changed. Visited Mob. Section	
	9th		Remounts arrive at railhead TINQUES.	
			Car supplied to me by OC. Train to meet Remounts.	
	10.		Inspected 1 Coy Train 3 Sect DAC C/49 units with mange. Sent away 40 horses from 3 Sect DAC. as suspicious. These animals have been done extremely badly right through the winter up to the present & the officer in charge is responsible for the condition of the horses of C/49.	
			The three units with mange stand out by themselves as the units badly done during the winter.	
	13th		Inspected 46 BAC & find remarkable improvement in animals.	
			Inspected 47 BAC. Condition Good	
	14th		Inspected 48 BAC Condition Very Good & this unit is always good owing to the O.C. Capt Alexander.	[signature]

T2134. Wt. W708—776. 500000. 4/15. Sir J. C. & S.

Instructions regarding War Diaries and Intelligence Summaries are contained in F. S. Regs., Part II. and the Staff Manual respectively. Title pages will be prepared in manuscript.

WAR DIARY
or
INTELLIGENCE SUMMARY.
(Erase heading not required.)

Army Form C. 2118.

A D V S 14th Div — MAY.

Place	Date	Hour	Summary of Events and Information	Remarks and references to Appendices
MAY.	14		Inspected 49 B A C. Condition Good.	
-	16		Inspected C R E. horses Poor	
			- 61 Coy RE The very best.	
			- 62 Coy - Fairly well done,	
			- 89. Coy - Very Good.	
			Visited No 1 Coy Train No 3 Section D A C C/49 RFA	
	17th		Visited No 1 Coy Train No 3 Section D A C C/49 RFA	
	18th		Mange parasite found in H D of 1/1 Highland Div Heavy Artillery but the animal has been isolated since his arrival from the Base. so does not affect the unit. No in contacts or other horses sent away.	
	19th		Capt Wein 26 M.V.S. admitted to Hospital with injury to arm. Lieut Crowe who is i/c 47 Bde R F A in that district takes charge of M V S.	[illegible]
	20		D D V S 3rd Army inspects animals of D A C.	
	21.		Inspected C/283 Bde RFA. 56th Div.	

T2134. Wt. W708—776. 500000. 4/15. Sir J. C. & S.

Instructions regarding War Diaries and Intelligence Summaries are contained in F. S. Regs., Part II. and the Staff Manual respectively. Title pages will be prepared in manuscript.

Army Form C. 2118.

WAR DIARY
or
INTELLIGENCE SUMMARY.
(Erase heading not required.)

ADVS. 14th Div. MAY. 1916

Place	Date	Hour	Summary of Events and Information	Remarks and references to Appendices
MAY	21st		Inspected 47 Bde RFA. Good.	
	22		Inspected 48 Bde - Good	
	23		Surplus horses in D.A.C., after doing away with BACs & increasing establishment of DAC, shown to 51st Div. but were not accepted. Eleven only were taken.	
	24		Inspected 41st Inf Bde Transport except 7th KRR. These units including Machine Gun Coy were good. Visited No 1 Coy Train No 3 Sect DAC. & C/49 RFA	
	25		Inspected 42nd Inf. Bde Transport & found them extremely good & very well turned out	
	26		Inspected 43 Inf Bde Transport & found them in competition with the 42 Inf Bde & looking extremely well turned out.	
	27		Pte Shea ASC arrives as clerk to replace AVC. Clerk who in his turn a month ago was sent to me because I was not allowed an ASC clerk.	[illegible]

Instructions regarding War Diaries and Intelligence Summaries are contained in F. S. Regs., Part II. and the Staff Manual respectively. Title pages will be prepared in manuscript.

WAR DIARY
or
INTELLIGENCE SUMMARY.

Army Form C. 2118.

A D V S. 14th Div. *(Erase heading not required.)* MAY.

Place	Date	Hour	Summary of Events and Information	Remarks and references to Appendices
May.	27th		Visited Mob Vety Sect. & took over charge of same from Lieut Crowe admitted to Hospital injured.	
			Took over charge of 47th Bde R F A. fr Lt Crowe.	
			Judged horses of 5th Div. Show.	
.	28th		Inspected 49th Bde R.F.A. Condition & general management much improved.	
.	29th		Visited M V S. paid personnel & prepared evacuation of horses.	
			Visited 47th Bde R F A.	
.	30th		Mob Vety Sect. & 47th Bde R.F.A.	
	31st		Visited Mob Vety Sect & 47th Bde R.F.A.	
			47th Bde R F A to be taken over by Capt O'Carroll.	
			During the month the fine weather & change of temperature has done a tremendous lot to improve the condition of both the horses & their surroundings. Animals have cast their coats. Picketting lines have become dry & animals & harness can be kept clean.	W B Bennett

T2134. Wt. W708—776. 500000. 4/15. Sir J. C. & S.

Instructions regarding War Diaries and Intelligence Summaries are contained in F. S. Regs., Part II. and the Staff Manual respectively. Title pages will be prepared in manuscript.

WAR DIARY
or
INTELLIGENCE SUMMARY.
(Erase heading not required.)

Army Form C. 2118.

ADVS 14th DW — MAY. 1916

Place	Date	Hour	Summary of Events and Information	Remarks and references to Appendices
			During the month the RA of the Division has been reorganised The B.A.C. of each RFA Brigade has been done away with & the D.A.C. raised from three Section to four sections one for each Brigade under the Colonel of DAC. Surplus horses have been returned to Abbeville. The changes in Veterinary Equipment of the Division have been carried out according to D.D.V.S Letter 6/261/16 27-4-16 There have been some cases of abdominal trouble in horses that would point to the food being cause. The work and surroundings being normal. I have reports of Alfalfa being the cause and this is being closely watched. Some trusses of Alfalfa have big quantities of Locusts embedded in them which also may be the cause. Alfalfa has been fed to horses for months together in previous days without ill effect. No Castor oil beans have been found in the oats up to now.	[signature]

T2134. Wt. W708—776. 500000. 4/15. Sir J. C. & S.

Army Form C. 2118.

Instructions regarding War Diaries and Intelligence Summaries are contained in F. S. Regs., Part II. and the Staff Manual respectively. Title pages will be prepared in manuscript.

WAR DIARY
or
INTELLIGENCE SUMMARY.
(Erase heading not required.)

A.D.V.S. 14th Div. MAY. 1916

Place	Date	Hour	Summary of Events and Information	Remarks and references to Appendices
			All the horses of the Division have been taken out of buildings except temporary buildings erected by the troops & are picketted in the open. The forage supply is good and supply of horse shoes nosebags etc has been well maintained. In connection with economy in horse shoes care is being taken to remove shoes & have them refitted to the opposite feet & the caulkings of heavy shoes are "knocked up" into bigger caulkings before being put on for use.	L. B. Barrett

T2134. Wt. W708—776. 500000. 4/15. Sir J. C. & S.

Warrant Officers, N

invited to notify to this Office

that the Address Book may be an u

desirous of communicating with a

address by enquiry from this Offi

The Common

Woolwich S.E.18.

June 1916

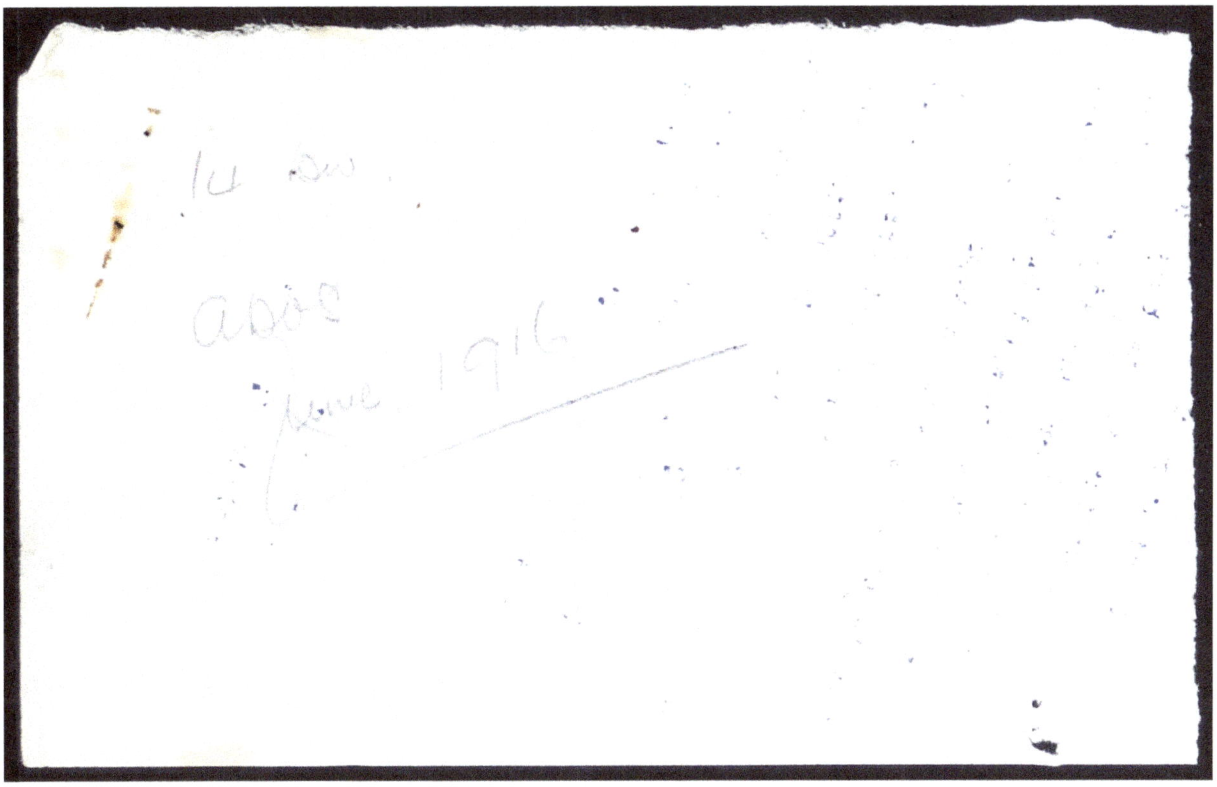

Instructions regarding War Diaries and Intelligence Summaries are contained in F. S. Regs., Part II. and the Staff Manual respectively. Title pages will be prepared in manuscript.

WAR DIARY
or
INTELLIGENCE SUMMARY.
(Erase heading not required.)

Army Form C. 2118.

ADVS 14th Div. June 1916 85

Place	Date	Hour	Summary of Events and Information	Remarks and references to Appendices
June	2nd		Captain Weir returned from Hospital & takes charge of 26 MVS	
"	16th		Lieut J L CLARK. TC arrived to replace Lieut Crowe sent to England sick.	
	29th		Capt Weir goes on leave. Mobile Section handed over to Lieut Clark whose units are in the same area as the Mob Vety Sect. The Division has remained in the same area during the month with a few minor changes of location of a few units. The usual inspection of all the units of the Division has been carried out by me during the month & the health of the animals is very good. With the warmer weather animals look well but there has been a considerable fall of rain regularly & the standings for horses in the open have not tended to help in the case of horses as one would wish to expect at this time of year. The presence of men and cost is a drawback	

T2134. Wt. W708—776. 500000. 4/15. Sir J. C. & S.

Instructions regarding War Diaries and Intelligence Summaries are contained in F. S. Regs., Part II. and the Staff Manual respectively. Title pages will be prepared in manuscript.

WAR DIARY
or
INTELLIGENCE SUMMARY.
(Erase heading not required.)

Army Form C. 2118.

ADVS 14th Div June 1916 86

Place	Date	Hour	Summary of Events and Information	Remarks and references to Appendices
			to the good appearance of horses in the open.	
			The sick list - A 2000 calls for no special remarks	
			except cases sent down as suspicious of Mange. In all	
			these cases no parasite has been found after careful	
			examination but as the animals show irritation of the skin	
			it is advisable to send them to the Base for dipping.	
			These cases all appear a class of under mange.	
			The Remount supply has been good and forage & stores	
			very good	
			Horses of Ammunition Column have been worked hard	
			during the month - others have not.	
			There has been a marked improvement in the turnouts	
			of units during the month - probably due to the proposal	
			to hold a Horse show in the near future	
			As regards Horses & turnouts the Division may be considered	[initials]
			very good.	

T2134. Wt. W708—776. 500000. 4/15. Sir J. C. & S.

Instructions regarding War Diaries and Intelligence Summaries are contained in F. S. Regs., Part II. and the Staff Manual respectively. Title pages will be prepared in manuscript.

WAR DIARY
or
INTELLIGENCE SUMMARY
(Erase heading not required.)

ADVS 14th Div June 1916

Army Form C. 2118.

85

Place	Date	Hour	Summary of Events and Information	Remarks and references to Appendices
June	2nd		Captain [illegible] returned from Hospital & takes charge of the MVS	
	16th		Lieut J L CLARK. TC arrived to replace Lieut [illegible] sent to England sick.	
	29th		Capt [illegible] goes on leave. Mobile Section handed over to Lieut Clark whose units are in the same area as the Mob Vety Sect. The Division has remained in the same area during the month with a few minor changes of location of a few units. The usual inspection of all the units of the Division has been carried out by me during the month & the health of the animals is very good. With the warmer weather animals look well but there has been a considerable fall off in [illegible] & the standing for horses in the open have not tended to keep up the care of horses [illegible] at this time of year.	[illegible]

WAR DIARY
or
INTELLIGENCE SUMMARY.
(Erase heading not required.)

Instructions regarding War Diaries and Intelligence Summaries are contained in F. S. Regs., Part II. and the Staff Manual respectively. Title pages will be prepared in manuscript.

Army Form C. 2118.

A.D.V.S. 11th Div. June 1916 86

Place	Date	Hour	Summary of Events and Information	Remarks and references to Appendices
			to the good appearance of horses in the open. The sick list A 2000 calls for no special remarks except cases sent down as suspicious of mange. In all these cases no parasite has been found after careful examination but as the animals show irritation of the skin it is advisable to send them to the base for dipping. These cases all appear a class of [illegible]. The Remount supply has been good and forage also very good Some of Ammunition Columns have been worked hard during the month — others have not. There has been a marked improvement in the turnouts of units during the month — probably due to the proposal to hold a Horse Show in the near future. As regards Horses & turnouts the Division may be considered very good	[illegible initials]

T2134. Wt. W708—776. 500000. 4/15. Sir J. C. & S.

Army Form C. 2118.

Instructions regarding War Diaries and Intelligence Summaries are contained in F. S. Regs., Part II. and the Staff Manual respectively. Title pages will be prepared in manuscript.

WAR DIARY
or
INTELLIGENCE SUMMARY.
(Erase heading not required.)

A.D.V.S. 14th Division July 1916

Place	Date	Hour	Summary of Events and Information	Remarks and references to Appendices
July	1st		Inspected 43rd Bde Inf Transport Visited Mob Vety Section Inspected RA spare riders, surplus due to Cycles being drawn (four per Battery) in lieu of horses. Those inspected were principally the poorest of the draught animals so they were sent back to units.	
	2nd		Visit Arras to see Civilian animals affected with mange & being treated Arrangement made to have buildings disinfected by the Divisional Sanitary Section.	
	3rd		Inspected No 1 Sect D.A.C. and visited the villages of WANQUETIN and DUISANS.	
	4th		Inspected Nos 2 and 3 Sections D.A.C.	

Instructions regarding War Diaries and Intelligence Summaries are contained in F. S. Regs., Part II. and the Staff Manual respectively. Title pages will be prepared in manuscript.

WAR DIARY
or
INTELLIGENCE SUMMARY.
(Erase heading not required.)

Army Form C. 2118.

A D V S 14th Division July 1916

Place	Date	Hour	Summary of Events and Information	Remarks and references to Appendices
July	14th		Returned from special leave. Inspected 41st Inf Bde Transport & reported badly to the 7th KRR upon the condition of the animals & recommended closer attention to details of stable management.	
	15th		Inspected No 4 Coy Train	
	16th		Visit Mob Vety Section Inspected Transport 8th Liverpool Regt Visit North Hants Yeomanry & arranging for Vety attendance.	
	17th		Inspected 48th Bde R F A lines Inspected No 1 Coy Div Train.	
	18th		Inspected 42nd Inf Bde Transport Reported necessity of a shoeing smith for Bde HQ Quarters	

T2134. Wt. W708—776. 500000. 4/15. Sir J. C. & S.

Instructions regarding War Diaries and Intelligence Summaries are contained in F. S. Regs., Part II. and the Staff Manual respectively. Title pages will be prepared in manuscript.

WAR DIARY
or
INTELLIGENCE SUMMARY.
(Erase heading not required.)

Army Form C. 2118.

ADVS 14th Divn July 1916

Place	Date	Hour	Summary of Events and Information	Remarks and references to Appendices
July	19th		Inspected 49th Bde R F A	
			Visited Mob Vety Section.	
			Received orders to take over No 10 Vety Hosp at the Base.	
	20th		Inspected 47th Bde R F A	
			Visited Northamptonshire Yeomanry & arranged to take over nine Riders as remounts for 14th Division	
			Visited Mob Vety Sect.	
			Indian Cavalry moved up to this area	
	21st		Vety Officers came to Hd Quarters with weekly returns	
			Inspect Horses RA Hd Quarters.	
			Issued circular memo to V.O.s re mange necessity for further vigilance & precautionary measures.	
	22nd		Visit 46th Bde R F A for inspection of horses but owing to misunderstanding units were out. Inspected lines & forage arrangements & horses.	
	23rd		Took over Remounts at MOBIGNY for the Division.	

T2134. Wt. W708—776. 500000. 4/15. Sir J. C. & S.

Instructions regarding War Diaries and Intelligence Summaries are contained in F. S. Regs., Part II. and the Staff Manual respectively. Title pages will be prepared in manuscript.

WAR DIARY
or
INTELLIGENCE SUMMARY.
(Erase heading not required.)

Army Form C. 2118.

ADVS 14th Div. July

Place	Date	Hour	Summary of Events and Information	Remarks and references to Appendices
July	24		Memo received from DDVS. 3rd Army reads — Ref V.O. allotted to Corps Headquarters & Corps H.A. please note that ~~these~~ under instructions from DVS these officers are not under the administration of ADVS but will be under them for supervision only — All returns & correspondence should be rendered to DDVS 3rd Army direct. They might be checked in your office. Inspected B/48 RFA & C/48 RFA both batteries in excellent condition & well done throughout.	
July	26		Took over from Major Bartlett who has now left the Division. Visited M.V.S.	
July	27		Visited M.V.S. Also saw A.D.V.S. XI Div. in charge of units in area.	
July	28		Inspected 43 Infy Bgde. K.O.Y.L.I. D.L.I. D.C.L.I. 89 Field Coy RE. 61 Field Coy RE No 1 Sect D.A.C. All animals were in very good condition. Found one case of mange in 43 Machine Gun Coy sent to 21 Div. M.V.S.	

T2134. Wt. W708—776. 500000. 4/15. Sir J. C. & S.

Instructions regarding War Diaries and Intelligence Summaries are contained in F. S. Regs., Part II. and the Staff Manual respectively. Title pages will be prepared in manuscript.

A.D.V.S.

WAR DIARY
or
INTELLIGENCE SUMMARY.
(Erase heading not required.)

Army Form C. 2118.

Place	Date	Hour	Summary of Events and Information	Remarks and references to Appendices
July	26		Took over from Major Bartlett who has now left the Division. Visited M.V.S.	
July	27		Visited M.V.S. Also saw A.D.V.S. XI Div. re charge of units in area.	
July	28		Inspected 43 Infy Bgde KOYLI DLI & CLI. 88 Field Coy RE. [illegible] Field Coy RE. [illegible] D.A.C. All animals were in very good condition. Found one case of Mange in [illegible] Machine Gun Coy sent to [illegible] M.V.S.	

Instructions regarding War Diaries and Intelligence Summaries are contained in F. S. Regs., Part II. and the Staff Manual respectively. Title pages will be prepared in manuscript.

WAR DIARY
or
INTELLIGENCE SUMMARY.
(Erase heading not required.)

ADVS 14th Div

Army Form C. 2118.

Place	Date	Hour	Summary of Events and Information	Remarks and references to Appendices
July	29		Inspected 14 Signal Coy R E Condition of animals very good. One case of mange sent to M.V.S. Shoeing of mules indifferent	
July	31		Div on move. Notice of horses left behind to be sent to [illegible] & all V.Os	

T2134. Wt. W708—776. 500000. 4/15. Sir J. C. & S.

CONFIDENTIAL

WAR DIARY

OF

A.D.V.S., 14TH (LIGHT) DIVISION.

August, 1916.

(Volume).

Instructions regarding War Diaries and Intelligence Summaries are contained in F. S. Regs., Part II. and the Staff Manual respectively. Title pages will be prepared in manuscript.

WAR DIARY

or

~~INTELLIGENCE SUMMARY.~~

(Erase heading not required.)

A.D.V.S. 14th Div

Army Form C. 2118.

Place	Date	Hour	Summary of Events and Information	Remarks and references to Appendices
Aug	1		Division on march.	
"	2		Inspected 9 K.R.R. 42 M.G.C. 3 Coy A.S.C. Ox & Bucks L.I. Condition good also shoeing	
"	3		Inspected 8 R.B. Very good. Visited D.A. 25 horses surplus ordered for inspection only 5 produced on arrival. One sent away sick (pneumonia)	
"	4		A.D.V.S. visited. Office all morning. Visited No 4 Coy 14 Div Train A.S.C. Found horses in good condition. Only two horses out of the four I wanted to see in. Called at D.L.I. Two animals there not suitable. One old & worn out recommended the T.O. to send in application for casting. Saw also K.O.Y.L.I. transport. Very good condition	
"	5		Went out again to farm where 4 Coy billet. The horse inspected mange and other debilitated. Sent both to M.V.S. Saw Capt Weir & made arrangements for evacuation.	
	6		Marched to RANNEVILLERS with divisional mounted troops less R.A. Billeted for night	
	7		Marched to BUIRE sur L'ANCRE. In camp.	
	8.		Visited Mob. Vety Section. Office. Remounts inspected. Visited M.V.S. again in afternoon to see about drugs available for issue. Also to see Capt Weir with regard to position of M.V.S	

Instructions regarding War Diaries and Intelligence Summaries are contained in F. S. Regs., Part II. and the Staff Manual respectively. Title pages will be prepared in manuscript.

WAR DIARY
or
INTELLIGENCE SUMMARY.
(Erase heading not required.)

A.D.V.S. 14 Divn

Army Form C. 2118.

Place	Date	Hour	Summary of Events and Information	Remarks and references to Appendices
Aug	9th		Remounts received. Distributed to various units who had indented for them. D.D.R. 4th Army was present. Animals arrived in very good condition	
	10th		Inspected 8 K.R.R. Condition good. Office in afternoon.	
	11th		Rode out and saw Divn Transport, RFA and D.A.C. in the morn. The horses seemed to be all in pretty good condition. Saw the Adjt. D.A.C. and had a talk re the last remounts. Office all afternoon. Checked V.O.s returns.	
	12th		Inspected one horse a charger 7 R.B. for suspected mange, sent him back to duty. Called and saw A.D.V.S. 17 Divn. Visited M.V.S.	
	13th		Moved to ALBERT. Bellevue Farm.	
	14th		Inspected 46 Bgde R.F.A. Saw A.B.C.D. batteries. Very good condition. Standings good, but somewhat spoilt by rain. Ground very slippery. Also inspected 47 Bgde RFA. Condition good. C battery have their horses too bunched together.	
	15th		Inspected 14th D.A.C. All sections looking very well.	
	16th		Inspected 48th Bgde RFA. Very good condition except A battery. Condition very fair however. Also 11th Kings Liverpool. Very good lot of horses. Conference at 2.30 pm. Lt Col Hunt D.D.V.S. Nothing much arrived at. Discussed mange & evacuations	

T2134. Wt. W708—776. 500000. 4/15. Sir J. C. & S.

Instructions regarding War Diaries and Intelligence Summaries are contained in F. S. Regs., Part II. and the Staff Manual respectively. Title pages will be prepared in manuscript.

WAR DIARY
or
INTELLIGENCE SUMMARY. 14th Div
(*Erase heading not required.*)

A.D.V.S

Army Form C. 2118.

Place	Date	Hour	Summary of Events and Information	Remarks and references to Appendices
Aug	17		Inspected 49th Bgde R.F.A. A. B & C batteries Condition fair. Inspected all Hd Qr Staff horses. Office	
	18		Inspected A. S. Corps Train 1.2.3 & 4 Coy. 1 Coy particularly good. 4 Coy horses not such a good class.	
			26 Mobile Vety Section in afternoon	
Aug	19		Inspected 8 R.B. 7 R. Brigade & 8th K.R.R.C. also Machine Gunners	
			Afternoon 89th Field Coy R.E.	
			26 Mobile Vety Section in afternoon.	
Aug	20		Office. and Visited D.A.C.	
Aug	21		Inspected 42 & 43 Infty Bgdes. Horses & mules good.	
	"		Inspected 61, 62 & 89 Field Coys R.E. 62 not very good.	
			V M Section in afternoon.	
	22		Inspected 26. V. M. Section. 17 M.V.S. having left. Place very dirty. Manure not burnt.	
	23		Remounts (19) arrived. Distributed to various units. Arranged for animals for inspection by D.D.R. to be sent to M.V.S.	
	24		Visited 43 Infty Bgde.	

Instructions regarding War Diaries and Intelligence Summaries are contained in F. S. Regs., Part II. and the Staff Manual respectively. Title pages will be prepared in manuscript.

WAR DIARY
or
INTELLIGENCE SUMMARY.
(Erase heading not required.)

A.D.V.S. 14 Div

Army Form C. 2118.

Place	Date	Hour	Summary of Events and Information	Remarks and references to Appendices
	25	Aug	Batch of remounts received on 9.8.16 having come from a depot where glanders has been discovered, made arrangements to test all of them.	
	26	Aug.	Inspected 42 43 & 44 Field Ambulances. The horses are in very good condition especially those in 42. They are rather a better class.	
			Visited M V Section.	
	27	Aug	Visited advanced post. Very few casualties have been taken in.	
	28	Aug	Visited M. Vety Sect. Office	
	29	Aug	Visited M. Vety Sect.	
	30	Aug	Visited M. Vety Sect and arranged for movement of Sect & evacuation of all cases unfit to travel. Capt Thornmwille to accompany first group moving. Artillery left in the line. Very wet & cold day.	
	31	Aug	Moved by car to BELLOY St LAURENCE.	

Instructions regarding War Diaries and Intelligence Summaries are contained in F. S. Regs., Part II. and the Staff Manual respectively. Title pages will be prepared in manuscript.

WAR DIARY
or
A.D.V.S. INTELLIGENCE SUMMARY. 14 Divn
(Erase heading not required.)

Army Form C. 2118.

Place	Date	Hour	Summary of Events and Information	Remarks and references to Appendices
	1st Sept		Transport arrived in evening. March arrangements not good. Horses not fed from early morning till they got in at night.	
	3rd Sept.		Inspected 42 Bgde M.G.C & Hd Qrs lines. Also Div Hd Qrs horses & M.M.P. Sent two Chargers to M. Vety Section.	
	4th Sept		Inspected Oxford & Bucks. Shrop. L.I. Visited Mobile Vety Sect.	
	5th Sept.		Inspected 9 KRR and 9th R.B. Water supply indifferent. No good water available in district. Visited M.V.S in afternoon.	
	6th Sept		Inspected 14th Signal Coy.	
	7th Sept		Inspected 7 KRR. 8 R.B. Bgde. Condition of animals very good. Good stream running near to their waggon lines.	
	8th "		Rode to Bettencourt on receipt of wire from D.D.V.S. 4th Army to say two horses were left by N.Z. D.A.C. No horses were left. Interviewed Maire. Visited M.V.S in afternoon.	
	9th "		Remounts arrived. Arranged for distribution of some. Others to be brought along by No 4 Coy A.S.C. (train) as the units were too scattered to receive animals before the march.	

T2134. Wt. W708—776. 500000. 4/15. Sir J. C. & S.

Instructions regarding War Diaries and Intelligence Summaries are contained in F. S. Regs., Part II. and the Staff Manual respectively. Title pages will be prepared in manuscript.

Army Form C. 2118.

WAR DIARY
or
INTELLIGENCE SUMMARY.
(Erase heading not required.)

A.D.V.S. 14th Division

Place	Date	Hour	Summary of Events and Information	Remarks and references to Appendices
	10th Sept		Horses and transport Hd Qrs marched to Buire.	
	11th Sept		Hd Qrs moved to Buire.	
	12th Sept		Inspected Meaulte with Capt Weir as to location of M.V.S. Decided on site N. of Dernacourt	
	13 Sept		Moved office to M.V.S. N of DERNACOURT. No room available at Fricourt with Hd Qrs. Visited 10 D.L.I. and 4 Coy A.S.C. Train.	
	14th Sept		Inspected 43 Field Ambulance, K.O.Y.L.I. Visited Fricourt (Hd Qrs)	
	15th Sept		Inspected 2.3.&4 Coys A.S.C. Div Train. Distributed eight HD Remounts.	
	17th Sept.		~~[illegible]~~. M.V.S. moved to Buire. Advanced Sect. at BECORDEL.	
	18th Sept		Conference Meaulte.	
	19th Sept		Inspected 43 Infty Bgde Hd Qrs, M.G. Coy. K.O.Y.L.I. D.L.I. Somerset L.I.	
	20 Sept		Remounts arrived for Division. Issued them to units concerned at EDGEHILL. D.W.R. present. D.A.C. didnt turn up. Had to send six L.Ds to M.V.S.	
	21st Sept		Marched to TALMAS.	
	22nd Sept		Marched to Le CAUROY.	

T2134. Wt. W708—776. 500000. 4/15. Sir J. C. & S.

Instructions regarding War Diaries and Intelligence Summaries are contained in F. S. Regs., Part II. and the Staff Manual respectively. Title pages will be prepared in manuscript.

WAR DIARY
or
INTELLIGENCE SUMMARY.
(Erase heading not required.)

Army Form C. 2118.

A.D.V.S. 14th Division

Place	Date	Hour	Summary of Events and Information	Remarks and references to Appendices
	23	Sept	Visited 26 M.V.S at BELLVILLERS. Capt Evans reported for duty.	
	24	"	Routine office work. Visited 14th Signal Coy RE. 9th K.R.R	
			Issued 3 LDs.	
	25	"	Visited M.V.S. & King Liverpools. Their animals looking fairly well.	
	26	"	Marched HdQrs. mounted party to GOUY.	
	27	"	Visited 14th Signal Coy.	
	[illegible] "	"	Rode to WARLUS to see A.D.V.S. 12th Division	
	28	"	Marched Hd Qrs mounted party to WARLUS.	
	29	"	Inspected 7 R.B. & 8 K.R.R. at BEAUMETZ. Animals in very good condition	
			7 R.B. making standings. 8 K.R.R. in sheds and barns in the village.	
	30	"	Visited 26 M.V.S at FOSSEUX. Receiving animals from 12th Div. as well	
			as our own. Fair standings. Good head cover but floors not too good.	
				[signature] Major A.D.V.S. 14 Divn.

T2134. Wt. W708—776. 500000. 4/15. Sir J. C. & S.

WAR DIARY

of

A.D.V.S., 14th (Light) Divn.

October 1st - October 31st '16.

Instructions regarding War Diaries and Intelligence Summaries are contained in F. S. Regs., Part II. and the Staff Manual respectively. Title pages will be prepared in manuscript.

WAR DIARY
or
INTELLIGENCE SUMMARY.
(Erase heading not required.)

Army Form C. 2118.

A. D. V. S. 14th Division

Place	Date	Hour	Summary of Events and Information	Remarks and references to Appendices
	1st	Oct.	Inspected 43 Machine Gun Coy. 11 Kings Liverpool Rgt. O& Bucks L.I. 89 Coy R.E. 62 Coy R.E. 14th Signals. One of Kings Liverpools horses sent away for debility. Condition of other units good. 14 Signals not as good as they might be.	
	2nd	Oct.	Visited Mobile Vety Section. Issued one pack pony to 42 Infy Bgde. One L.D. to 14th Train A.S.C. Office in afternoon.	
	3rd	Oct.	Inspected 41st M.G. Coy. 7 K.R.R. and 8 R.B. 7 K.R.R. fair condition 8 R.B. very good. Standings not completed for 7 K.R.R. and M.G.C.	
	4th	Oct.	O.C. 26 M.V.S. appointed Town Major, Fosseux. Visited Fosseux	
	5th	Oct.	Inspected 42 Infty Bgde. M.G.C. 5 O&B. K.S.L.I. 9 K.R.R. 9 R.B. Condition fairly good. All in Standings. Afternoon inspected 2 3 & 4 Coys of Train. Condition good. Standings very good. Not finished in places.	
	6th	Oct.	Inspected 46th R.F.A. Brigade. Picked out forty nine horses for debility. Afternoon inspected D.A.C. Picked out thirteen for evacuation for debility.	
	7th	Oct.	Inspected 48th R.F.A. Bgde. Picked out twenty three for debility. Lines very poor. Very dirty and muddy.	

T2134. Wt. W708—776. 500000. 4/15. Sir J. C. & S.

Army Form C. 2118.

Instructions regarding War Diaries and Intelligence Summaries are contained in F. S. Regs., Part II. and the Staff Manual respectively. Title pages will be prepared in manuscript.

WAR DIARY
or
INTELLIGENCE SUMMARY.
(Erase heading not required.)

Place	Date	Hour	Summary of Events and Information	Remarks and references to Appendices
	8th	Oct	Visited Mobile Vety Section. Office routine in afternoon.	
	9th	Oct	Office routine. Returns sent to A.D.V.S. 12 & 33 Divisions.	
	10th	Oct	D.D.V.S. inspected D.A. 46. 47 Bigades.	
	11th	Oct	Proceeded on leave for 10 days to England	
	20th	Oct	Returned to duty from leave. Arrived 12 midnight. First frost of year	
	21st	Oct	Visited M.V.S.	
	22nd	Oct	Inspected Signal Coy. and went to M.V.S. in the afternoon.	
	23rd	Oct	Inspected C battery 48 Brigade R.F.A. Horses not too good. Also 43 Field Ambulance. Inspected 3rd Section D.A.C in afternoon	
	24th	Oct	Visited M.V.S. Office routine. Very wet.	
	25th	Oct	Inspected 14 Signal Coy R.E. 62nd and 89th Field Coys R.E. Stables dirty. Too much old wire about. 14 Signals done nothing to their stables since occupation. Reported matter to C.R.E.	
	26th	Oct	Office routine.	
	27th	Oct	Moved to Le Cauroy. Visited M.V.S.	
	28th	Oct	Visited 14th Signal Coy. One horse picked up nail. B. batty 46th R.F.A. where ringworm was suspected. Not ringworm, mud rash. Visited M.V.S.	

T2134. Wt. W708—776. 500000. 4/15. Sir J. C. & S.

Instructions regarding War Diaries and Intelligence Summaries are contained in F. S. Regs., Part II. and the Staff Manual respectively. Title pages will be prepared in manuscript.

WAR DIARY
or
INTELLIGENCE SUMMARY.
(Erase heading not required.)

Army Form C. 2118.

Place	Date	Hour	Summary of Events and Information	Remarks and references to Appendices
	29th	Oct	Routine Office work. Weekly returns prepared.	
	30th	Oct.	Office work. Wet.	
	31st	Oct.	Went to Peten and Maignes to investigate the reason why so many billets had been put out of bounds as regards Mange and Glanders. Went to 4 Coy A.S.C. in afternoon to distribute remounts. Fair sample but riders mostly small. Two very poor mules.	
			A.J. [illegible] Major A.V.C. 14 Div	

T2134. Wt. W708—776. 500000. 4/15. Sir J. C. & S.

Vol 13

Confidential

War Diary

of

Major Dalgleish A.V.C.

A.D.V.S. 14 Division

From 1st Nov. 1916 to 30 Nov. 1916

Volume X

Instructions regarding War Diaries and Intelligence Summaries are contained in F. S. Regs., Part II. and the Staff Manual respectively. Title pages will be prepared in manuscript.

WAR DIARY
or
INTELLIGENCE SUMMARY.
(Erase heading not required.)

Army Form C. 2118.

A. V. S. 14 Div

Place	Date	Hour	Summary of Events and Information	Remarks and references to Appendices
	Nov.	1.	Visited Mob. Vet. Sec. Latter St Quentin	
	"	2	Inspected 43 M. Gen Coy. Standing in open. Animals very good	
	"	3	14 Train H.Q. Interview Col Richards re extra forage. Visited Beaufort for	
	"		billets for M.V.S. no room. Visited Larbret. Inspected 61 Coy R.E. very good	
	"		good stabling.	
	"	4	Inspected B batty 46 Bgde and C 47 Bgde R.F.A. Also 3 sect D.A.C.	
	"		Horses fair. Inspected Water troughs. Very bad condition. Office Routine	
	"	5	Inspected 7 R.B. 7 KRR and 2 Coy Train. Horses very good.	
	"	6	Inspected 42 Field Ambulance 9th R. Bgde. Very good.	
	"		Visited 14 Signal Coy R.E.	
	"	7	Capt Beal arrived vice Lt Clark. Inspected 9 KRR very good condition	
			Office.	
	"	8	Visited 14th Train H.Q. Inspected 6 K.S.L.I. Condition mules fair.	
			44 Field Ambulance very good.	
	"	9	Visited M.V.S. Mont Joie Farm. Office.	
	"	10	Inspected 8 KRR 8 R.B. 41st H.Q. Very good.	

T2134. Wt. W708—776. 500000. 4/15. Sir J. C. & S.

Instructions regarding War Diaries and Intelligence Summaries are contained in F. S. Regs., Part II. and the Staff Manual respectively. Title pages will be prepared in manuscript.

WAR DIARY
or
INTELLIGENCE SUMMARY.
(Erase heading not required.)

Army Form C. 2118.

Place	Date	Hour	Summary of Events and Information	Remarks and references to Appendices
	25th	Nov.	Office. Visited 26 Mob Vet Section	
	26th	Nov.	Inspected Durham L. I. Good condition	
	27th	Nov.	Visited Mob. Vet Section	
	28th	Nov.	Office routine	
	29th	Nov.	Inspected 43 Machine Gun Coy. Very good	
	30	Nov.	Office routine. Visited 14 Signal Coy R.E. and 26 Mob. Vet Section	

[illegible]
Major
A.D.V.S.
14 Divn

Instructions regarding War Diaries and Intelligence Summaries are contained in F. S. Regs., Part II. and the Staff Manual respectively. Title pages will be prepared in manuscript.

WAR DIARY
or
INTELLIGENCE SUMMARY.
(Erase heading not required.)

Army Form C. 2118.

Place	Date	Hour	Summary of Events and Information	Remarks and references to Appendices
	11	Nov	Inspected 4 Coy A.S.C. 11 Kings Liverpools Very good.	
	12	Nov.	Inspected 84 Coy R.E and billets Mont-en-Ternois.	
	13	Nov.	Inspected 42 M.G.C. H.Q. 42. Office	
	14	Nov.	Office.	
	15	Nov	Inspected 1 Coy A.S.C. Condition Very good.	
	16	Nov.	M.V.S. Mont Joie Ferme.	
	17	Nov.	Visited 14 Signal Coy R.E.	
	18	Nov.	Inspected. 6 K.O.Y.L.I. Condition Very good. No Case Mange.	
	19	Nov.	Office.	
	20	Nov.	M.V.S and Office	
	21	Nov.	Liencourt. Inspected Surplus Animals D.A. Cast 22 debility cases. Office.	
	22	Nov.	Inspected 3 Coy Train A.S.C. Outbreak of Swine fever HENCOURT. Place put out of bounds.	
	23	Nov.	Office	
	24	Nov.	Inspected 2 Coy Train A.S.C. Lignereuil.	

T2134. Wt. W708—776. 500000. 4/15. Sir J. C. & S.

Vol 14

Confidential

War Diary
of
A.D.V.S. 14th Light Division

From 1st December 1916 to 31st December 1916

(Volume No. ~~10~~)

Instructions regarding War Diaries and Intelligence Summaries are contained in F. S. Regs., Part II. and the Staff Manual respectively. Title pages will be prepared in manuscript.

WAR DIARY
or
INTELLIGENCE SUMMARY.
(Erase heading not required.)

A.D.V.S. 14th Light Division

Army Form C. 2118.

Place	Date	Hour	Summary of Events and Information	Remarks and references to Appendices
LE CAUROY	Dec	1st	Office routine. Visited Mob. Vety Section	
	"	2	Inspected 14th Signal Coy R.E. and Div M.M.P. Office.	
	"	3	Inspected. 62 Field Coy R.E. Office.	
	"	4	Visited Mob. Vet Sec. Office	
	"	5	Inspected. 61st Coy R.E. Nosebags deficient. Office.	
	"	6	Inspected. 8 KRR. Transport. Office	
	"	7	Inspected. 7 KRR and 8 R.B. Transport. Office	
	"	8	Inspected 7 R.B Transport. Office	
	"	9	Visited Mob. Vet. Sec. Office routine	
	"	10	Visited MONT-EN-TERNOIS to inspect billets. Only one place available. Arranged with Capt Meeke as to disinfection.	
	"	11	Office routine. Inspected 1 and 3 Sections, D.A.C.	
	"	12	Office routine	
	"	13	Inspected. A 46 Bgde R.F.A. Visited Mob Vet Sec.	
	"	14	Visited 26 M.V.S. at Mont Joie Ferme.	
	"	15	Inspected. 48 Bgde R.F.A. Horses very good. On to C.O. A.V.C reported	

Instructions regarding War Diaries and Intelligence Summaries are contained in F. S. Regs., Part II. and the Staff Manual respectively. Title pages will be prepared in manuscript.

WAR DIARY
or
INTELLIGENCE SUMMARY.
(Erase heading not required.)

Army Form C. 2118.

Place	Date	Hour	Summary of Events and Information	Remarks and references to Appendices
Dec.	15th	Contd.	As not very efficient. Sent report to DDVS.	
	16th.		Visited M.V.S. Mont frie Ferme.	
	17th		Visited M.V.S. in conjunction with Col Afe. He thought approaches not good and recommended removal.	
			Visited Capt Beal 47th Bgde R.F.A.	
	18th.		Inspected 47th Bgde R.F.A. Horses pretty good. One battery had clipped legs, which I reported to AA & QMG. 14th Div.	
	19th		Marched to Warlus. Took over from 12th Div. Moved office to A.D.V.S. office in Warlus.	
	20th		Office routine	
	21st		Visited M.V.S. which has moved to Fosseux.	
	22nd		Visited 14 Signal Coy R.E.	
	23		Office routine.	
	24th		Visited M.V.S at Fosseux. Office.	
	25th		Office.	
	26th		Office. Visited 89 Field Coy R.E. Much mud. Unsanitary	

T2134. Wt. W708—776. 500000. 4/15. Sir J. C. & S.

Instructions regarding War Diaries and Intelligence Summaries are contained in F. S. Regs., Part II. and the Staff Manual respectively. Title pages will be prepared in manuscript.

WAR DIARY
or
INTELLIGENCE SUMMARY.
(Erase heading not required.)

Army Form C. 2118.

Place	Date	Hour	Summary of Events and Information	Remarks and references to Appendices
Dec.	27		Visited 26 M.V.S. at Fosseux. Office routine.	
	28.		Office. Visited 14 Signal Coy R.E. One case of mange found which I sent to M.V.S. No others apparently. Had harness etc. thoroughly disinfected.	
	29		Visited M.V.S. Office.	
	30		Visited M.V.S. Inspected sick cases there. Office.	
	31		Visited M.V.S. Inspected fresh horses which had arrived. Capt O'Carroll has taken over during Capt Weir's absence on leave.	

[illegible signature]
Major
A.V.S. 14 Div.

T2134. Wt. W708—776. 500000. 4/15. Sir J. C. & S.

4/M 15

Confidential

War Diary
of
A.D.V.S. 14th Division

From 1st Jan. 1917 to 31st Jan 1917

(Volume No ~~44~~)

Instructions regarding War Diaries and Intelligence Summaries are contained in F. S. Regs., Part II. and the Staff Manual respectively. Title pages will be prepared in manuscript.

WAR DIARY
or
INTELLIGENCE SUMMARY.
(Erase heading not required.)

Army Form C. 2118.

A.D.V.S. 14th Light Division

Place	Date	Hour	Summary of Events and Information	Remarks and references to Appendices
1917.				
Jan	1		Visited 26th Mobile Vety Sect. Capt O'Carroll in charge. Office afternoon Routine	
	2		Visited 26 Mobile Vety Sect. Very debilitated horses sent in from 12 Dn. Office routine.	
	3.		Visited 26 Mobile Vety Sect. Office routine.	
	4		Visited detacht 14 Train Berneville. Somerset L.I. and 14 Coy Signals RE	
	5.		Visited 26 Mobile Vety Sect. Office routine.	
	6.		Visited 14 Signal Coy R.E. One horse tested for roaring. Visited Kings Liverpool Regt. Very muddy surroundings to stables. Office routine.	
	7		Visited 26 Mobile Vety Section and M. Mounted Police. Office routine	
	8.		Visited 26 Mobile Vety Section. 14 Signal Coy R.E. Office routine	
	9.		Visited 26 Mobile Vety Section. Office Routine	
	10		Visited 26 Mobile Vety Section. Office routine	
	11		Inspected D battery 46 Bgde R.F.A. D. Cornwalls L.I. one case of mange in heavy draught. Evacuated. D/46 in very poor condition. Reported to O.C. Bgde. Arranged for clipping all of the horses. Office routine	
	12		Visited 26 Mobile Vety Section. Office routine	
	13		Visited 26 Mobile Vety Section. Three debility cases very poor	

T2134. Wt. W708—776. 500000. 4/15. Sir J. C. & S.

Army Form C. 2118.

WAR DIARY
or
INTELLIGENCE SUMMARY.
(Erase heading not required.)

Instructions regarding War Diaries and Intelligence Summaries are contained in F. S. Regs., Part II. and the Staff Manual respectively. Title pages will be prepared in manuscript.

A.D.V.S. 14th Light Division.

Place	Date	Hour	Summary of Events and Information	Remarks and references to Appendices
	1917			
Jan	14		Visited 26 Mob. Vety Section. Office routine	
	15		Visited 26 Mob. Vety Section. Capt Weir has to give up his billet, XVII Corps having demanded the rooms. Stables to be retained.	
	16		Office routine	
	17		Office routine. Fall of snow. Bad going. Visited 14th Signals, and inspected two cases one sick one debility. Inspected Detachment A.S.C. Office routine	
	18		Visited Remounts farm at Frevent. Remounts for division on this side. Visited Barly Div. A.S.C. Standings poor and very dirty. Ordered disinfection to be carried out. Visited D.A.C at Gouy.	
	19		Visited Simoncourt D.A.C. Inspected C/48 at Monchiet. Good horses and condition good. Visited Barly a mange in civilian horses. Arranged for attendance by Capt Weir.	
	20		Simoncourt. B 48. M.M.P. and office	
	21		Visited 26 Mobile Vet. Section.	
	22		Visited Monchiet and Simoncourt. Office routine	
	23		Visited 14th Signal Coy and 89 F. Coy R.E. Sent one horse to M.V.S.	

T2134. Wt. W708—776. 500000. 4/15. Sir J. C. & S.

Instructions regarding War Diaries and Intelligence Summaries are contained in F. S. Regs., Part II. and the Staff Manual respectively. Title pages will be prepared in manuscript.

WAR DIARY
or
INTELLIGENCE SUMMARY.
(Erase heading not required.)

A.D.V.S. 14th Light Division.

Army Form C. 2118.

Place	Date	Hour	Summary of Events and Information	Remarks and references to Appendices
	1916			
	24 January		Visited 26 Mobile Vety Section	
	25th		Visited 14th Signal Coy R.E. Office routine Infantry Transport.	
	26th		Visited 26 Mobile Vety Section. Office routine.	
	27th		Visited B/46 Brigade Summit. Water troughs. Inspected 201st Coy R.E. Transport.	
	28th		Visited 26th M.V. Section. Office routine	
	29th		Visited 14th Signal Coy. Inspected Pioneer Batt. Kings Liverpool Regt. Office routine	
	30th		Visited two civilian cases in Wailes. Office routine.	
	31st		Proceeded on Div. Leave	

A. J. Dalgleish
Major
A.D.V.S.
14th Div

T2134. Wt. W708—776. 500000. 4/15. Sir J. C. & S.

Vol 16

Confidential

War Diary

of

A.D.V.S. 14th Division.

From February 1st to February 28th 1917

(Volume ~~#5~~)

Instructions regarding War Diaries and Intelligence Summaries are contained in F. S. Regs., Part II. and the Staff Manual respectively. Title pages will be prepared in manuscript.

Army Form C. 2118.

WAR DIARY
or
INTELLIGENCE SUMMARY.
(Erase heading not required.)

A.D.V.S. 14th Light Division

Place	Date	Hour	Summary of Events and Information	Remarks and references to Appendices
	1917			
Feb	11		Returned from leave Office routine.	
"	12		Visited 14th Train A.S.C. 26th M.V.S. Office	
"	13		Mobility M.P. inspected. Sent one horse away to M.V.S. Office	
"	14		Office Visited Le Gros Tison Farm to see a heifer with actinomycosis.	
"			Injury originally said to be caused by troops billetted.	
"	15th		Inspected 41st Infty Bgde.	
"	16		Inspected 42 Infty Bgde. Office	
"	17		Office routine. Weekly returns. General thaw.	
"	18		Visited 26 M.V.S. Office.	
"	19		Inspected D battery 46 Bgde R.F.A Poor condition.	
"	20		Visited 26 M.V.S and inspected 42nd 43rd and 44th Field Ambulances.	
			Horses good condition.	
"	21		Office	
"	22		Visited 26 M.V.S.	
"	23		Went to Le Gros Tison Ferme to see D battery 46 Bgde dipped. Office.	
"	24		Visited D battery 46 Bgde. No horses damaged through dipping.	

T2134. Wt. W708—776. 500000. 4/15. Sir J. C. & S.

Instructions regarding War Diaries and Intelligence Summaries are contained in F. S. Regs., Part II. and the Staff Manual respectively. Title pages will be prepared in manuscript.

Army Form C. 2118.

WAR DIARY
or
INTELLIGENCE SUMMARY.
(Erase heading not required.)

A.D.V.S. 14th (Light) Division

Place	Date	Hour	Summary of Events and Information	Remarks and references to Appendices
Feb.	25		Visited 26 M.V.S. Office routine.	
"	26		Inspected 14 Div Train Bavincourt. 1 & 4 Coys. very good. 2 and 3 good	
"			Condition, but not such good horses.	
"	27		Inspected A B & C batteries 46th R.F.A. C very good A good. B fair	
"			A is in the open. Office.	
"	28		Visited ~~14~~ Div. Train. 26 Cases of influenza have occurred in 4 Coy.	
"			Abdominal type.	
"	[illegible]			

[illegible signature]
Major
A.D.V.S.
14th Div.

T2134. Wt. W708—776. 500000. 4/15. Sir J. C. & S.

ADVS Mar 17

Confidential

War Diary

of

A.D.V.S. 14th Div.

—

Volume 46

(Mar: 1st to Mar 31st 1917)

Instructions regarding War Diaries and Intelligence Summaries are contained in F. S. Regs., Part II. and the Staff Manual respectively. Title pages will be prepared in manuscript.

WAR DIARY
or
INTELLIGENCE SUMMARY.
(Erase heading not required.)

A.D.V.S. 14th Light Division

Army Form C. 2118.

Place	Date	Hour	Summary of Events and Information	Remarks and references to Appendices
1917				
March	1		Visited 26th M.V. Section. Office.	
"	2		Visited 14th Div Train. M.V. Section.	
"	3		Inspected 179 Tunnelling Coy R.E. Sent three horses away for debility. Reported Condition of horses to A.A. & Q.M.G.	
"	4		Office.	
	5		Office. Fall of snow. Very Cold	
	6		Visited 26 M.V.S	
	7		Inspected. 47 Bgde R.F.A and 46. Bgde	
	8		Inspected 14 Div Train A.S.C	
	9		More Snow	
	10		Inspected 14 Div. Signal Coy	
	11		Visited 26 M.V.S.	
	12		Inspected 62. 63. & 89 Field Coys R.E., 11 Kings Liverpool & H.Q. A.S.C.	
	13		Visited 26 M.V.S.	
	14		Visited 26 M.V.S Inspected 2 and 4 Coys. D.A.C	
	15		Visited Train.	

Instructions regarding War Diaries and Intelligence Summaries are contained in F. S. Regs., Part II. and the Staff Manual respectively. Title pages will be prepared in manuscript.

WAR DIARY
or
INTELLIGENCE SUMMARY.
(Erase heading not required.)

A.D.V.S. 14 Light Division

Army Form C. 2118.

Place	Date	Hour	Summary of Events and Information	Remarks and references to Appendices
March	16		Visited 26 M.V.S. Office & 44 F.A.	
	17		Visited 26 M.V.S. Inspected 42, 43, & 44 F.A. Horses very good.	
	18.		Visited 14 Signal Coy. 46 Bgde R.F.A. Office	
	19.		Visited 26 M.V.S.	
	20		Visited 14 Coy Train A.S.C. Inspected all the horses. Influenza practically over.	
	21		Visited 26 Mob Vety. Sect. Office routine	
	22		Inspected D/46 Bgde R.F.A. Berneville	
	23		Inspected remainder of 46 Bgde R.F.A. at Berneville	
	24		Visited 26 M.V.S. at Bosseux. Office routine 14th Signal Coy.	
	25		Visited Hautville 3rd D.A.C. Office and Berneville	
	26		Inspected 33 Reserve Park at BARLY. Horses fair, report sent D.D.V.S. 3 Army	
			Inspected 14 Div Train Office routine	
	27		Inspected H.Q. horses. Sect Div Train A.S.C. at BERNEVILLE	
	28		Visited 26th M.V.S. Office	
	29		Inspected 232 Bdge R.F.A. Corps Artillery. Sent 40 horses away with debility. Saw town major Simoncourt re extra watering arrangements in his area. Office.	

T2134. Wt. W708—776. 500000. 4/15. Sir J. C. & S.

Instructions regarding War Diaries and Intelligence Summaries are contained in F. S. Regs., Part II. and the Staff Manual respectively. Title pages will be prepared in manuscript.

WAR DIARY
or
INTELLIGENCE SUMMARY.
(Erase heading not required.)

A.D.V.S. 14th Light Division

Army Form C. 2118.

Place	Date	Hour	Summary of Events and Information	Remarks and references to Appendices
Warlus	30		Visited 26 M.V.S. Inspected all cases for evacuation.	
"	31		Visited DAINVILLE with regard to advanced post for M.V.S. Saw Town Major. Visited SIMONCOURT in afternoon; called at D.A.C. Inspected 95 remounts which had arrived. Fairly good lot. Office	

A. J. [illegible] Major
A.D.V.S. 14 Div.

T2134. Wt. W708—776. 500000. 4/15. Sir J. C. & S.

Vol 18

Confidential

War Diary

of

ADVS. 14th Division

From April 1st to April 30th 1917

(Volume No 47)

Army Form C. 2118.

WAR DIARY
or
INTELLIGENCE SUMMARY.
(Erase heading not required.)

Instructions regarding War Diaries and Intelligence Summaries are contained in F. S. Regs., Part II. and the Staff Manual respectively. Title pages will be prepared in manuscript.

A.D.V.S. 14th (Light) Division

Place	Date	Hour	Summary of Events and Information	Remarks and references to Appendices
1917				
April	1		Inspected 48 Bgde R.F.A. BEAUMETZ. B. C good D. A battery fair.	
	2		Inspected 37th Bgde D.A. SIMONCOURT A. B. C battery fair. Also one sect 37 DAC.	
	3		Visited 26 Mobile Vety Section SIMONCOURT. Office routine. Inspected H.Q. horses.	
	4		Inspected 232 Bgde R.F.A. Fair.	
	5		Visited 26 Mobile Vety section 232 Bgde R.F.A. and interviewed Capt Bend A.V.C.	
	6		Inspected D battery 37 brigade R.F.A. Also 14 Div Train	
	7		Visited 26 Mob Vety Section. Advanced post DAINVILLE. Office routine.	
	8		Visited 26 M. Vety Section. Office	
	9		Visited 26 M.V.S. Evacuation at DOUY.	
	10		Visited 26 M.V.S. Office	
	11		Visited 26 M.V.S. Office	
	12		Visited 26 M.V.S. Inspected H.Q. horses and 11 Kings Liverpool. Evacuated two for debility	
	13		Visited 26 M.V.S. Inspected 14 Signal Coy R.E. Made 3 P.Ms at M.V.S	

T2134. Wt. W708—776. 500000. 4/15. Sir J. C. & S.

Instructions regarding War Diaries and Intelligence Summaries are contained in F. S. Regs., Part II. and the Staff Manual respectively. Title pages will be prepared in manuscript.

WAR DIARY
or
INTELLIGENCE SUMMARY.
(*Erase heading not required.*)

Army Form C. 2118.

A.D.V.S. 14 (Light) Division

Place	Date	Hour	Summary of Events and Information	Remarks and references to Appendices
	1917			
April	14.		26 Mobile Vety Section moved to LE CAUROY. Office. Inspected 1 and 3 sections DAC	
"	15		Office routine	
"	16		Office routine	
"	17		Visited 14 DAC SIMENCOURT and inspected H.Q horses	
"	18		Visited 26 M.V.S. at Le Cauroy. Office routine	
"	19		Visited GOUEY and 14 Signal Coy. Office routine	
"	20		Visited DAINVILLE. Office	
"	21		Visited 26 M.V.S. at Le Cauroy	
"	22		Office routine Visited 14 DAC 14 Signal Coy.	
"	23		Interviewed Capt O Carroll A.V.C. Office H.Q horses	
"	24		Head Quarters moved to BAIEULLMONT.	
"	25		Inspected 11 Kings Liverpool Regt. Transport. Horses poor. Feet neglected	
"	26		Head Quarters moved to ARRAS. 12 Boulevard Carnot. Visited 14 Signal Coy.	
"	27		Visited 26 Mob. Vety. Section at Berneville	
"	28		Visited 11 Kings Liverpool. Achicourt and looked for place for advanced collecting post	

T2134. Wt. W708—776. 500000. 4/15. Sir J. C. & S.

Instructions regarding War Diaries and Intelligence Summaries are contained in F. S. Regs., Part II. and the Staff Manual respectively. Title pages will be prepared in manuscript.

WAR DIARY
or
INTELLIGENCE SUMMARY.
(Erase heading not required.)

Army Form C. 2118.

A.D.V.S. 14th (Light) Division

Place	Date	Hour	Summary of Events and Information	Remarks and references to Appendices
April	29		Visited 26 Mob. Vety Section Bernville. Office routine.	
"	30		Visited advanced collecting post [illegible]. 14th Light Coy R.E. Capt Beal A.V.C. departed for London on expiration of service. Saw Capt [illegible] and arranged for him to look after 47th Bgde. R.F.A. temporarily.	

[illegible]
Major
A.D.V.S.
14 Div.

T2134. Wt. W708—776. 500000. 4/15. Sir J. C. & S.

Vol 19

Confidential

War Diary

of

A.D.V.S. 14th Div.

From 1st May to 31st May 1917

(Volume No 48)

Instructions regarding War Diaries and Intelligence Summaries are contained in F. S. Regs., Part II. and the Staff Manual respectively. Title pages will be prepared in manuscript.

WAR DIARY
or
INTELLIGENCE SUMMARY.
(Erase heading not required.)

Army Form C. 2118.

A.D.V.S. 14(Lt) Division

Place	Date	Hour	Summary of Events and Information	Remarks and references to Appendices
May	1st		Visited 26. Mobile Vety Section Bernaville Office	
"	2nd		Visited Active court. Inspected mule at North^d Germany. 11th (Kings) Liverpool Regt. and H.Q. horses. 11th Kings Liverpool transport going back in condition. Office	
"	3rd		Visited 26 Mobile Vety Section. Bernaville. Office	
	4th		Inspected 41st Infty Bgde. transport. 14th Div Tran Coys and 9th K.R.R.	
	5th		Visited 26 Mobile Vety Section Bernaville Office	
	6th		Visited 14th Signal Coy. R.E and H.Q. horses. Office.	
	7th		Sent to Borly VII Corps rest station.	
	21st		Returned to duty. Office	
	22nd		Visiting H.Q. and inspected horses. Office	
	23rd		Went to Aubigny and distributed 92 remounts for the division. H.D. poor. L.D. good. Rides moderate. Office.	
	24th		Office & 26th M.V.S. which is now at Agny.	
	25th		Visited H.Q. and 14th Div Signal Coy.	
	26th		Office routine 26 M.V.S.	
	27th		Visited H.Q. horses. Office routine. and 26 M.V. Section. 11th (Kings) Liverpool. They have improved.	

T2134. Wt. W708—776. 500000. 4/15. Sir J. C. & S.

Instructions regarding War Diaries and Intelligence Summaries are contained in F. S. Regs., Part II. and the Staff Manual respectively. Title pages will be prepared in manuscript.

WAR DIARY
or
INTELLIGENCE SUMMARY.
(Erase heading not required.)

Army Form C. 2118.

A.D.V.S. 14th Lt Division

Place	Date	Hour	Summary of Events and Information	Remarks and references to Appendices
May	28th		Visited 43 Field Ambulance. 26 M.V.S. Office.	
"	29th		Office. 26th Mobile Vety Section. Two operations.	
"	30th		26th Mobile Vety Section Office. Rain.	
"	31st		Inspected A.B.C. & batteries 46th Bgde. R.F.A. Improved very much. 26th M.V.S. Office.	

[illegible]
Major
A.D.V.S.
14th Div.

T2134. Wt. W708—776. 500000. 4/15. Sir J. C. & S.

Vol 20

Confidential

War Diary

of

D.A.D.V.S. 14th Div.

From June 1st to June 25th 1917

(Volume 49.)

Army Form C. 2118.

Instructions regarding War Diaries and Intelligence Summaries are contained in F. S. Regs., Part II. and the Staff Manual respectively. Title pages will be prepared in manuscript.

WAR DIARY
or
INTELLIGENCE SUMMARY.
(Erase heading not required.)

ADVS. 14th. (Lt) Division

Place	Date	Hour	Summary of Events and Information	Remarks and references to Appendices
1917 June	1st		Inspected C & D batteries 47th Bg. R.F.A. Horses have much improved. Their coats are still backward. Linseed cake is being issued and they are having grazing. 26th M.V.S. office	
	2nd		Inspected 44th Field Ambulance.	
	3rd		Visited Mobile Vety Section and Div H.Q.	
	4th		Visited Mobile Vety Section	
	5th		Inspected B Echelon and 2 Sect. D.A.C.	
	6th		Inspected remounts at D.A.C. fair condition.	
	7th		Inspected 1 Section D.A.C. dirty standing. Mules fair. Visited H.Q.	
	8th		Mobile Vety Section, and 14th Signal Coy R.E. Operations at M.V.S.	
	9th		Visited Mobile Vety Section	
	10th		Marched to Marieux.	
	11th		Inspected various sites for proposed horse show. Inspected H.Q. horses	

A5834 Wt. W4973 M687 750,000 8/16 D. D. & L. Ltd. Forms/C.2118/13.

Instructions regarding War Diaries and Intelligence Summaries are contained in F. S. Regs., Part II. and the Staff Manual respectively. Title pages will be prepared in manuscript.

Army Form C. 2118.

WAR DIARY
or
INTELLIGENCE SUMMARY.
(Erase heading not required.)

A.D.V.S. 14th (Light) Division

Place	Date	Hour	Summary of Events and Information	Remarks and references to Appendices
June	12		Office work. Held meeting to consider arrangements for horse show.	
"	13		Inspected Shropshire L.I. and 9th K.R.R.C. Also 42 M.G.C. Showing indifferent teams. 9th R.B. 42 H.Q. and M.M.P. detachment.	
"	14th		Inspected Ox & Bucks L.I. and 62 Field Coy R.E.	
"	15th		Inspected 41 M.G.C. 7 K.R.R.C. Malleined 2 Coy Train and ½ 3 Coy Train 14 Div Train. Inspected 8 K.R.R.C and 8 R.B.	
	16th.		Inspected 7 R.B. Meeting of Committee of horse show. Visited M.V.S Office.	
	17		Inoculated with Mallein 43 Bgde Infantry Transport animals. M.V.S.	
	18		Inspected Malleined animals. No reactions. Inoculated in afternoon remaining animals which were working on the 17th.	
	19.		Inspected 43 Bgde. Inspected D.C.L.I. and 9 R.B. for best animals.	
	20		Inspected 42 Bgde S.L.I and 9 K.R.R. again for best animals.	

A5834 Wt. W4973 M687 750,000 8/16 D. D. & L. Ltd. Forms/C.2118/13.

Army Form C. 2118.

WAR DIARY
or
INTELLIGENCE SUMMARY.
(*Erase heading not required.*)

Instructions regarding War Diaries and Intelligence Summaries are contained in F. S. Regs., Part II. and the Staff Manual respectively. Title pages will be prepared in manuscript.

A.D.V.S 14th Light Division

Place	Date	Hour	Summary of Events and Information	Remarks and references to Appendices
June	21st		Inoculated 43 M.G. Coy. T.M.B. and part H.Q. Inspected 89 Field Coy R.E.	
"	22nd		Inspected tested animals this morning. No reactors.	
"	23		Office. M.V.S.	
"	24th		M.V.S. Visited 14 Signal Coy R.E.	
"	25th		Spent all day on Show ground arranging areas for competitions.	

F. J. Weir. Capt. A.V.C.
for D A D V S

Vol 21

Confidential

War Diary

of

D. A. D. V. S. 14th Div.

July 1st to July 31st 1917

(Volume 50)

Army Form C. 2118.

WAR DIARY
or
INTELLIGENCE SUMMARY.
(*Erase heading not required.*)

Instructions regarding War Diaries and Intelligence Summaries are contained in F. S. Regs., Part II. and the Staff Manual respectively. Title pages will be prepared in manuscript.

D.A.D.V.S 14 Light Division

Place	Date	Hour	Summary of Events and Information	Remarks and references to Appendices
8th July			Returned from ten days leave	
9th "			Visited 26 Mobile Vety Section. Inspected H Q horses.	
10th "			Visited 26 Mobile Vety Section. Moving to Doullens.	
11th July			H. Q moved to St Jan Cappel by train	
12th July			Arrived St Jan Cappel. Horses travelled well, no casualties	
13th "			Visited M. V. S. & H Q horses	
14th July			Visited 14 Signal Coy. M. V. S. Capt Weir went on leave	
			Capt Evans left for base	
15th July.			Inspected Somerset L. I. 4 Coy Train. 2 Coy Train and M. V. S.	
16th July			Office routine	
17th July			Inspected 43 Bgde (Infty). Office	
18th July			Inspected 46 Bgde R. F. A. with Lt Col Bartlett. Also 89 Coy R.E.	

A5834 Wt. W4973 M687 750,000 8/16 D. D. & L. Ltd. Forms/C.2118/13.

Army Form C. 2118.

Instructions regarding War Diaries and Intelligence Summaries are contained in F. S. Regs., Part II. and the Staff Manual respectively. Title pages will be prepared in manuscript.

WAR DIARY or D.A.D.V.S. INTELLIGENCE SUMMARY. 14 Lt Division

(Erase heading not required.)

Place	Date	Hour	Summary of Events and Information	Remarks and references to Appendices
19 July	1917.		Office 26 Mob. Vet. Sect	
"	20		26th Mob Vety sect. Inspected 41st Bgde H. Q. and 7th and 8th Rifle Bgdes. Also 42 and 43 M. Gun Coys.	
"	21		Office. Returns. Visited Ox & Bucks L. I. 26th Mob. Vet Sect. H. Quarters.	
"	22		Visited 43 Infty Bgde H.Q. 42 M G Coy M.V.S. 9th Rifle Bgde	
"	23		Visited 249 M. Gun Coy. A new addition from England. Very good mules. 26th Mob. Vet. Sec. Saw 46th Bgde D battery dipped. Also 43 H. Q. transport & 5/S.L.I. transport dipped.	
"	24		Visited H. Q. and 26 Mob. Vet Sec	
"	25		Visited B(3) D.A.C. and 1 Coy D.A.C. 1 Coy Train and 26 M.V.S.	
"	26		Visited 5/K.S.L.I. & 26 M.V.S. Office	

Army Form C. 2118.

Instructions regarding War Diaries and Intelligence Summaries are contained in F. S. Regs., Part II. and the Staff Manual respectively. Title pages will be prepared in manuscript.

WAR DIARY
or
INTELLIGENCE SUMMARY.
(Erase heading not required.)

D.A.V.S. 14th Lt Division

Place	Date	Hour	Summary of Events and Information	Remarks and references to Appendices
	27th July 1917.		Visited 26 M.V.S. Remount at Station 17 received for Divn. Visited 7 R.B. and 7 K.R.R.	
	28th July		Visited 11/Kings Liverpool Regt. Horses & Mules looking very well.	
	29th July		Office. Returns. Visited A.D.V.S. IX Corps.	
	30th July		14th Signal Coy & H.Q. horses	
	31st July		21st M.V. Sect. Evacuated 24 horses. Capt Thornwell on leave.	

A. J. [illegible] Major
D.A.V.S. 14th Div.

A5834 Wt. W4973 M687 750,000 8/16 D. D. & L. Ltd. Forms/C.2118/13.

Vol 22

Confidential

War Diary

of

D.A.D.V.S. 14th Div.

From Aug. 1st to Aug. 31st 1917.

(Volume no 51)

Army Form C. 2118.

WAR DIARY
or
INTELLIGENCE SUMMARY.
(Erase heading not required.)

Instructions regarding War Diaries and Intelligence Summaries are contained in F. S. Regs., Part II. and the Staff Manual respectively. Title pages will be prepared in manuscript.

DADVS 14th (Lt) Division

Place	Date	Hour	Summary of Events and Information	Remarks and references to Appendices
1 Aug	1917		Visited 4 Coy Train ASC. 43 F Ambulance	
"	2nd		Inspected 10/D.L.I. and visited 26 Mob Vet Sec	
	3rd		Visited 26 Mob Vet Sec. and saw surplus horses of division with the DDR. 2 Army	
	4th		Visited 26 Mob Vet Sec. & 5/K.S.L.I.	
	5th		Inspected A. Q horses & M.M.P	
	6th		Moved to CAESTRE	
	7th		Inspected 61st 62 & 89 Field Coys R.E. also 11 K Liverpool with the C.R.E. Visited D.C.L.I.	
	8th		Inspected Ox Bucks L.I. & 26 M.V.S. at BORRE	
	9th		Visited 61st Coy R.E. to inspect forage. Visited Remount Section	
	10th		Visited 26 Mob Vet Sec. Steenvoorde to short horse left by 18 Divn	
	11th		Visited 7 KRR and Mt Horse	

A5834 Wt. W4973 M687 750,000 8/16 D. D. & L. Ltd. Forms/C.2118/13.

Instructions regarding War Diaries and Intelligence Summaries are contained in F. S. Regs., Part II. and the Staff Manual respectively. Title pages will be prepared in manuscript.

WAR DIARY
or
INTELLIGENCE SUMMARY.
(Erase heading not required.)

Army Form C. 2118.

DDVS — 14th (Lt) Division

Place	Date	Hour	Summary of Events and Information	Remarks and references to Appendices
August	12	1917	Visited 26 Mob Vet Sec	
"	13		Visited KSLI & 10/DLI. the Lines, a jibber sent to M.V.S	
"	14		Visited 8 CLRI KOYLI 9 KRRC. 4 Coy Train	
"	15		Moved to REDINGHELST.	
"	16		Visited 26 Mob Vet Sec. 2/Corps HQ. and 14th Signals	
"	17		Visited 26 Mob Vet Sec & 56 M.V.S. also ADVS 2/Corps	
"	18		Visited 14 DAC. Capt Beal taken over from Capt ? Carroll	
"	19		Inspected 47 Bgde RFA.	
"	20		Visited 26 Mob Vet Sec	
"	21		Inspected D/46 Bgde RFA and No 1 Coy ASC. Also visited 26 Mob Vety Section	

A5834 Wt. W4973 M687 750,000 8/16 D. D. & L. Ltd. Forms/C.2118/13.

Instructions regarding War Diaries and Intelligence Summaries are contained in F. S. Regs., Part II. and the Staff Manual respectively. Title pages will be prepared in manuscript.

WAR DIARY
or
INTELLIGENCE SUMMARY.
(*Erase heading not required.*)

D.A.D.V.S. 14 (Light) Division

Army Form C. 2118.

Place	Date	Hour	Summary of Events and Information	Remarks and references to Appendices
1917	Aug. 22		Inspected A/B/C batteries 46 Bgde R.F.A. Horses fairly good. D battery is very poor.	
	" 23		Visited 26 Mob. Vety Section and inspected horses for evacuation.	
	" 24		Visited H. Q horses at Dickebusch.	
	" 25		Went to Proven for the purpose of inspecting remounts 30 for 14 Div. Train	
	" 26		Conference at 11 Corps, 26 M. V. Section.	
	" 27		Went to Proven 80 remounts received.	
	" 28		Visited 26 Mob. Vety Section.	
	" 29		Went to Proven. 34 horses received. Marched to Berthen.	

A5834 Wt. W4973 M687 750,000 8/16 D. D. & L. Ltd. Forms/C.2118/13.

Army Form C. 2118.

WAR DIARY
or
INTELLIGENCE SUMMARY.
(Erase heading not required.)

Instructions regarding War Diaries and Intelligence Summaries are contained in F. S. Regs., Part II. and the Staff Manual respectively. Title pages will be prepared in manuscript.

D.A.V.S. 14 (Light) Division

Place	Date	Hour	Summary of Events and Information	Remarks and references to Appendices
1916 Aug	30		Visited 26 Mob. Vet Section at Fletre. Went to 42 Bgde H.Q.	
Aug	31		Went to Meteren to see 14 Div. H.Q. Train re surplus horses.	

[illegible]
Major
D.A.V.S.
14 Div

A5834 Wt. W4973 M687 750,000 8/16 D. D. & L. Ltd. Forms/C.2118/13.

WO 95/ 23

Confidential

War Diary

of

D.A.D.V.S. 14th Division

September 1st to 30th 1917.

(Volume No 52)

Army Form C. 2118.

Instructions regarding War Diaries and Intelligence Summaries are contained in F. S. Regs., Part II. and the Staff Manual respectively. Title pages will be prepared in manuscript.

WAR DIARY
or
D.A.D.V.S. INTELLIGENCE SUMMARY. 14th Light Division
(Erase heading not required.)

Place 1917	Date	Hour	Summary of Events and Information	Remarks and references to Appendices
Sept	1		Marched to RAVELSBURG ROAD Camp.	
	2.		Inspected H. Q horses. Office routine.	
	3		Office. Visited 14 Signal Coy R.E.	
	4		Office. Visited 26 Mob. Vet Section at BULLER Camp	
	5		Visited 26 Mob Vet Section	
	6		Visited 26 Mob. Vet Section and H. Q Train and No 1 Coy A.S.C.	
	7		Inspected 7/KRR Corps. 41st M. G. Coy. And 249 M. Gun Coy. Also 42 Field Ambulance	
	8.		Office routine	
	9		Visited 26 Mob. Vet Section.	
	10		Visited 26 Mob Vet Sec. Inspected three horses with opthalmia with Lugols Solution. Office.	

A5834 Wt. W4973 M687 750,000 8/16 D. D. & L. Ltd. Forms/C.2118/13.

Army Form C. 2118.

WAR DIARY
or
INTELLIGENCE SUMMARY.
(Erase heading not required.)

Instructions regarding War Diaries and Intelligence Summaries are contained in F. S. Regs., Part II. and the Staff Manual respectively. Title pages will be prepared in manuscript.

D.A.D.V.S. 14 (Light) Division

Place	Date	Hour	Summary of Events and Information	Remarks and references to Appendices
1917. Sept.	11		Visited 26 Mob Vet Sec. The animals operated on seem better. Visited Train re Surplus animals.	
	12		Looked for a site for Div. Clipping power station	
	13		Visited 26 Mob. Vet Sect	
	14		Inspected C and D battery 47 Brigade R.F.A. D is somewhat improved. Five cases for evacuation for debility	
	15.		Conference at Flêtre. Capt Beal returned from leave	
	16		Selected site for Clipping. Saw 44 F.A. horses.	
	17.		Inspected 26 Brigade A.F.A. Capt Taylor in Vety Charge.	
	[illegible]		Saw one case of mange.	
	18.		Inspected 41 M. Gun Coy and 42 F. Ambulance.	
	19		Laid up with "necrotic dermatitis" on neck & ankle.	

A5834 Wt. W4973 M687 750,000 8/16 D. D. & L. Ltd. Forms/C.2118/13.

Army Form C. 2118.

Instructions regarding War Diaries and Intelligence Summaries are contained in F. S. Regs., Part II. and the Staff Manual respectively. Title pages will be prepared in manuscript.

WAR DIARY
or
INTELLIGENCE SUMMARY.

D.A.D.V.S. 14th Division

(Erase heading not required.)

Place	Date 1917	Hour	Summary of Events and Information	Remarks and references to Appendices
Sept	20		Office routine. Unable to go out of camp.	
Sept	24.		Ordered to bed by M.O. Abscess in leg.	
Sept	25–30.		Office routine carried out in bed.	

[illegible]
Major
D.A.D.V.S.
14 Division

A5834 Wt. W4973 M687 750,000 8/16 D. D. & L. Ltd. Forms/C.2118/13.

Vol 24

Confidential

War Diary

of

D.A.D.V.S. 14th Div

From Oct. 1st to Oct 31st 1917

(Volume No 53)

Appendix I

Copy of letter sent to Q 14th Div on the subject of clipping of Artillery horses.

Q
14 Div.

Ref my No 681 V of 17th Nov. 1917.

The following telegrams have been received from the Veterinary Officers of the 46th & 47th Bdes R.F.A.

From VO i/c 46th Bde.-
Begins - 326 horses in 46th Bde R.F.A. and 34 in No 1 Coy. 14 Divl. Train clipped aaa clipping all stopped in RFA - e

From VO i/c 47th Bde -
Begins - clipping not completed in 47th R.F.A. nor in 14th D.A.C. - ends.

In connection with the latter telegram I have wired for definite figures.

From the figures to hand it would appear as if clipping operations had not been carried out with that expedition essential to have completed work by Nov 15th.

Sd. R. J. Stordy Major
DADVS 14th Div

Appendix II

Copy

To AA & QMG.
14th Div

Ref. your memo of 24th inst. forwarding Second Army No QC/134 of 23rd inst.

Have the honour to offer the following remarks & suggestions.

1. Horsemastership So long as the horsemastership obtaining in the 14th Division is maintained at its present high standard I feel confident that nothing will be left undone for the animals welfare.

2. Clipping. The horses of the Division are now all clipped and their condition is extremely satisfactory. Mules have not been clipped. Their condition is also satisfactory.

3. Rugs. Rugs have been issued for all horses. The rugging of mules is worthy of consideration.

Capt Thornewill A.V.C. VO/c 46th Bde RFA. communicates the result of an experiment in connection with the tarring of horse rugs, carried out by Captain Bleach of C Batty of that Bde. The tar is applied to the outside of the rug. The following advantages are claimed.

Appendix II (Contd)

ⓐ The rug is made practically waterproof
ⓑ Wind is kept out better – superior wind shield.
ⓒ The worst rug eaters won't touch the tarred article.
ⓓ Its cheapness

A Copy of Captain Thornewill's letter has already been forwarded to the A.D.V.S. VIII Corps together with recommendations for the institution of a more extended trial of what appears to be a very excellent and practical suggestion.

4. Shelters. While shelters are extremely desirable for animals working in the front area, I am of the opinion that good standings are of first importance.

To allow horses freedom of movement – to be fed and groomed properly – to have their legs attended to (more particularly the feathered legs of our H.D's) – is to do more for the comfort and welfare of the animals than erecting overhead shelters with standings such as only permit of animals standing up to their bellies in mud.

5. Picket Lines. The custom of fastening horses, head to head, to one picket line is wrong. Stable management under such conditions is well nigh impossible for, horses keep fretting & biting each other, feeding & grooming is unsatisfactory and the shy feeder is placed at the mercy of its more voracious neighbours; this latter being a frequent cause of debility. Only one side of a picket line should

Appendix II (Contd)

be used. In cases where the single line is insufficient, a second line should be erected, leaving an interval of at least 5' to 6' between and in this way every animal can be satisfactorily inspected and attended to.

6. Shoeing. The shoeing in the Brigades is of a higher standard than in those units where only cold shoeing is adopted. Recommendations will be made later with the hope that all the animals of the Division will be hot shod.

Correspondence is returned herewith.

Sgd. Robt. J. Stordy Major
DADV.S. 14th Division

26.XI.17.

Instructions regarding War Diaries and Intelligence Summaries are contained in F. S. Regs., Part II. and the Staff Manual respectively. Title pages will be prepared in manuscript.

Army Form C. 2118.

WAR DIARY
or
D.A.D.V.S. INTELLIGENCE SUMMARY. 14th Lt Division

(Erase heading not required.)

Place	Date	Hour	Summary of Events and Information	Remarks and references to Appendices
	1917			
Oct	1st		In bed. Abscess healing. Conducted Office routine from bed.	
	2		Got up today. Office, and lunched at H.Q. mess.	
	3		Went to Hazebrouck with Col Lewis to look at clipping machinery. Took Horsemastership Officer with us, who was very anxious and disinclined to help.	
	4		Went out for a little ride. Felt very weak	
	5		Rode down to M.V.S and to 14 Sig. Coy to see their animals	
	6		Went to M.V.S. Saw various cases there. Also rode to H.Q. Train.	
	7		Visited A/47 Bty R.F.A. and saw some horses with Beal. Also looked at a mule inoculated with mallein by Thornwell. No reaction	
	8		Rode to Train H.Q. at La Creche.	

Instructions regarding War Diaries and Intelligence Summaries are contained in F. S. Regs., Part II. and the Staff Manual respectively. Title pages will be prepared in manuscript.

Army Form C. 2118.

WAR DIARY
or
INTELLIGENCE SUMMARY.

(*Erase heading not required.*)

D.A.D.V.S. 14th Lt Division

Place	Date	Hour	Summary of Events and Information	Remarks and references to Appendices
Oct	9th		Marched to Westoutre. Another abcess forming on left leg. Quite lame.	
"	10th		Rode up to M.V.S. who are in the fields. No standings	
"	11th		Marched to La Clytte. Very lame. Scarcely sit on horse.	
	12th		Remained in bed. Capt O'Carroll reported	
	13th–18th		In bed. Temp varying. Abscess burst and healing up. Serum injected	
	19th		Went on ten days leave	

[illegible] Capt AVC

for DADVS 14th Div

Vol 25

Confidential

War Diary

of

DADVS. 14th Division

from November 3rd to November 30th
1917.

(Volume No 54).

Instructions regarding War Diaries and Intelligence Summaries are contained in F. S. Regs., Part II. and the Staff Manual respectively. Title pages will be prepared in manuscript.

WAR DIARY
or
~~INTELLIGENCE~~ ~~SUMMARY~~.
(Erase heading not required.)

Army Form C. 2118.

Place	Date 1917	Hour	Summary of Events and Information	Remarks and references to Appendices
BERTHEN	November 3rd		Arrived at Divisional Hdqts. to assume duties of DADVS. 14th DIVISION. Along with Major Watson, DAQMG, visited Divisional Clipping Station.	BERTHEN SHEET 27 R22
	4th		Visited 26th M.V.S. Reported myself to ADVS XI Corps. Captain F. J. WEIR AVC. proceeded to 23rd Veterinary Hospital. Office routine.	
	5th		Visited Divisional Clipping Station. Horses are being clipped at the rate of 50 per diem. Office routine.	
	6th		Office routine.	
	7th		Inspected horses of the MMP. ordered destruction of Bay mare with suppurating open joint (fetlock) evacuated Bay gelding for debility	
	8th		Visited Divisional Clipping Station. Progress very satisfactory. Inspected following Units of the 41st BRIGADE :- No 2 Coy. Div Train, 7th R.B., 8th R.B., 7th KRR, 8th KRR, M.G. Co, 42nd Field Ambulance and the 6th D.C.L.I., belonging to the 43rd Bde. Condition of animals highly satisfactory, shoeing fair, grain & forage good, no contagious disease. Discussed number of questions relating to Veterinary Services with the DAQMG. Office routine.	
	9th		Inspected 26th M.V.S. found all in good order. Inspected Div Hdqts. horses, condition good. In view of Division moving back Div Clipping Stn. closed down.	
	10th		Received Administrative Orders relating to Division moving to ST. OMER area. In anticipation	ST. OMER SHEET 27A X5

A5834 Wt. W4973 M687 750,000 8/16 D. D. & L. Ltd. Forms/C.2118/13.

Instructions regarding War Diaries and Intelligence Summaries are contained in F. S. Regs., Part II. and the Staff Manual respectively. Title pages will be prepared in manuscript.

WAR DIARY
or
~~INTELLIGENCE SUMMARY.~~
(Erase heading not required.)

Army Form C. 2118.

Place	Date 1917	Hour	Summary of Events and Information	Remarks and references to Appendices
BERTHEN (CONTD)	November 10th contd.		anticipation of move obtained sanction of ADVS. to evacuate all sick from 26th MVS. at HOPOUTRE siding receiving and issuing 44 remounts to Units of 14th DIVISION.	HOPOUTRE SHEET 27
	11th		All sick animals evacuated from 26th M.V.S. Office routine.	
WIZERNES	12th		Divisional Headquarters moved to WIZERNES. Office of DADVS. opened.	WIZERNES SHEET 36D F2
	13th		26th M.V.S. in charge of Captain J O'CARROLL, AVC. arrived. Arranged for Section to be located at Mill on outskirts of WIZERNES village. Office routine.	
	14th		Interviewed AA QMG. in regard to Div. Clipping Stn. In this connection visited Area Commandant at AUSTRA, who stated that site was available at SETQUES for Div. Clipping Stn. Visited site suggested, considered standings impossible and work necessary to renovate too great. in view of small amount of clipping to be undertaken.	AUSTRA SHEET 36D E5
	15th		Reported result of visit to SETQUES to AA QMG. recommending that clipping operations be completed in Units. Recommendation accepted. Visited 23rd Veterinary Hospital. O.C. MAJOR YOUNG, AVC., office routine.	SETQUES SHEET 36D E5
	16th		Visited Hdqrts 42nd Bde. at HALLINES evacuated case of CELLULITIS. Visited Hdqrts VIII Corps to discuss Veterinary matters with ADVS. Instructed that in accordance with G.R.O. 2622 mules would not be clipped.	HALLINES SHEET 36D F1
	17th		Despatched weekly returns. Inspected horses and mules of 14th Div. Signals. Some poor	

A5834 Wt. W4973/M687 750,000 8/16 D. D. & L. Ltd. Forms/C.2118/13.

Instructions regarding War Diaries and Intelligence Summaries are contained in F. S. Regs., Part II. and the Staff Manual respectively. Title pages will be prepared in manuscript.

WAR DIARY
or
~~INTELLIGENCE SUMMARY.~~
(Erase heading not required.)

Army Form C. 2118.

Place	Date 1917	Hour	Summary of Events and Information	Remarks and references to Appendices
WIZERNES	November 14th contd.		in condition, evacuated 3. Visited 26th M.V.S. Letter from Capt. THORNEWILL, A.V.C. in regard to the tarring of horse rugs.	
	18th		Clipping Station closed and personnel returned to respective units. Interviewed Acty. DAQMG in matter of duties and authority of DADVS. of a Division, asking that orders might be transmitted through DADVS. to O.C. 26th M.V.S. Telegrams received in connection with the clipping of horses of the 46th & 47th Bdes R.F.A. Forwarded details to DAQMG.	APPENDIX I
	19th		Visited 14th Div Signals to enquire into cause of death of a mule. Found that animal had been rolling during the night, fell into a brick lined drain, which ran close to the standing, and was strangulated. Inspected horses of Div Hdqrs. All in good condition and comfortably housed. Inspected 43rd Field Ambulance at LA WATTINE and No 4 Coy. Div. Train at QUERCAMP. All animals in good condition.	LA WATTINE SHEET 27A P32 QUERCAMP SHEET 27A V1
	20th		Forwarded statement on the clipping of horses by the O.C. 26th MVS. to DAQMG. The Divisional Units having been somewhat split up, clipping operations have had to be undertaken within the Units themselves. Rugs have been issued for all clipped animals. Visited 23rd Veterinary Hospital.	
	21st		In company with the B.T.O. inspected the following Units of the 43rd Bde:—	

Army Form C. 2118.

Instructions regarding War Diaries and Intelligence Summaries are contained in F. S. Regs., Part II. and the Staff Manual respectively. Title pages will be prepared in manuscript.

WAR DIARY
or
~~INTELLIGENCE SUMMARY.~~
(*Erase heading not required.*)

Place	Date 1917	Hour	Summary of Events and Information	Remarks and references to Appendices
WIZERNES	November 21st contd.		Bde. Hdqrts., M.G. Coy., 6th KOYLI, 6th D.C.L.I., 6th S.L.I., 10th D.L.I. and transport of Trench Mortar Battery. With the exception of a mare and mule belonging to 10 D.L.I. and a mare belonging to 6th D.C.L.I., found animals in very satisfactory state. The excellent condition of the H.Ds. is worthy of special reference. Shoeing good. Grain & Forage good. No contagious disease.	
	22nd		Office routine.	
	23rd		Visited Hdqrts. 41st Brigade at LONGUENESS found Chestnut Mare, property of French farmer, to be grossly mange infected. Placed Chateau Grounds "out of Bounds", arranged for disinfection of Bde. transport mare which was stabled in close proximity to infected animal. The disinfection of mare, harness, stable utensils, cart etc. was carried out at No. 23 Veterinary Hospital.	LONGUENESS SHEET 27A X15
	24th		26th M.V.S. carried out disinfection of stables at 41st Bde. Hdqrts. Mare has been removed by owner & placed under treatment of a Civil Veterinary Surgeon. Wrote to Signals re the non delivery of an urgent telegram addressed to Captain THORNEWILL, 16th BDE R.F.A.	
			To VIII Corps Hdqrts. to attend weekly Veterinary Conference.	
	25th		Held inspection of 26th M.V.S. The condition & cleanliness of the animals and equipment and the	

Instructions regarding War Diaries and Intelligence Summaries are contained in F. S. Regs., Part II. and the Staff Manual respectively. Title pages will be prepared in manuscript.

WAR DIARY
or
~~INTELLIGENCE SUMMARY.~~
(Erase heading not required.)

Army Form C. 2118.

Place	Date 1914	Hour	Summary of Events and Information	Remarks and references to Appendices
WIZERNES	November 25th contd.		the smartness of NCOs and men reflect the greatest credit on the Officer Commanding - Captain J. O'CARROLL. Memo from AAQMG. forwarding Second Army Circular letter No QC/134 with ref to the necessity for greatest care of horses & mules in view of Army's inability to obtain further supply of horses from America. AAQMG. asks for remarks and suggestions.	
	26th		Interviewed DAQMG in regard to Remount Demand and made the necessary alterations in accordance with the reduction in the animal establishment of the D.A.C. Office routine.	
	24th		Replied to AAQMG's Memo. of the 25th inst. Captain THORNEWILL AVC. proceeded on leave	APPENDIX II
	28th		Office routine. Captain THORNEWILL writes that the tarring of horses legs is very successful.	
	29th		OC Signals replies that he has traced telegram addressed to Captain THORNEWILL to 2nd Army Signals but as their copy has been destroyed no further trace can be made. Chateau Stables at LONGUENESS again disinfected. Area Commandant informed that Chateau Stables & grounds should remain out of bounds for horses & mules for sometime to come. Visited 224 M.G. Co. at VAL D'ACQUIN. One or two mules in poor condition, evacuated two with foot lameness. Visited BEUVEINGHEM, ALQUINES and inspected A.B.C.D. Batteries 162 Bde. R.F.A. 33rd Division. The condition of a number of the horses	BEUVEINGHEM HAZEBROUCK 5A A 4.

Instructions regarding War Diaries and Intelligence Summaries are contained in F. S. Regs., Part II. and the Staff Manual respectively. Title pages will be prepared in manuscript.

WAR DIARY
or
~~INTELLIGENCE SUMMARY.~~
(Erase heading not required.)

Army Form C. 2118.

Place	Date	Hour	Summary of Events and Information	Remarks and references to Appendices
WIZERNES	1917 November 29th contd		horses leaves much to be desired. The Batteries have been resting for nearly a month and the animals should be looking in the "pink" instead of which a fair percentage of them were found poor light in condition and dirty. With some three exceptions none of the horses have been clipped. This in great measure accounts for the condition of the animals. Enquiries as to why no horses had been clipped elicited the statement that those in command were not in favour of the operation. G.R.O. No 2622 of the 15th Sept 1917 lays down "that horses may be clipped once at the discretion of the G.Os C. Armies. Second Army Routine Order No 1250 of 23rd Oct. 1917 states "All horses and mules will be clipped out" These orders have been published after careful consideration of the whole question of clipping by those responsible for the health of the horses and mules of our Army. It would be well with the animals had these orders been carried out — orders founded on expert opinion and framed for the guidance of all entrusted with the care of animals in the field. Visited JOURNY to interview Capt GORDON AVC. V.O. i/c 156 Bde. RFA. He reports several suspicious cases of mange and has established isolated lines for the reception	

Instructions regarding War Diaries and Intelligence Summaries are contained in F. S. Regs., Part II. and the Staff Manual respectively. Title pages will be prepared in manuscript.

WAR DIARY
or
~~INTELLIGENCE SUMMARY.~~
(Erase heading not required.)

Army Form C. 2118.

Place	Date 1914	Hour	Summary of Events and Information	Remarks and references to Appendices
WIZERNES	November 29th contd.		perception of suspected cases. Instructed Capt. GORDON to send in scrapings at once for microscopic examination. Should parasitic skin disease assume epizootic proportions in the present unfitted condition of the animals it will demand the most stringent measures to effect its eradication.	
			Cases of Stomatitis have occurred in A & B Battery horses. The animals are segregated. The disease would appear to be running a benign course.	
	30th		visited Divisional Signals, examined a case of lameness. Office routine.	

Robt. J. Stordy Major
D.A.D.V.S. 14th Division.

A5834 Wt. W4973 M687 750,000 8/16 D. D. & L. Ltd. Forms/C.2118/13.

Vol 26

Confidential

War Diary

of.

D.A.D.V.S. 14th Div.

Decr. 1st to Decr 31st 1917

(Volume No 55)

Instructions regarding War Diaries and Intelligence Summaries are contained in F. S. Regs., Part II. and the Staff Manual respectively. Title pages will be prepared in manuscript.

WAR DIARY
or
~~INTELLIGENCE SUMMARY.~~
(Erase heading not required.)

Army Form C. 2118.

Place	Date 1914 DECEMBER	Hour	Summary of Events and Information	Remarks and references to Appendices
MERSEY CAMP 28·H·1·A·4·5·	1		Attended weekly Veterinary Conference at VIII Corps.	
"	2		In company with DADVS. VIII Division visited MOBILE VETERINARY SECTION LOCATION. The standings are very bad. It would appear as if any place was good enough to which to evacuate sick or wounded animals.	28·G·11·a·5·6·
"	3		Inspected animals of No. 2 and S.A.A. Section VIII Div D.A.C. Horses and mules in excellent condition, all provided with good standings. 14th Division arrived Front area.	
"	4		Inspected animals of 3rd Batt. 45th Bde RFA. 8th Div. Animals in good condition. New sheltered standings in course of erection; 5th Batt. 45th Bde RFA. 8th Div. Animals in fair condition, standings bad; 1st Batt 45th Bde RFA. 8th Div. Horses & mules in only fair condition, standings bad new ones being erected; 57th Batt. 45th Bde RFA. Animals in fair condition, few old horses & mules in poor condition brick standings; 32nd Batt. 33rd Bde RFA. 8th Div. horses & mules in bad condition, standings bad. Great lack of horsemastership.	
"	5		Inspected animals of Hdqrs. 14th Div. all in order, housed in good sheltered standings. Visited Area Commandant with a view to obtain better location for M.V.S.	
"	6		Inspected 'B' Batt. 47th Bde RFA. 14th Div animals very fair condition, standings under repair. Complaint made in regard to No. 15 Mule stamped shoe. The shoe is too long more particularly for animals working on plank roadways and if shortened the front cog hole is much weakened. Referred matter to A.D.V.S. VIII Corps; "A" Batt. 46th Bde RFA. 14th Div. Animals in fair condition. Good standings, number of horses unclipped; 'C' Batt. 46th Bde RFA. 14th Div. animals in good condition, mud standings. This battery has only had 10 days out of the line in 12 months; 'D' Batt. 46th Bde RFA. 14th Div. animals in good condition. Good standings. The Battery	

A5834 Wt. W4973 M687 750,000 8/16 D. D. & L. Ltd. Forms/C.2118/13.

Instructions regarding War Diaries and Intelligence Summaries are contained in F. S. Regs., Part II. and the Staff Manual respectively. Title pages will be prepared in manuscript.

WAR DIARY
or
~~INTELLIGENCE SUMMARY.~~
(Erase heading not required.)

Army Form C. 2118.

Place	Date 1914 DECEMBER	Hour	Summary of Events and Information	Remarks and references to Appendices
MERSEY CAMP	6th contd.		has suffered considerably from shelling. NO horses clipped; D.A.C. 14th Div animals in good condition. The animals in Section III are in excellent condition all have been clipped and the horsemastership of the Section leaves nothing to be desired. New standing of excellent design are in course of erection.	
	7th		Visited advanced Hdqrs. 14th Div along with ADVS. VIII Corps to discuss with "Q" site for M.V.S. Conference of Veterinary Officers held at Mersey Camp.	
	8th		Attended weekly Veterinary Conference at VIII Corps.	
	9th		Visited 26th M.V.S. Evacuation now take place by rail which means greater comfort to sick & wounded animals & enabled small MVS Personnel to deal with larger number of animals. Number of unclipped horses have been evacuated to MVS with suspected skin disease condition due to dirt only.	
	10th		OC 21st MVS and Capt BEAL V.O. i/c 47th Bde RFA called to discuss few questions. Visited 44th Bde AFA. but as the Veterinary Officer Capt. CHAGNON was absent I did not carry out an inspection.	
	11th		Inspected 64th Bde AFA. The general condition of the animals was bad and the animals of the B.A.C. were the worst of all units inspected. Very large number of animals will require to be evacuated. Standings were fair from good in one or two batteries; D Batt. 38th AFA. animals in fair condition but good percentage of them require rest: fair standings. Forwarded report on inspection of AFA Bdes. to ADVS VIII Corps. From inspections made it would appear that some Veterinary Officers are too	

A5834 Wt. W4973/M687 750,000 8/16 D. D. & L. Ltd. Forms/C.2118/13.

Instructions regarding War Diaries and Intelligence Summaries are contained in F. S. Regs., Part II. and the Staff Manual respectively. Title pages will be prepared in manuscript.

WAR DIARY
or
~~INTELLIGENCE SUMMARY.~~
(Erase heading not required.)

Army Form C. 2118.

Place	Date 1917 DECEMBER	Hour	Summary of Events and Information	Remarks and references to Appendices
MERSEY CAMP	11th contd		prone to retain animals which should be sent to base to recuperate. It is false economy to keep animals in poor condition on the strength of unit. 26th M.V.S. takes over animals for evacuation from the 43rd M.V.S. 33rd Div. on the latter moving to another area.	
	12th		Inspected 41st M.G. Co. animals in fair condition; inspected 42nd Bde. Transport, animals in good condition; No. 3 Coy. Train 14th Div. animals in excellent condition. Capt. THORNEWILL returned from leave.	
	13th		Inspected "A" Batt. 47th Bde. RFA. 14th Div. animals fair, 4 cases of mange evacuated, 6 cases of debility; good standings in course of erection; "C" Batt. 47th Bde. RFA. animals very good condition; "D" Batt. 47th Bde. RFA. animals good. In Sub Section E several in light condition, these are receiving special attention. Visited VIII Corps. to discuss some matters with A.D.V.S. Visited advanced Hdqts. to see "Q" re reduction in D.A.C. animals. Wired A.D.V.S. II Corps in regard to dipping number of in-contacts.	
	14th		Held weekly Conference of Veterinary officers. 70 animals from D.A.C. 14th Div. handed over to 64th Bde. A.F.A.	
	15th		Attended Veterinary Conference at VIII Corps. Capt. BLYTH A.V.C. attached VIII Div. proceeded on leave.	
	16th		O.C. 26th M.V.S. reports case of Stomatitis evacuated from 64th Bde. A.F.A., reported matter by wire to A.D.V.S. case placed in strict isolation.	
	17th		Visited D.A.C. Hdqts. in regard to animals handed over to 64th Bde. A.F.A. Bde. Transport and Divisional Units. Inspected 89th Coy. R.E. animals in good condition.	

A5834 Wt. W4973/M687 750,000 8/16 D. D. & L. Ltd. Forms/C.2118/13.

Instructions regarding War Diaries and Intelligence Summaries are contained in F. S. Regs., Part II. and the Staff Manual respectively. Title pages will be prepared in manuscript.

WAR DIARY

or

~~INTELLIGENCE SUMMARY.~~

(Erase heading not required.)

Army Form C. 2118.

Place	Date 1914 DECEMBER	Hour	Summary of Events and Information	Remarks and references to Appendices
MERSEY CAMP	18th		Inspected "B" Batt R.F.A. 14th Div. animals with one or two exceptions in good condition. Shelters good but standings very bad, no system of drainage. Office routine	
	19th		Visited Hdqrs 14th Div. Animals visited 26th M.V.S. Ouderdom & advanced Hdqrs.	
	20th		Inspected No 1 Train, 14th Div. animals in good condition, good standings; 61st Field Coy R.E. animals in good condition, good standing. But inspected in forward area; 62nd Field Coy R.E. animals in good condition, good stables; 43rd Field Ambulance animals very good, good stabling. Replied to Memo. No A 689 from A.A.Q.M.G. Memo. had reference to the Veterinary Administration in the forward area and what, if any improvements were considered desirable. Pointed out that the arrangement of having two Mobile Sections in one location was a distinct success for the VOs in charge were given time to classify & arrange their cases for evacuation to the Base & that congestion of Section was avoided. The improvements suggested were :- (a) improved standings and shelters for horses & mules, (b) advantageous to adopt hot shoeing in all units (c) chaff cutters to be supplied to all units of 25 animals or over (d) that clipping regulations be strictly adhered to (e) that tarring of horse rugs was both successful and economical (f) that, in order to prevent as far as possible injury to horses feet through the animals picking up discarded SAA. that orders be issued calling attention to the danger of dropping SAA on the main thoroughfares (g) that increased transport facilities be granted the D.A.D.V.S.	
	21st		Held conference of Veterinary Officers.	

A5834 Wt. W4973 M687 750,000 8/16 D. D. & L. Ltd. Forms/C.2118/13.

Army Form C. 2118.

Instructions regarding War Diaries and Intelligence Summaries are contained in F. S. Regs., Part II. and the Staff Manual respectively. Title pages will be prepared in manuscript.

WAR DIARY
or
INTELLIGENCE SUMMARY.
(Erase heading not required.)

Place	Date 1917 DECEMBER	Hour	Summary of Events and Information	Remarks and references to Appendices
MERSEY CAMP.	22		Attended Conference at VIII Corps. New regulations promulgated in regard to evacuation of all animals suffering from Ophthalmia.	
	23		Discussed with O.C. 26th M.V.S. & Capt. THORNEWILL the effect of evacuating all ophthalmic cases. Periodic Ophthalmia is fairly prevalent throughout the Division & if all cases are to be sent to Base there will be grave danger of some units becoming immobile. Advised officers to use most careful discretion in the matter. Enemy bombed the horse lines heavily between Ypres and Vlamertinghe.	
	24		Reported that some fifty horses were killed by last night bombing. Only casualties in 14th Divisional Units were two horses wounded belonging to Hdqrs. 46th Bde R.F.A. One case tetanus destroyed at "A" Batt 47th RFA	
	25		Office routine. Very heavy snow fell.	
	26		Inspected new stables at "A" Batt. 47th Bde. Construction excellent.	
WIZERNES.	27		Division moved to Wizernes. Frost & snow made travelling difficult and dangerous.	
	28		Office routine.	
	29		Weekly returns submitted. Visited Ordnance in regard to reserve supply of front crop mail.	
	30		At Hdqrs to see "Q" regarding Brood Mares selection Committee.	
	31		Visited Hdqrs animals. All comfortably housed. Office routine.	

Robt. J. Hardy Major.
D.A.D.V.S.
14th Division.

A5834 Wt. W4973 M687 750,000 8/16 D. D. & L. Ltd. Forms/C.2118/13.

Vol 27

Confidential

War Diary

of

D.A.D.V.S. 14th Div

January 1st to 31st. 1918

(Volume No 56.)

Instructions regarding War Diaries and Intelligence Summaries are contained in F. S. Regs., Part II. and the Staff Manual respectively. Title pages will be prepared in manuscript.

WAR DIARY
or
~~INTELLIGENCE SUMMARY.~~
(*Erase heading not required.*)

Army Form C. 2118.

Place	Date 1918 JANUARY	Hour	Summary of Events and Information	Remarks and references to Appendices
WIZERNES	1		Inspected Hdqtrs horses. Office routine.	
"	2		Office routine. Captain Beal returned from leave.	
MERICOURT SUR SOMME	3		To MERICOURT-SUR-SOMME. Division came under administration of XVIII Corps.	
"	4		Office opened at Mericourt-sur Somme. Visited 26th Mobile Vety Section at Bray	
"	5		Visited Units at Sailly LAURETTE, BRAY, CAPPY, SUZANNE. Inspected 42nd Field Ambulance, 42nd M.G. Coy., visited 26th M.V.S., Capt. Thornhill, V.O. i/c 46th Brigade R.F.A. arrived from ST. OMER area.	
"	6		Inspected Hdqtrs & M.M.P. horses. Sent off returns to Corps.	
"	7		14th Division came under administration of VII Corps. Capt. O'Carroll proceeded on leave.	
	8		Inspected 224th M.G. Co. Office routine.	
	9		Visited A.D.V.S. VII Corps, Lt.Col. CONDER, at TEMPLEUX LA FOSSE to discuss number of Veterinary Questions.	
	10		Visited 26th M.V.S. Gave instructions in regard to disinfection of stables and animals at Bray and Mericourt. Bad case of mange evacuated from "A" 47th Bde. Visited M.V.S.	
	11		Held conference of Veterinary Officers. Ordnance report shortage of foot-wraps. The 169th Bde A.F.A. comes under administration of 14th Division.	
	12		At Conference at VII Corps. Visited ETINEHEM to inspect "A" 47th Bde.	

A5834 Wt. W4973 M687 750,000 8/16 D. D. & L. Ltd. Forms/C.2118/13.

Instructions regarding War Diaries and Intelligence Summaries are contained in F. S. Regs., Part II. and the Staff Manual respectively. Title pages will be prepared in manuscript.

WAR DIARY
or
~~INTELLIGENCE SUMMARY.~~
(Erase heading not required.)

Army Form C. 2118.

Place	Date 1918 JANUARY	Hour	Summary of Events and Information	Remarks and references to Appendices
MERICOURT SUR SOMME	13		Issued instructions re disinfection of horses & stables at Mericourt. At Field Remount Park – VILLERS CARBONNEL – selecting remounts. Hard frost prevails.	
"	14		Disinfection of animal stables completed. Capt. BEAL reports 2 cases of mange at Convalescent Farm, CERISY.	
"	15		With a view to locating all centres of mange among animal property of Civilians visited VAUX-SUR-SOMME, SAILLY LE SEC, SAILLY LAURETTE, CERISY, MORCOURT, PROYARD, CHIGNOLLES, CHUIGNES. Inspected transport of 7th K.R.R., 61st Field Coy. R.E., 44th Field Ambulance, 41st M.G. Coy, 8th R.B., No 2 Coy. Div. Train, 46th Reserve Park ASC., 7th R.B. & X DLI. French Civilians anxious to have their animals treated & only desire facilities for so doing. Risk run by animals of British Army located in BRAY area cannot be overestimated.	
"	16		Inspected "A" Batt. 46th Bde. R.F.A. in which cases of mange have occurred, at Field Reserve Park distributing remounts & visited 26th M.V.S.	
	17		Inspected 376th 378th 377th Batts & B.A.C. of 169th Bde A.F.A. consider 100 to 120 evacuations will be necessary. Animals much run down.	
	17		Inspected X DLI. Five cases of skin disease placed under observation. Discussed Veterinary matters with AA & QMG to whom a report on mange had been submitted.	
	18		Held conference of Vety. Officers.	

A5834 Wt. W4973 M687 750,000 8/16 D. D. & L. Ltd. Forms/C.2118/13.

Army Form C. 2118.

WAR DIARY
or
INTELLIGENCE SUMMARY.
(Erase heading not required.)

Instructions regarding War Diaries and Intelligence Summaries are contained in F. S. Regs., Part II. and the Staff Manual respectively. Title pages will be prepared in manuscript.

Place	Date 1918 JANUARY	Hour	Summary of Events and Information	Remarks and references to Appendices
MERICOURT SUR SOMME	19		D.D.V.S. 5th Army, Col. TATAM CMG. visited area. Discussed number of question with him. He inspected 169th Bde AFA. with exception of No 377th Batt.	
"	20		Inspected 11th King's Liverpool Regt. transport, 377 Batty 169th Bde. AFA. & D.C.L.I. Visited M.V.S. Discussed question of disinfecting stables in new area with the AA & QMG & ordered necessary material for same. Spoke to Capt. Beal re Mange in "D" Batt 47th & called upon him to exercise every care. Wrote to AA&QMG asking that a D.R.O. should be published forbidding the occupation of stables & standings in CLASTRES area & en route to same.	
	21		Issued instructions in regard to the disinfection of stables in which cases of mange had occurred. Had standings placarded.	
	22		Visited 36th M.V.S. to inspect animals prior to evacuation. Inspected "D" Battery. 47th Bde RFA. placed 4 cases of skin disease in working isolation.	
	23		Interviewed AA & QMG. in regard to the disinfection of stables & standings in new area. Wrote to D.D.V.S. in regard to Mange in Bray area, & to the ADVS. III Corps to warn the Division about to enter the area to exercise greatest care.	
GUISCARD	24		Moved with Div Hdqrs. to GUISCARD.	
	25		Informed ADVS III Corps of my office location. Captain O'CARROLL returned from leave. Visited, to inspect suspect skin cases, No 1 Coy. Div. Train.	

Instructions regarding War Diaries and Intelligence Summaries are contained in F. S. Regs., Part II. and the Staff Manual respectively. Title pages will be prepared in manuscript.

WAR DIARY
or
~~INTELLIGENCE SUMMARY.~~
(Erase heading not required.)

Army Form C. 2118.

Place	Date 1918 JANUARY	Hour	Summary of Events and Information	Remarks and references to Appendices
GUISCARD	25th	contd.	Visited FLAVEY-LE-MARTEL to find that creosol for disinfecting purposes had arrived. Issued instructions re disinfection in forward area.	
	26th		Visited JUSSY to select site for 26th M.V.S. Visited MONTESCOURT and CLASTRES.	
	27th		Inspected all the horses of No 1 Div. Train. Issued instructions to B.T.Os informing them that all standings and stables would be inspected by competent authority before occupation. Accompanied by Captains O'CARROLL and THORNEWILL visited CLASTRES, MONTESCOURT and REMIGNY to inspect disinfecting operations.	
JUSSY	28th		Moved with Div. Hdqrs. to JUSSY. A.A. & Q.M.G. brought Captain GUFFROY Veterinary Major 2nd Class of the 154th Infantry Division French Army to see me with reference to the prevalence of mange in CLASTRES area. Captain GUFFROY was good enough to give me much valuable information in regard to contagious animal disease.	
	29th		Accompanied by Captain GUFFROY and M. HEV of the French Mission visited all stables & standings lying within Divisional area. Every building or horse line in which cases of mange had been located were placarded. On account of tactical reasons the 26th M.V.S.	

A5834 Wt. W4973 M687 750,000 8/16 D. D. & L. Ltd. Forms/C.2118/13.

Instructions regarding War Diaries and Intelligence Summaries are contained in F. S. Regs., Part II. and the Staff Manual respectively. Title pages will be prepared in manuscript.

WAR DIARY
or
~~INTELLIGENCE~~ SUMMARY.
(Erase heading not required.)

Army Form C. 2118.

Place	Date 1918 JANUARY	Hour	Summary of Events and Information	Remarks and references to Appendices
JUSSY	29th contd.		is ordered South of the Canal.	
	30th		Inspected new site for 26th M.V.S. Visited REMIGNY, CLASTRES and MONTESCOURT. Disinfecting operations well in hand. Found 43rd Inf. Bde. had occupied stables without my authority. Visited Hdqts. & discussed the matter with A.A.Q.M.G. who informed me that owing to aerial activity on the part of the enemy it was considered expedient to place animals under cover. To III Corps with A.A.&Q.M.G. Visited PETIT DETROIT with GENERAL PERKINS, C.R.A. to select stabling for heavy Battery animals.	
	31st		Visited 26th MVS. Sent in report on Contagious disease in CLASTRES area to A.A.Q.M.G. Office routine.	APPENDIX I

Robt. J. Stordy Major
DADVS 14th Div.

A5834 Wt. W4973 M687 750,000 8/16 D. D. & L. Ltd. Forms/C.2118/13.

APPENDIX I

Copy.

D.A.D.V.S.
14th DIV.
No. 770 V
Date 31·1·18

To. AA + QMG.
14th Div.

Contagious Animal Disease in Clastres Area

Accompanied by Captain Guffroy, Divisional Veterinary Officer to the 154th Infantry Division, French Army and M. Amouric of the French Mission I visited, on Tuesday last all stables and standings lying within the 14th Divisional Area.

Captain Guffroy was good enough to give me the following data, in regard to Contagious Animal disease which is now submitted for your information and disposal.

CLASTRES

The worst village in the area for Mange. 150 cases evacuated recently to Noyon Veterinary Hospital.

LE BURGUET CHATEAU a number of mange cases. Stabling good but situated in swampy location

MONTESCOURT Mange in 3 standings

LIZEROLLES Number of stables with mange cases. Some grossly infected.

FLAVEY-LE-MARTEL No cases of Mange. During "taking over" the animals of French Regimental transport have occupied the stables in the village therefore all animal accomodation must receive every attention.
PETIT DETROIT Two farms, with standings for 150 horses, infected.
DETROIT BLEU One stable with 2 cases of Mange. Standings for 800 horses.
DETROIT d'ANNCIS 2 cases of Mange accommodation for 150 horses.
BEAUMONT 1 farm infected, accommodation for 500 horses. Water only obtainable from wells. pumps required.
REMIGNY This area lies outside the 15th Divisional Area. Reported to have a number of cases of mange
JUSSY. No cases of Mange
FERME MAURETAS No cases.

Every stable & standing, in which cases of mange have been located have been placarded or clearly marked "MANGE"

Instructions have been issued through D.R.C. & direct from this office to all V.O's., B.T.O.'s., & officers in charge of animals in regard to disinfection of stables, standings, water troughs, harness sheds & harness and saddle racks and that no stables or standings shall be occupied until passed by competent authority.

The disinfection of the stables of Divl. H.Q., Signals, Divl. Train HQ., 43rd Inf Bde, 89th Fd. Coy. R.E. & 43rd Fd Amb. is completed. Disinfection of other locations is well in hand & should be finished by 14th prox.

Practically all the mange met with in this area is of the sarcoptic variety. The French Army only evacuate animals in advanced stages, the newly or slightly infected are put into teams and placed in "working isolation".

It should be pointed out that in many instances the horses of a unit occupy one row of stabling - 1 or 2 empty stalls forming the boundary line between clean & infected animals. Further, healthy & mangey drink at same trough.

The greatest care is therefore necessary to ensure that all stables & standings about to be used by our animals be absolutely cleaned.

None of the French horses are clipped as horse rugs are not issued.

The winter coat around root of the tail is removed to enable one of the primary seats of mange infection to be kept under observation.

Glanders no cases. All horses are Mallein tested every 4 months.
Ulcerative Cellulitis very few cases.
Epizootic Lymphangitis 4 cases in stables at Lizerolles. Stable will be destroyed.
Specific Opthalmia Few cases. Reget's treatment - the injection of Lugol's Solution into supraorbital fat - is adopted.
Tetanus. 2 cases during January at LIZEROLLES.
Strangles none.
Anthrax no cases.

Surgical Cases. Severe cases or cases likely to take a long time to recover are slaughtered, the flesh being issued as rations to German Prisoners.

Sgd. Robt. J. Stordy Major

DADVS 40th Division

Confidential

War Diary

of

D.A.D.V.S. 14 Div

February 21st to 28th

(Volume No 57)

Instructions regarding War Diaries and Intelligence Summaries are contained in F. S. Regs., Part II. and the Staff Manual respectively. Title pages will be prepared in manuscript.

WAR DIARY
or
~~INTELLIGENCE SUMMARY.~~
(Erase heading not required.)

Army Form C. 2118.

Place	Date 1918 FEBRUARY	Hour	Summary of Events and Information	Remarks and references to Appendices
JUSSY	1st		Held conference of V.Os. Visited Div. Depot Battn. and D.A.C. to enquire into disinfection operations. At III Corps to discuss several matters with A.D.V.S.	
	2nd		Visited 26th M.V.S. Visited 169th A.F.A. 182nd Infantry Transport lines. Nos 2,3,4 Coys Div Train re disinfection. Discussed number of Veterinary Questions with "Q". Visited A.D.V.S. III Corps.	
	3rd		26th M.V.S. moved to new location North of Canal. A lot of work required before location is in ship shape order. Visited Div. Hdqrs at Clastres. Enemy bombed "A" Batt. horse lines killing one horse and wounding 13 horses & mules, of which 4 had to be destroyed. Bombs used are of the lateral explosive type - detrimental to most field structures at present made of tarred felting supported on wire netting. Horses were wounded at distance of 80 to 100 yds. Had interview with the G.O.C. Sir VICTOR COUPER K.C.B. in regard to the stabling of animals - placing them under cover - in view of enemy aerial activity. Expressed the opinion that animals should not be stabled until disinfection had been carried out. In my opinion it was better to lose a few animals from air chance than to having mange rampant in Div. Units.	

Instructions regarding War Diaries and Intelligence Summaries are contained in F. S. Regs., Part II. and the Staff Manual respectively. Title pages will be prepared in manuscript.

WAR DIARY
or
~~INTELLIGENCE SUMMARY.~~
(Erase heading not required.)

Army Form C. 2118.

Place	Date 1918 FEBRUARY	Hour	Summary of Events and Information	Remarks and references to Appendices
TUGNY	3rd contd.		Disinfection operation going on apace & the great majority of the animals will be treated within the next few days.	
	4th		Lt STEINER proceeded on leave. To Veterinary Conference at III Corps.	
	5th		At Clastres, Montescourt, Detroit d'Annois & BIEV... re disinfection. Enemy bombed 1/2nd Infty. Transport Lines at MONTESCOURT resulting in death of 2 mules & minor injuries to 15 horses & mules. Stables and standings are now disinfected & will be occupied. Suspected debility cases in 376th, 377th, 378th & 379th Batts. 169th A.F.A. At Hdqrs discussing transport questions. Wrote to A.D.V.S. III Corps re what if carcases of horses & mules killed or destroyed could be put to any economic use.	
	6th		Enemy shelled REMIGNY resulting in wounding 2 mules which had to be destroyed. At Div. Hdqrs with Col. RICHARDS O.C. Train to go into question with Q re the formation of a Div. Troops Reserve Park. Visited Petit DETROIT with Q to inspect location of Transport Lines. To III Corps accompanied A.D.V.S. to CREPIGNY, GRANDRU, DAMPCOURT to assist in the selection of a location for a Vety C.C. Station. Garden situated out side of [illegible] off main road near to railhead - APILLY - and	

A5834 Wt. W4973 M687 750,000 8/16 D. D. & L. Ltd. Forms/C.2118/13.

Instructions regarding War Diaries and Intelligence Summaries are contained in F. S. Regs., Part II. and the Staff Manual respectively. Title pages will be prepared in manuscript.

WAR DIARY
or
INTELLIGENCE SUMMARY.
(Erase heading not required.)

Army Form C. 2118.

Place	Date 1918 FEBRUARY	Hour	Summary of Events and Information	Remarks and references to Appendices
JUSSY	6th contd.		and offering considerable accommodation was considered a very suitable location.	
	7th		Visited 26th M.V.S., Inspected site at FLAVEY LE MARTEL for Div. Transport Reserve Park. Selected stable & standing.	
	8th		Visited 5 DLI and inspected transport animals prior to them being taken over by the 18 Division. Evacuated one charger with skin disease and one mule with sprained fetlock joint. Inspected animals to be evacuated to Base from 26th M.V.S. Issued order to T.O. 5 DLI to occupy no stables or standings while en route to 5 D.W. Held conference of V.Os., placed animals belonging to Hdqrs 298th Bde A.F.A. under mallein test — four cases of glanders having been discovered in the Bde animals at GUIVRY.	
	9th		A.D.V.S. III Corps visited the following Divisional Units:- No 3 Section D.A.C., 26th M.V.S., 46th & 47th Bdes R.F.A., 41st Infantry Transport, 3/6th & 3/7th Batt. 169th A.F.A. At conclusion of inspection he expressed himself as satisfied with all he had seen. 10 tons of material for horse washing stables arrived.	

A5834 Wt. W4973 M687 750,000 8/16 D. D. & L. Ltd. Forms/C.2118/13.

Instructions regarding War Diaries and Intelligence Summaries are contained in F. S. Regs., Part II. and the Staff Manual respectively. Title pages will be prepared in manuscript.

WAR DIARY
or
~~INTELLIGENCE SUMMARY.~~

(Erase heading not required.)

Army Form C. 2118.

Place	Date 1918 FEBRUARY	Hour	Summary of Events and Information	Remarks and references to Appendices
Tussy	10th		Suspected animals under mallein test at 298th Bde Hdqrts: no reactions so far. Placed 4 H.Ds. belonging to Div Train (attached to Bde) under test.	
	11th		Inspected transport animals of 9th Scottish Rifles and 49th R.R., and No 1 Section D.A.C. evacuated 2 H.Ds. from D.A.C. with [illegible] disease.	
	12th		At 21st M.V.S. inspecting evacuated animals. Inspected doubtful reaction at 298th Hdqrts — one of the A.S.C. H.D. — placed animal under counter test.	
	13th		Visited 160th Bde R.F.A. evacuated 13 animals for debility. Since the arrival of this Bde in the Clastres Area the condition of the animals is much improved. Inspected the newly disinfected Transport lines at Flavy le Martel, at Divisional Train Hdqrts. Discussed with the S.S.O. the question of Salt ration for animals. Can find no authority for its issue. Referred matter to A.D.V.S. III Corps. Visited 26th M.V.S.	
	14th		The mallein placed under counter test has again exhibited a pronounced reaction with a thermal rise of 2°. Despatched telegram to A.D.V.S. III Corps advising its destruction. Held weekly Veterinary Conference at conclusion of which the D.G.O. — Capt. ATKINSON — gave a demonstration of anti gas	

A5834 Wt. W4973 M687 750,000 8/16 D. D. & L. Ltd. Forms/C.2118/13.

Instructions regarding War Diaries and Intelligence Summaries are contained in F. S. Regs., Part II. and the Staff Manual respectively. Title pages will be prepared in manuscript.

WAR DIARY
or
INTELLIGENCE SUMMARY.
(Erase heading not required.)

Army Form C. 2118.

Place	Date 1918 FEBRUARY Hour	Summary of Events and Information	Remarks and references to Appendices
JUSSY	14th contd.	appliances for animals.	
	15th	Visited Flowy. le Martel to inspect transport lines. At Hdqrs. to discuss several matters with the DADVS. Destroyed & held post mortem exam. on reactor to mallein. NO glanders lesions found but reaction on primary & mallein test so definite, its destruction was justified. The animals of No 1 Coy. Train, with which the reacting horse had come in contact, were placed under the mallein test this afternoon, put into working isolation and separate watering troughs provided. The authorities concerned were notified of measures taken. Reported No. 20076 – Private PERKINS – of 43rd M.G.C. to his Commanding Officer for maltreating a mule, and called for disciplinary action. The 298th Bde AFA arrived in CLASTRES AREA. This Brigade has been recently tested for Glanders 5 reactors destroyed and the entire Brigade placed in working isolation until a retest is made. Retesting will be undertaken on or about 14.3.18.	

A5834 Wt. W4973 M687 750,000 8/16 D. D. & L. Ltd. Forms/C.2118/13.

Army Form C. 2118.

Instructions regarding War Diaries and Intelligence Summaries are contained in F. S. Regs., Part II. and the Staff Manual respectively. Title pages will be prepared in manuscript.

WAR DIARY
or
~~INTELLIGENCE SUMMARY.~~

(Erase heading not required.)

Place	Date 1918 FEBRUARY	Hour	Summary of Events and Information	Remarks and references to Appendices
JUSSY	16th		Captain MORLAND A.V.C. Veterinary Officer attached to the 298th Bde A.F.A, after full discussion was instructed by the measures to be adopted in regard to the Brigade during its period of working isolation. Issued instructions to O.C. 298th Bde. and requested that the instructions be issued in Brigade Orders. Inspected 49th Field Coy R.E. to ensure that thorough disinfection of stables had been carried out. Visited 26th M.V.S. 2 horses and 1 mule had to be destroyed - 1 horse & 1 mule with suppurating open joints and those for serious front injuries - These cases should never have been sent in but destroyed in the Unit lines. Such lack of judgment on the part of members of the Field Staff tends to convert the M.V.S. into an animal graveyard. Visited Ordnance to arrange for various supplies for 298th Bde. Issued disinfecting materials to the Bde. and informed the A.P.M of the regulations governing the Bde during its isolation.	

A5834 Wt. W4973 M687 750,000 8/16 D. D. & L. Ltd. Forms/C.2118/13.

Army Form C. 2118.

Instructions regarding War Diaries and Intelligence Summaries are contained in F. S. Regs., Part II. and the Staff Manual respectively. Title pages will be prepared in manuscript.

WAR DIARY
or
~~INTELLIGENCE SUMMARY.~~
(Erase heading not required.)

Place	Date 1918 FEBRUARY	Hour	Summary of Events and Information	Remarks and references to Appendices
JUSSY	17th		Inspected watering arrangements for 298th Bde. A.F.A. Visited 26th M.V.S. No reactions among the 478 animals tested belonging to No 1 Co. 14th Div. Train. Received telegram authorising salt ration for horses and mules.	
	18th		Inspected A B C Batteries 298th Bde. A.F.A. number of skin disease cases, several cases of ophthalmia, number poor in condition. Ordered evacuation of some 14 animals. In company with the D.A.D.V.S. inspected the Battalion Transport of the 10th D.L.I. and 6th K.S.L.I. Visited III Corps to discuss number of Veterinary personnel. Complaint lodged by O.C. 7th Vety. Hospital in regard to the evacuation conducted by 26th M.V.S. on 8th inst.	
	19th		Visited Railhead to supervise entraining of sick animals proceeding to Base. Inspected D Batt. and B.A.C. 298th Bde. A.F.A. Two doubtful reactions to Mallein among A.S.C. horses attached to B.A.C. Ordered counter test — intradermal — Inspected No 2 Coy. 14th Div. Train.	

A5834 Wt. W4973 M687 750,000 8/16 D. D. & L. Ltd. Forms/C.2118/13.

Instructions regarding War Diaries and Intelligence Summaries are contained in F. S. Regs., Part II. and the Staff Manual respectively. Title pages will be prepared in manuscript.

WAR DIARY
or
~~INTELLIGENCE SUMMARY.~~

(Erase heading not required.)

Army Form C. 2118.

Place	Date 1918 FEBRUARY	Hour	Summary of Events and Information	Remarks and references to Appendices
JUSSY	19th contd.		Lt. Elmer A.V.C. returned from leave. Forwarded report from O.C. 26th M.V.S. on the Complaint raised by O.C. No 4 Veterinary Hospital.	
	20th		Inspected debility cases at 116th Bde. AFA animals have so much improved that it may be hoped that very few evacuations may be necessary. Discussed a few Veterinary matters with "Q". Visited 26th M.V.S. and went carefully over a number of skin cases. Report received from G.H.Q. in regard to the use of Coopers dip in the treatment of mange ringworm & lice. The dip has been found to be even more successful than Calcium sulphide. I advocated its adoption in August 1914. East African Experience proved the dips value in the treatment of skin disease.	
	21st		Held conference of Vety. officers. Captain Morland reports reactions in 2 horses retested by him. Gave instructions to have them destroyed. At III Corps to attend Veterinary Conference.	
	22nd		Proceeded on leave.	

R. J. [illegible] Major
DADVS 14th Division.

A5834 Wt. W4973 M687 750,000 8/16 D. D. & L. Ltd. Forms/C.2118/13.

1.4

DADVS + 26 MVS Vol 34

26th MOBILE VETERINARY SECTION
Army Form C. 2118.
Date............

Instructions regarding War Diaries and Intelligence Summaries are contained in F. S. Regs., Part II, and the Staff Manual respectively. Title pages will be prepared in manuscript.

WAR DIARY
or
INTELLIGENCE SUMMARY.
(Erase heading not required.)

Place	Date	Hour	Summary of Events and Information	Remarks and references to Appendices
Jussy –	1/3/18		Evacuated fourteen animals to the base from Flavy-le-Martel	
– " –	2/3/18		Went to Div. H.Q.; drew 550 francs and paid NCO's and men.	
	3/3/18		Saddle and rifle inspection	
	4/3/18		Visited by ADVS III Corps.; No1012 Pte Johnson J.R. A.V.C. proceeds on one months leave from 4/3/18 — 3/4/18.	
	5/3/18		Evacuated twenty six animals to the base	
	6/3/18		Building of Sick Stable continues very satisfactorily	
	7/3/18		Nothing to report.	
	8/3/18		Washing and oiling of waggons.	
	9/3/18		Visited by ADVS. Usual routine	
	10/3/18		D.A.D.V.S. returns from leave; Saddle and rifle and anti gas appliance inspection.	
	11/3/18		Visited by DADVS.	
– " –	12/3/18		Evacuated 47 animals to the base. In the afternoon went with the DADVS to find a suitable site for the MVS around PETIT DETROIT.	W. Carroll

DIRECTOR GENERAL ARMY VETERINARY SERVICES 1? JUN 1918 WAR OFFICE

D. D. & L., London, E.C. (A8004) Wt. W1771/M2·31 750,000 5/17 Sch. 52 Forms/C2118/14

Instructions regarding War Diaries and Intelligence Summaries are contained in F. S. Regs., Part II. and the Staff Manual respectively. Title pages will be prepared in manuscript.

WAR DIARY
or
INTELLIGENCE SUMMARY.
(Erase heading not required.)

26th MOBILE VETERINARY SECTION
Army Form C. 2118.
Date..........

Place	Date	Hour	Summary of Events and Information	Remarks and references to Appendices
JUSSY.	13/3/18	—	Visited by the AA+QMG. who is awfully pleased and surprised with the improvements made in the camp. — Sent to Corps H.Qrs for No 27253 PTE BULL AVC Skinner attached to the Division	
	14/3/18	—	Visited by DADVS and OC Div Train. My RSPCA ambulance out of action for the want of a wheel. Received orders to move to PETIT. DETROIT.	
	15/3/18	—	Evacuated 30 animals to the base	
	16/3/18	—	Usual routine; Sent a party of men to clean up and prepare new camp.	
	17/3/18	—	Routine as usual	
PETIT. DETROIT.	18/3/18	—	Moved to PETIT DETROIT. Had to leave ambulance at Jussy awaiting the arrival of a wheel from ordnance.	
— " —	19/3/18	—	Evacuated 17 animals to the base. Visited by CRE. who is going to carry out necessary repairs.	
— " —	20/3/18		Routine as usual. During the course of the day all units around me had orders to stand to: but I received no such orders.	
— " —	21/3/18		Enemy bombardment commenced at 4.30 Am. wounded animals coming in all the morning DADVS wounded and evacuated & take over his duties. attended a number of wounded at Jussy during the morning. — wired to Corps if I could evacuate my animals to the 18th Div M.V.S.	W. Hand..

(A8004) Wt. W1771/M2 31 750,000 5/17 Sch. 52 Forms/C2118/14 H. D. & L., London, E.C.

Instructions regarding War Diaries and Intelligence Summaries are contained in F. S. Regs., Part II. and the Staff Manual respectively. Title pages will be prepared in manuscript.

WAR DIARY
or
INTELLIGENCE SUMMARY.
(Erase heading not required.)

Army Form C. 2118.

26th MOBILE VETERINARY SECTION

Place	Date	Hour	Summary of Events and Information	Remarks and references to Appendices
	21st (contd).		then at Grand Ru. but received no reply. — At 2 P.M. the 42nd Fd Ambulance alongside me received orders to move to Beaumont en Beine. and so I began to make preparations for I had then forty wounded to deal with. At 3 PM I received orders to move to BUSSY. With the exception of one mule (destroyed) I brought along all the wounded. Arrived BUSSY at 11 PM. — My ambulance left at Jussy was completely destroyed by shell fire — None of the DADVS stationery could be got away from Jussy.	
BUSSY.				
— " —	22/3/18 —		Notified ADVS III Corps of my move, also Q of my move and the evacuation of Noyon Siding. Went to Corps HQ. to see ADVS: but only could find his corporal in charge, who told me that he had not received my wire of the day before with reference to my evacuating my animals from PETIT DETROIT to Grand Ru. He also informed me that: that was the scheme and that I should have received those instructions. —: Sent to Noyon and ordered six trucks for the following day.	
— " —	23/3/18		Evacuated forty animals from Noyon. — Sent portion of the Section to Cuy; keeping the remainder at Bussy. This I did without orders from the Division: for in the event of Noyon being closed as a railhead there was no other course open to me. — I informed OC 14th Div Train of this move.	[illegible]

Instructions regarding War Diaries and Intelligence Summaries are contained in F. S. Regs., Part II. and the Staff Manual respectively. Title pages will be prepared in manuscript.

WAR DIARY
or
INTELLIGENCE SUMMARY.
(*Erase heading not required.*)

26th MOBILE VETERINARY SECTION
Army Form C. 2118.
Date..............

Place	Date	Hour	Summary of Events and Information	Remarks and references to Appendices
CUY.	24/3/18		Moved my advanced post back to Cuy. In the afternoon I went with my Staff Sgt and some men to establish an advanced post at QUESMY for the AFA Bdes attached to the Division in accordance with instruction received from the AA & QMG. Just before reaching Quesmy I met the AFA Bdes on the move withdrawing from there; so I decided to return with my men and put up a post the following day when I hoped things would be more settled.	
BOURMONT	25/4/18		Received orders to move to BOURMONT. — Arrived BOURMONT at 2PM. Reported my arrival to OC 14th Div Train. — Stood to awaiting orders to move — all night.	
	26/4/18		Orders received at 2PM to move to ______ near COMPIEGNE; arrived there at 6PM.	
ESTREES ST DENIS	27/4/18		Moved to ESTREES ST DENIS at 10Am; and arrived there at 5PM.	
—"—	28/4/18		Wounded animals attended to during the day. Received orders to move at 8Pm to PONT STMAXENCE where I was to meet a Staff Officer from whom I would receive further instructions as to billeting. Reached PONT ST MAXENCE at 2AM; no Staff officer to be seen at appointed place. Waited there a considerable time and eventually billetted at BEAUREPAIRE arriving there at 3.30 Am everyone all wet for it had been raining all the night through.	W Connell

D. D. & L., London, E.C. (A8600) Wt. W5329/M2 350,000 5/17 Sch. 52 Forms/C2118/14.

Instructions regarding War Diaries and Intelligence Summaries are contained in F. S. Regs., Part II. and the Staff Manual respectively. Title pages will be prepared in manuscript.

WAR DIARY
or
INTELLIGENCE SUMMARY.
(Erase heading not required.)

Army Form C. 2118.

Place	Date	Hour	Summary of Events and Information	Remarks and references to Appendices
RANTIGNY	29/4/18		Notified Div HQ: also OC 14th Div Train of my location — Moved at 1 PM. to RANTIGNY. where billeted for the night.	
AVRECHY.	30/4/18		again on the move — through rain — to Avrechy where Section was billetted with Train HdQrs.	
BOURSINES	31/4/18		Moved at 12 noon to BOURSINES — a distance of 28 kilometres —	

J W Carroll

D. D. & L., London, E.C.
(A8004) Wt. W1771/M2-31 750,000 5/17 Sch. 52 Forms/C2118/14

Confidential

War Diary

of

D.A.D.V.S. 14th Div.

from April 4th to April 30th

(Volume No)

Army Form C. 2118.

Instructions regarding War Diaries and Intelligence Summaries are contained in F. S. Regs., Part II. and the Staff Manual respectively. Title pages will be prepared in manuscript.

WAR DIARY
or
INTELLIGENCE SUMMARY.
(*Erase heading not required.*)

Place	Date	Hour	Summary of Events and Information	Remarks and references to Appendices
Aubigny	4.4.18.	2.45.	Reported arrival to Advanced Headquarters, 14th Division, at Aubigny	
Amiens	4.4.18		Took over duties of D.A.D.V.S. 14th Division, in place of Major Stordy D.S.O. evacuated, wounded. Found all office papers & equipment had been destroyed, during bombardment at Jussy 21.4.18.	
"	5.4.18		Office work which had been suspended recommenced – casualty figures made out.	
"	6.4.18		26. M.V.S. evacuating – 30 animals despatched from Saleux to Rouen. Interviewed Capt. Beal A.V.C. V.O. i/c 47 Bgde R.F.A. – he at present attached to another division	
"	7.4.18		Received instructions from A.D.V.S. III Corps to evacuate animals to 4th Army V.C.C.S. at PICQUIGNY. Sent 24 animals	
"	8.4.18		8 Animals evacuated to V.C.C.S. Moved 10.30 A.M. from AMIENS to FRESNOY AU VAL (26 Kilos)	
FRESNOY AU VAL	9.4.18		Moved 10.0 A.M. from FRESNOY AU VAL to FRUCOURT – arrived there 6.30 P.M. (33 Kilos) A.F. A 2000 for week ending 21.3.18 made out	
FRUCOURT	10.4.18		Moved from FRUCOURT 10.A.M to FEUQUIERES (18 Kilos). A.F.A. 2000 for week ending 28.3.18 made out, and despatched to 4th Army. Copies sent to III Corps.	
FEUQUIERES	11.4.18		A.F.A. 2000 for week ending 4.4.18 made out and sent to 4th Army and III Corps. Entrained at 6.0 P.M. for MARESQUEL	

D. D. & L., London, E.C. (A8004) Wt. W1771/M2 31 750,000 5/17 Sch. 52 Forms/C2118/14

Army Form C. 2118.

Instructions regarding War Diaries and Intelligence Summaries are contained in F. S. Regs., Part II. and the Staff Manual respectively. Title pages will be prepared in manuscript.

WAR DIARY
or
INTELLIGENCE SUMMARY.
(Erase heading not required.)

Place	Date	Hour	Summary of Events and Information	Remarks and references to Appendices
MARESQUEL	12.4.18		Arrived MARESQUEL 2.30 A.M. and left there for HEUQUELIERS, arriving 5.30 A.M. OFFICE opened – arranged Vety. attendance of units. A.D.V.S. XIII Corps called	
HEUQUELIERS	13.4.18		Inspected Div H.Q. animals. M.M.P. & 14 Signal Coy R.E. Rode over to M.V.S. at PREURES & inspected them. Also SAA section 14th D.A.C.	
" "	14.4.18		26 M.V.S moved from PREURES to ECQUIRRE.	
" "	15.4.18		Moved from HEUQUELIERS to ECQUEDECQUES	
ECQUEDECQUES	16.4.18		Office opened. As practically all Divisional transport back, arranged so as to be more central to move to ECQUIRRE. Notified A.D.V.S. XIII Corps of move.	
ECQUIRRE	17.4.18		Inspected No 3. Coy Train & No 4. Coy Train also 2 K.R.R. & 8 R.B. Arranged Vety Charge of Units	
" "	18.4.18		Office routine AFA 2000 for week ending 11.4.18. finished and rendered to A.D.V.S XIII Corps.	
" "	19.4.18		Inspected 14 Signal Coy. 9 R.B. 7 KRR. and 42 Bgde Headquarters All transport in back area moved to Carron area. M.V.S. to move there too. Received instructions from Q. to rejoin Div. Headquarters at ECQUEDECQUES Established advanced post 26 M.V.S at MAZINGHEM X ROADS. Notified A.D.V.S. XIII Corps	

D. D. & L., London, E.C. (A8094) Wt. W1771/M2 31 750,000 5/17 Sch. 52 Forms/C2118/14

Army Form C. 2118.

WAR DIARY
or
INTELLIGENCE SUMMARY.
(Erase heading not required.)

Instructions regarding War Diaries and Intelligence Summaries are contained in F. S. Regs., Part II. and the Staff Manual respectively. Title pages will be prepared in manuscript.

Place	Date	Hour	Summary of Events and Information	Remarks and references to Appendices
ECQUEDECQUES	20.4.18		Notified A.D.V.S. XIII Corps of change of office	
			Inspected No 4. Coy. Train. 43 Field Ambulance. 44 Field Ambulance 11 Kings Liverpools, 7. R.B. 5 Oxford & Bucks. 43. Brigade H.Q. and 61 R.E. Coy	
" "	21.4.18		Inspected animals of Portuguese Brigade, & forwarded special report to A.D.V.S XIII Corps and to Q office	
			A.D.V.S XIII Corps called	
			Moved with Div. H.Q. to COYECQUE.	
COYECQUE	22.4.18		Visited 47 Brigade R.F.A. "D" & "A" Batteries at Delette which had arrived from AMIENS the day before. Capt Thornewill V.O. i/c 46 Bgde R.F.A. called, & Capt. O'Carroll V.O. i/c 26 M.V.S.	
			Arranged for an advanced post of 26. M.V.S. to be established at DELETTE to serve Artillery Brigades while there.	
" "	23.4.18		Inspected 47. Bgde R.F.A. H.Q. "B" & "C" batteries. No 2 section of D.A.C. and "A.B.C.D" batteries of 46 Bgde R.F.A.	
			Advanced post of 26 M.V.S. established just outside DELETTE	

D. D. & L., London, E.C. (A8004) Wt. W1771/M2 31 750,000 5/17 Sch. 52 Forms/C2118/14

Instructions regarding War Diaries and Intelligence Summaries are contained in F. S. Regs., Part II. and the Staff Manual respectively. Title pages will be prepared in manuscript.

WAR DIARY
or
INTELLIGENCE SUMMARY.
(Erase heading not required.)

Army Form C. 2118.

Place	Date	Hour	Summary of Events and Information	Remarks and references to Appendices
COYECQUE	24.4.18		Inspected 26 M.V.S. 42 Field Ambulance. No 2 Coy Train + No 3. Coy Train 42 Inf. Bgde H.Q. 7 K.R.R. 9. R.B. 8 K.R.R. 8 R.B. 6 Somerset L.I. and D.H.T. Park	
"	25.4.18		Inspected Advanced Post M.V.S Mazinghem, 43 Field Amb. No 4 Coy Train 9 K.R.R. 43 Bgde H.Q. 61 Coy R.E. 5. Ox. & Bucks. 7 R.B. 44 Field Amb. H.Q. Train. 43 Bgde Signals. 11 Kings Liverpools. Portuguese attached to 11 King's Liverpools.	
"	26.4.18		37 Animals Evacuated by advanced post 26 M.V.S. DELETTE to St OMER and 10 animals evacuated by " " " MAZINGHEM to " " Met D.D.V.S. 1st Army + A.D.V.S. XIII Corps who inspected animals 47 Bgde R.F.A at DELETTE + No I D.A.C. Inspected No 2 Coy Train A.F.A. 2000 for week ending 26. 4. 18 Sent to XIII Corps.	
"	27.4.18		Office Routine	
"	28.4.18		Inspected animals of 14 Div. H.Q. Warned to be ready to move 46 + 47th Bgdes R.F.A. moved out of 14 Division	
"	29.4.18		Moved to TORCY. Informed A.D.V.S XIII Corps. Inspected 43 Field Ambulance. Ordered advanced Posts at MAZINGHEM and DELETTE to return to 26 M.V.S at CHYRON	
TORCY	30.4.18		Inspected Portuguese Bgde att. 14 Division 62 Coy R.E + 44 Field Ambulance Advanced headquarters 14 Div. at MOLLINGHEM. Rear H.Q. at TORCY.	

J. F. Blakeway Major
D.A.D.V.S. 14 Division

D. D. & L., London, E.C. (A8094) Wt. W1771/M2 31 750,000 5/17 Sch. 52 Forms/C2118/14

Confidential

War Diary

of

D.A.D.V.S. 14 Div

from 1st to 31st May 1918

Instructions regarding War Diaries and Intelligence Summaries are contained in F. S. Regs., Part II. and the Staff Manual respectively. Title pages will be prepared in manuscript.

WAR DIARY
or
INTELLIGENCE SUMMARY.
(Erase heading not required.)

Army Form C. 2118.

Place	Date	Hour	Summary of Events and Information	Remarks and references to Appendices
TORCY	1.5.18		Office Routine. The Brigades in the Division again ordered to move. The order later cancelled, + put off till tomorrow. Rain	
"	2.5.18		The Brigades move into a fresh area. 26 M.V.S. come from CAYRON to TORCY. My own chargers arrive from No 4. Advanced Remount Depot in good condition.	
"			Inspected Divisional M.M.P. 4th Cavalry Reserve, No 2 Coy Train and Head Quarters of the Train. Fine and sunny.	
"	3.5.18		Inspected 26 M.V.S. No 3. Coy Train + 14 Signals Coy. A.F. A 2000 made out + sent A.D.V.S. XIII Corps. Fine + warm	
"	4.5.18		Inspected 42 Field Ambulance, 7 R.B. 8 K.R.R. 8 R.B. and 43 Field Amb. Raw and cold	
"	5.5.18		Office Routine. V.O. i/c Scots Greys called. Showery but warm.	
"	6.5.18.		Left XIII Corps for administration. Now in XI Corps. Informed A.D.V.S.s of both. Inspected 43 Bgde Hdqts at QUILEN. 6 Somerset L.I. and 11 King's Liverpools at CLENLEU, and 7. K.R.R at St MICHEL. Dull in morning, afterwards turning out fine + warm	
"	7.5.18.		Had orders from Q at 10.0A.M. that they were leaving for advanced Headquarters. Also that animals of the Divisional Transport are going in a day or two.	

D. D. & L., London, E.C. (A8004) Wt. W1771/M2 31 750,000 5/17 Sch. 52 Forms/C2118/14

Instructions regarding War Diaries and Intelligence Summaries are contained in F. S. Regs., Part II. and the Staff Manual respectively. Title pages will be prepared in manuscript.

WAR DIARY
or
INTELLIGENCE SUMMARY.
(Erase heading not required.)

Army Form C. 2118.

Place	Date	Hour	Summary of Events and Information	Remarks and references to Appendices
TORCY	7.5.18		Wired A.D.V.S XI Corps to this effect, and asked if all animals are to be malleined before moving. Sent away Capt Beal's application for transfer. A.D.V.S. XI Corps called. Said horses need not be malleined. Inspected, 26.M.V.S. TORCY, No2 Coy Train ROYON, H.Q Train ROYON 14 Signals, LEBIEZ, and NO3. Coy. Train LEBIEZ Heavy rain morning, afterwards fine & brilliant sunshine.	
"	8.5.18		Had wire from D.D.V.S 1st Army saying Capt A.E. Froggart was reporting for duty with 14 Div. Capt O'Carroll, 26 M.V.S to proceed to No. 19. V.H. CALAIS. Capt Froggart reported at this Office 3.30 P.M. He will take over the duties of Capt E. Steiner, A.V.C. attached to 14th Divisional Train, & sent him to LEBIEZ for this purpose. Inspected 42 Inf. Bgde H.Q. and 9. RB at SEMPY. 5 Oxford & Bucks at HUMBERT 9 K.R.R at ST DENCEUX and 42 Field Ambulance at BOUBERS. Fine all day and hot.	
"	9.5.18		Capt E. Steiner handed over to Capt A.E. Froggart A.V.C. Inspected 41 Bgde H.Q. 8 K.R.Rs 7 RB and 8 RB at EMBRY Inspected and judged animals of No2 Coy Train at ROYON. Summer weather all day. A.F. A 2000 sent to A.D.V.S. XI Corps.	
"	10.5.18		No42 Field Ambulance at BOUBERS leave 14th Division for 77th American Division at NORTKERQUE. (This order was cancelled later in the day). Office Routine. Fine but cold. Capt. Steiner takes over No26. M.V.S. from Capt O'Carroll.	
"	11.5.18		Capt. J O'Carroll A.V.C. i/c 26. M.V.S. left 14th Division for duty at No. 19. V.H. Calais. Informed Q. XI Corps & 1st Army of his departure. Office routine. Inspection report for week sent in. Fine.	

D. D. & L., London, E.C.
(A8004) Wt. W1771/M2 31 750,000 5/17 Sch. 52 Forms/C2118/14

Instructions regarding War Diaries and Intelligence Summaries are contained in F. S. Regs., Part II. and the Staff Manual respectively. Title pages will be prepared in manuscript.

WAR DIARY
or
INTELLIGENCE SUMMARY.
(Erase heading not required.)

Army Form C. 2118.

Place	Date	Hour	Summary of Events and Information	Remarks and references to Appendices
TORCY	12.5.18		Surplus transport animals of 14th Division leave for CUCQ to be there handed over to Americans. The animals struck off the strength of this Division from today. Sent Capt A.E. Froggatt A.V.C. in veterinary charge, with orders to report back here after the handing over is completed. Inspected 61 R.E. MOLLINGHEM. 89 R.E. at CORNET BRASSART. No 4 Coy. Train at L'OBLOIS WOOD. 62 R.E + 44 Field Ambulance at ECQUEDECQUES, and the animals of the Portuguese attached 14 Division. Sent special report in to "Q" + Principal Liaison Officer, Portuguese Mission, respecting waste of forage going on in the latter. Weather fine + cold.	
TORCY	13.5.18		Office Routine. Raining all day	
"	14.5.18		Received memo from A.D.V.S saying that as Capt. Steiner A.V.C only held an Hony. Commission he was not eligible for 26 M.V.S. Wired Capt Froggatt to return as soon as he had handed over surplus Divisional Transport at CUCQ with a view to placing him in charge of Mobile Section. Inspected 41 Bgde HQ. at Embry, 7 R.B. 8 R.B and 8 K.R.R. at EMBRY and 42 Field A. at ROUBERS. Weather - fine all day + hot	

D. D. & L., London, E.C. (A8004) Wt. W1771/M2 31 750,000 5/17 Sch. 52 Forms/C2118/14

Army Form C. 2118.

Instructions regarding War Diaries and Intelligence Summaries are contained in F. S. Regs., Part II. and the Staff Manual respectively. Title pages will be prepared in manuscript.

WAR DIARY
or
INTELLIGENCE SUMMARY.
(Erase heading not required.)

Place	Date	Hour	Summary of Events and Information	Remarks and references to Appendices
TORCY.	15.5.18.		Inspected 43 Field Amb. at RIMBOVAL. 7 K.R.R. at St. MICHEL, 43 Bgde H.Q. at QUILEN. 11 Kings and 6 Somersets at CLENLEU 41st Inf Brigade left EMBRY for AIRE area Beautifully fine all day	
"	16.5.18		Had wire from A.D.V.S. XI Corps, saying Capt. Beal A.V.C. to be put in charge 26. M.V.S. As he is at present under 3rd Division for administration wired A.D.V.S. XI Corps for instructions whether to order him here. Also wrote for instructions re Capt. Froggatt Inspected 26 M.V.S at TORCY and Train H.Q. at ROYON Fine all day & hot.	
"	17.5.18.		Had orders to move to advanced H.Q. at St. Quentin, which I did. 26. M.V.S. still remaining at TORCY Orders from A.D.V.S. XI Corps to send for Capt Beal, wired for him to proceed to TORCY and take over charge 26. M.V.S. Fine and Hot Bombed heavily at night, starting 11 PM & lasting an hour	
St. Quentin	18.5.18		Wire from A.D.V.S. XI Corps to say he calls at 3 PM. Saw A.D.V.S & visited Corps with him. Fine A.F.A 2000 forwarded	
" "	19.5.18		Office Routine. Fine - very hot.	
" "	20.5.18		Inspected 14 Div. Signal Coy. MOULIN LE COMTE 41st Inf. Bgde H.Q. BOESEGHEM. 7 R.B 8 R.B & 8 K.R.R Very hot all day. 61 R.E. lost 7 Animals through Shell Fire at MOLLINGHEM	

D. D. & L., London, E.C.
(A8004) Wt. W1771/M2 31 750,000 5/17 Sch. 52 Forms/C2118/14

Instructions regarding War Diaries and Intelligence Summaries are contained in F. S. Regs., Part II. and the Staff Manual respectively. Title pages will be prepared in manuscript.

WAR DIARY
or
INTELLIGENCE SUMMARY.
(Erase heading not required.)

Army Form C. 2118.

Place	Date	Hour	Summary of Events and Information	Remarks and references to Appendices
St. Quentin	21.5.18		Inspected 26. M.V.S. at TORCY in company with A.D.V.S. XI Corps. Had memo from Capt. Froggatt to say he has been ordered to stay at CCCQ by Commandant there. Wrote A.D.V.S. XI Corps for instructions on this. Very hot all day	
" "	22.5.18		Inspected No 2 Coy Train L'OBLOIS WOOD, 61 RE, MOLLINGHAM 89. RE at CORNET BRASSART and DIV. Hdqrs at St QUENTIN. Fine all day.	
" "	23.5.18		Capt Beal AVC took over 26 MVS at TORCY. Inspected with A.D.V.S. XI Corps the Portuguese Units in 14 Division. Also went with him to TORCY and interviewed Capts Steiner and Beal. Very strong wind all day, but fine. Inspected 44 Field Ambulance at Ecquedecques	
" "	24.5.18		Office Routine. A.F.A 2000 sent to Corps. Raining most of day.	
" "	25/5/18		Inspected 43 Bgde H.Q. at Torcy, 11 Kings; Torcy, 5th Ox & Bucks Royon, 9 RB. Royon, 9 K.R.R. Royon, 42nd Inf. Bgde H.Q. Royon, 7 K.R.R. Sains les Fresin, Somerset L.I. Sains les Fresin. Fine all day.	
" "	26/5/18		Inspected 432 Field Coy RE at St. Quentin, & Train H.Q. at Lambres. Office Routine. Fine & warm.	

(A8004) D. D. & L., London, E.C. Wt. W1771/M2 31 750,000 5/17 Sch. 52 Forms/C2118/14

Army Form C. 2118.

Instructions regarding War Diaries and Intelligence Summaries are contained in F. S. Regs., Part II. and the Staff Manual respectively. Title pages will be prepared in manuscript.

WAR DIARY
or
INTELLIGENCE SUMMARY.
(Erase heading not required.)

Place	Date	Hour	Summary of Events and Information	Remarks and references to Appendices
St QUENTIN	27/5/18		Inspected 41 Brigade H.Q at BOESEGHEM. 8 K.R.R 7 R.B at LES CISEAUX, 14 Signal Coy at MOULIN LE COMTE & 43rd Field Ambulance at LES CISEAUX. Heard from Capt Froggatt that he had been posted to No 3. Vety Hospital for duty. "Q" office take up the matter of his return to the Division. Also memo from A.D.V.S. XI Corps saying Capt. Steiner should proceed to 47 Bgde R.F.A. "Q" office know nothing of it, & enquiries being made. Fine	
"	28.5.18		43rd Field Ambulance & 44th Field Ambulance leave the 14th Division. Inspected and drew remounts for 14th Division. Fine	
"	29.5.18		Visited A.D.V.S. XI Corps. re Capts. Froggatt & Steiner. Also visited Portuguese Artillery & XI Corps V.E.S. at GLOMENGHEM. "Q" office called for all correspondence re Capt. Froggatt. A.V.C. Fine.	
"	30.5.18		Inspected M.M.P. 14th Division at St QUENTIN. Order received for Capt. Steiner A.V.C. to proceed to 47th ~~Division~~ Brigade R.F.A for duty. Fine.	
"	31.5.18		Inspected 43 Brigade H.Q. TORCY, 11 Kings, TORCY, 26. M.V.S. TORCY, 5th ~~Ox~~ Bucks ~~Royon~~, 9 R.B. Royon, 42 Inf Brigade H.Q ROYON, 9. K.R.R. LEBIEZ, 9 K.R.R & Somerset L.I at SANS, LES FRESIN 62 R.E. ECQUEDECQUES and 61st R.E. at LOBLOIS WOOD. Fine. A.F.A 2000 forwarded.	

J. Blakeway Major
D.A.D.V.S. 14 Division
31.5.18.

D. D. & L., London, E.C.
(A8004) Wt. W1771/M2 31 750,000 5/17 Sch. 52 Forms/C2118/14

11

Instructions regarding War Diaries and Intelligence Summaries are contained in F. S. Regs., Part II. and the Staff Manual respectively. Title pages will be prepared in manuscript.

WAR DIARY
or
INTELLIGENCE SUMMARY.
(Erase heading not required.)

Army Form C. 2118.

DADVS 14 D
Vol 32

Place	Date	Hour	Summary of Events and Information	Remarks and references to Appendices
ST QUENTIN	1.6.18		Capt. Steiner A.V.C. left for duty with 47 Brigade R.F.A. Informed "Q" office, A.D.V.S. "X" Corps and Camp Commandant. 14th Division leave XI Corps for X Corps administration tomorrow at Noon. Wired A.D.V.S. Corps to this effect. Office Routine. Rearranged work now Capt. Steiner has gone. Fine & hot.	
"	2.6.18		Inspected M.M.P. 14 Division ST QUENTIN, & 41st Bgde H.Q BOESEGHEM. Fine all day and hot. Moved into X Corps.	
"	3.6.18		Inspected 14th Div. Signal Coy at MOULIN LE COMTE, Train H.Q at LAMBRES, and 5th Royal Irish Fus. at MANQUERILL. The latter just arrived from Palestine, via MARSEILLES. 8 Days on the boat, & 3 in Train. Condition of animals satisfactory. Fine but cooler.	
"	4.6.18		Inspected No 2 Coy Train, L'OBLOIS WOOD, 89 R.E. Cornet Brassart, 43 Bgde H.Q at ROYON, 26 M.V.S. at TORCY, 11 Kings, TORCY, 6th Somersets and 7 K.R.R. at SAINS LES FRESIN. A.D.V.S. X Corps called. Fine	
"	5.6.18		Inspected Divisional M.M.P. at ST QUENTIN. Fine	
"	6.6.18		Inspected 61 R.E. at L'OBLOIS WOOD. Fine	

D. D. & L., London, E.C.
(A8004) Wt. W1771/M2 31 750,000 5/17 Sch. 52 Forms/C2118/14

Army Form C. 2118.

Instructions regarding War Diaries and Intelligence Summaries are contained in F. S. Regs., Part II. and the Staff Manual respectively. Title pages will be prepared in manuscript.

WAR DIARY
or
INTELLIGENCE SUMMARY.

(Erase heading not required.)

11

Place	Date	Hour	Summary of Events and Information	Remarks and references to Appendices
ST. QUENTIN	7.6.18		Inspected 8 KRR at BOESEGHEM Now Coy Train at LES CISEAUX and 43. Brigade H.Q. at FONTES 5 Connaught R. 6th Innis. Fusiliers, 6th Leinsters, 5 Irish Fus. and 2/4 Somerset L.I. arrive from Palestine and come under the administration of 14th Division. Fine. A.F. A 2000 sent.	
" "	8.6.18		Inspected 5th Connaught R. at LA ROUPIE, 6th Innis. Fus. Le PIRE, 6th Leinsters at LA ROUPIE, 5th Irish Fusiliers at HAM and 2/4 Somerset L.I. at ESPLIMLY FARM. Fine. Also 23rd Inf Batt. Machine Gun Section 12 Inf Batt. Field Ambulance, Train H.Q. of Portuguese Division at ECQUEDECQUES. 62 Field Coy RE at ECQUEDECQUES, + Mobile Veterinary Section of Portuguese at LIERES. Fine.	
" "	9.6.18		Office Routine. Fine 13th Yorks arrive from CUCQ.	
" "	10.6.18		Inspected Divisional M.M.P. at ST QUENTIN. Rain morning, fine afternoon.	

D. D. & L., London, E.C. (A8004) Wt. W1771/M2 31 750,000 5/17 Sch. 52 Forms/C2118/14

Army Form C. 2118.

Instructions regarding War Diaries and Intelligence Summaries are contained in F. S. Regs., Part II. and the Staff Manual respectively. Title pages will be prepared in manuscript.

WAR DIARY
or
INTELLIGENCE SUMMARY.
(Erase heading not required.)

Place	Date	Hour	Summary of Events and Information	Remarks and references to Appendices
ST QUENTIN	11.6.18		Inspected 43 Bgde H.Q. at FONTES, 13 Yorks. at L'OBLOIS WOOD, No 2 Coy. Train at L'OBLOIS WOOD, 5th Connaught R. at L'OBLOIS WOOD, 41st Inf. Bgde H.Q. at BOESECHEM and No 4 Coy. Train at LES CISEAUX.	
			36 M.V.S. arrives from TORCY & function at L'OBLOIS WOOD. Fine.	
" "	12.6.18		Inspected 14 Divisional Signal Coy at MOULIN LE COMTE + 14 Divisional Train H.Q at LAMBRES. A.D.V.S. X Corps called. Fine	
	13.		14 Div. proceeded to England.	

D.A.D.V.S., 14th DIVISION. No. .... Date 4/9/18

J. Blakeway
Major.
D.A.D.V.S. 14 Div

D. D. & L., London, E.C. (A8004) Wt. W1771/M2 31 750,000 5/17 Sch. 52 Forms/C2118/14

6

Instructions regarding War Diaries and Intelligence Summaries are contained in F. S. Regs., Part II. and the Staff Manual respectively. Title pages will be prepared in manuscript.

WAR DIARY
or
~~INTELLIGENCE SUMMARY.~~
(Erase heading not required.)

Army Form C. 2118.

DADVS 14 D
Vol 33

Place	Date	Hour	Summary of Events and Information	Remarks and references to Appendices
WIERRE EFFROY	4.7.18		Left England this morning from Folkestone at 9.30 A.M. – reached Boulogne 11.30. Had been in England 16 days to refit. Left Boulogne afternoon of 4th for Wierre Effroy. Arrived there 4.30 P.M.	
" "	5.7.18		Informed A.D.V.S. 7th Corps of arrival – Office routine.	
" "	6.7.18		A.D.V.S 7th Corps called when I was out	
" "	7.8.18		Location table of Units received at definite situations. Office routine.	
" "	8.8.18		A.D.V.S 7th Corps called Inspected 42 Bgde H.Q Signal Section, No 3. Coy Train Argyle & Sutherlands, Wilts & Manchesters.	
" "	9.8.18		Inspected 43 Brigade H.Q. Signal Section, 43 Field Ambulance Suffolks, Middlesex, H.L.I. & 14. Signal Squadron.	
" "	10.8.18		Inspected 41st Brigade H.Q. Signal Section, Durhams, Yorks & Lancs. and 33 London Regt	

D. D. & L., London, E.C.
(A8004) Wt. W1771/M2 31 750,000 5/17 Sch. 52 Forms/C2118/14

Army Form C. 2118.

WAR DIARY
or
~~INTELLIGENCE~~ SUMMARY.
(Erase heading not required.)

Instructions regarding War Diaries and Intelligence Summaries are contained in F. S. Regs., Part II. and the Staff Manual respectively. Title pages will be prepared in manuscript.

Place	Date	Hour	Summary of Events and Information	Remarks and references to Appendices
Wierre Effroy	11.7.18.		Orders received for move.	
EPERLECQUES	12.7.18		Division move into the EPERLECQUES AREA	
" "	13.7.18.		Visited A.D.V.S 7th Corps. Office Routine.	
" "	14.7.18.		Visited & saw arrangements made for 26.M.V.S.	
" "	15.7.18		Inspected 41 Bgde HQ Durham L.I 43 Field A. Divisional Signal Squadron Train H.Q. No 4 Coy Train. No 3. Coy. Train, 43 Bgde H.Q.	
" "	16.7.18.		Office Routine	
" "	17.7.18.		Inspected S.A.A section, No 2 Coy. Train, 26. M.V.S.	
" "	18.7.18		Inspected A.B.C. & D. Coys Machine Gun Battalion and H.Q. of Machine Gun Batt. Middlesex, 89 R.E. 62 R.E. and Wilts.	
" "	19.7.18.		Inspected Suffolks & 42 Field A.	

D. D. & L., London, E.C.
(A8004) Wt. W1771/M2 31 750,000 5/17 Sch. 52 Forms/C2118/14

Instructions regarding War Diaries and Intelligence Summaries are contained in F. S. Regs., Part II. and the Staff Manual respectively. Title pages will be prepared in manuscript.

WAR DIARY
or
INTELLIGENCE SUMMARY.
(Erase heading not required.)

Army Form C. 2118.

Place	Date	Hour	Summary of Events and Information	Remarks and references to Appendices
EPERLECQUES ~~WIERRE EFFROY~~	20.7.18		Inspected 61 RE 14 Argyle & Sutherlands, 10. H.L.I. 42 Bgde H.Q and 16 Manchesters: also Div. H.Q & Div. M.M.P.	
" "	21.7.18		Office Routine.	
" "	22.7.18		Inspected 61 RE 26 M.V.S. 10 H.L.I. 18 Yorks & Lancs	
" "	23.7.18.		Inspected 41 Bgde H.Q. 43 Field Ambulance Wilts.	
" "	24.7.18.		Inspected Middlesex, - Office routine.	
" "	25.7.18		Inspected 42 Bgde H.Q 16 Manchesters, 14 Argyle & Sutherlands. S.A.A section, 42 Field Ambulance & 12 Suffolks.	
" "	26.7.18		Inspected No 4. Coy Train, Train H.Q Div H.Q. Divisional Signal Squadron & Div. M.M.P.	
" "	27.7.18		Office Routine	

D. D. & L., London, E.C.
(A8004) Wt. W1771/M2 31 750,000 5/17 Sch. 52 Forms/C2118/14

Army Form C. 2118.

Instructions regarding War Diaries and Intelligence Summaries are contained in F. S. Regs., Part II. and the Staff Manual respectively. Title pages will be prepared in manuscript.

WAR DIARY
or
INTELLIGENCE SUMMARY.
(Erase heading not required.)

Place	Date	Hour	Summary of Events and Information	Remarks and references to Appendices
EPERLECQUES	28.7.18		Inspected 14 Argyle & Sutherlands & 16 Manchesters. Also SAA section	
" "	29.7.18		Inspected 12 Suffolks & 14 Divisional Signals.	
" "	30.7.18.		Inspected H.Q. Train, No 2 Coy. No 3. Coy No 4 Coy.	
" "	31.7.18.		Inspected 89 Field Coy RE & 20th Middlesex.	

J. Blakeway
Major
D.A.D.V.S. 14 Div.

D.A.D.V.S.,
14th DIVISION.
No. ....
Date 31.7.18.

D. D. & L., London, E.C.
(A8004) Wt. W1771/M2 31 750,000 5/17 Sch. 52 Forms/C2118/14

24

Instructions regarding War Diaries and Intelligence Summaries are contained in F. S. Regs., Part II. and the Staff Manual respectively. Title pages will be prepared in manuscript.

WAR DIARY
or
INTELLIGENCE SUMMARY.
(Erase heading not required.)

Army Form C. 2118.

DADVS 14 D
W.D. 34

Place	Date	Hour	Summary of Events and Information	Remarks and references to Appendices
Eperlecques.	1.8.18.		Office Routine – Course of horsemastership started at 26. M.V.S. by me, with the idea of improving the standard of same in the Division.	
" "	2.8.18.		A.D.V.S. visited 26. M.V.S.	
" "	3.8.18.		Office Routine –	
" "	4.8.18.		Office Routine.	
" "	5.8.18.		14 Divisional Horse Show. Won open class for chargers. 26 M.V.S. won 1st Prize for best Single Horse Turn out, + 2nd for best H.D.	
" "	6.8.18.		A.D.V.S. 7th Corps visited 26 M.V.S. Inspected 33 Londons, Div. M.M.P. Div. H.Q. + 26. M.V.S.	
" "	7.8.18.		Inspected 14 Divisional Signals, 43 Field A. 12 Suffolks, 20. Middlesex, No 4 Coy. Train. Train H.Q. No 3. Coy. Train, H.Q 43 Bgde.	
" "	8.8.18.		Inspected H.Q 41 Bgde 44 Field Ambulance, and York + Lancs. + 26. M.V.S.	

D. D. & L., London, E.C.
(A8004) Wt. W1771/M2 31 750,000 5/17 Sch. 52 Forms/C2118/14

Army Form C. 2118.

Instructions regarding War Diaries and Intelligence Summaries are contained in F. S. Regs., Part II. and the Staff Manual respectively. Title pages will be prepared in manuscript.

WAR DIARY
or
INTELLIGENCE SUMMARY.
(Erase heading not required.)

Place	Date	Hour	Summary of Events and Information	Remarks and references to Appendices
Eperlecques.	9.8.18.		Inspected S.A.A Section, Manchesters, "A.B.C. & D" Coys of 14 Machine Gun Batt. Wilts, H.Q. 42 Bgde.	
" "	10.8.18		Visited 26 M.V.S. – Office Routine.	
" "	11.8.18		Visited by A.D.V.S. 7th Corps – Office routine.	
" "	12.8.18.		Visited 33 Londons, Yorks & Lancs, 20 Middlesex 29. Durhams, 43 Field Ambulance,	
" "	13.8.18		Office Routine.	
" "	14.8.18.		Visited 89. Field Coy R.E. 14 Div Signal Squadron, Argyle & Sutherlands 42 Field Ambulance, 26. M.V.S	
" "			Examined men at 26. M.V.S. for 1st Course of Horsemastership	
" "	15.8.18		Visited Durham L.I., Loyal North Lancs, Wilts, Manchesters. 42 Bgde H.Q.	

D. D. & L., London, E.C.
(A8094) Wt. W1771/M2 31 750,000 5/17 Sch. 52 Forms/C2118/14

Army Form C. 2118.

Instructions regarding War Diaries and Intelligence Summaries are contained in F. S. Regs., Part II. and the Staff Manual respectively. Title pages will be prepared in manuscript.

WAR DIARY
or
INTELLIGENCE SUMMARY.
(Erase heading not required.)

Place	Date	Hour	Summary of Events and Information	Remarks and references to Appendices
Eperlecques	16.8.18		2nd Course of Horsemastership starts at 26 M.V.S. Visited 14 Div Sig[na]l Squadron, 62 Field Coy R.E. Div M.M.P. Argyle & Sutherlands. Div H.Q.	
" "	17.8.18		Warning order received to move. Inspected Train H.Q. & No 4 Coy. Train. Office Routine.	
" "	18.8.18		Brigades in Division start to move	
" "	19.8.18		Office Routine – Destroyed D.A.D.M.S. charger – back broken by stable falling in.	
Chateau Couthove	20.8.18		14 Divisional H.Q. move to Chateau Couthove, outside Poperinghe.	
" "	21.8.18		Visited A.D.V.S. II Corps & reported.	
" "	22.8.18		Visited 26. M.V.S.	
" "	23.8.18		Visited Suffolks, H.L.I. 20 Middlesex, 41 Bgde H.Q. 33 Londons, York Lancs, No 2 Coy. Train	

D. D. & L., London, E.C.
(A8094) Wt. W1771/M2 31 750,000 5/17 Sch. 52 Forms/C2118/14

Instructions regarding War Diaries and Intelligence Summaries are contained in F. S. Regs., Part II. and the Staff Manual respectively. Title pages will be prepared in manuscript.

WAR DIARY
or
INTELLIGENCE SUMMARY.
(Erase heading not required.)

Army Form C. 2118.

Place	Date	Hour	Summary of Events and Information	Remarks and references to Appendices
Chateau Coulhove	24.8.18		Visited Durham L.I. 89 Field Coy RE Div M.M.P. Div. H.Q	
" "	25.8.18		Visited A.D.V.S II Corps for Conference. Visited H.Q. A B. C & D. Coys of 14 Machine Gun Batt	
" "	26.8.18		Visited 42 Bgde H.Q. Wilts, Manchesters, & Argyle & Sutherlands.	
" "	27.8.18		Visited 41 Bgde H.Q. Durhams, 33 Londons, Yorks & Lancs. 89 Field Coy. R.E. S.A.A. Section; & 26 M.V.S. Went to Calais & saw Remounts for the Division.	
" "	28.8.18		Visited 14 Div. M.M.P. Div. H.Q. No 4. Coy. Train	
" "	29.8.18		Visited No 3. Coy. Train. Examined men at 26. M.V.S. for 2nd Course in horse mastership	
" "	30.8.18		A.D.V.S. II Corps visited office. A.F. 2000 sent	
" "	31.8.18		Office Routine – monthly reports sent.	

D.A.D.V.S., 14th DIVISION.
No. ....
Date 31.8.18

J. Blakeway Major
D.A.D.V.S 14 Div.

D. D. & L., London, E.C. (A8094) Wt. W1771/M2 31 750,000 5/17 Sch. 52 Forms/C2118/14

Confidential

War Diary

of

D.A.D.V.S. 14 Div

September 1st to 30th 1918

Instructions regarding War Diaries and Intelligence Summaries are contained in F. S. Regs., Part II. and the Staff Manual respectively. Title pages will be prepared in manuscript.

WAR DIARY
or
INTELLIGENCE SUMMARY.
(Erase heading not required.)

D.A.D.V.S., 14th DIVISION.
No. ...
Date – 9. 18

Army Form C. 2118.

Place	Date	Hour	Summary of Events and Information	Remarks and references to Appendices
Chateau Couthove	1.9.18		Office Routine	
"	2.9.18		Inspected Durhams, Londons, 41. Bgde HQ 18 York & Lancs. 62 R.E A.B.C & D. Coys. 14. Machine Gun Batt 89 R.E. Loyal North Lancs. Detachment of 42 Field A. Manchesters, Argyle & Sutherlands, 61. R.E 43. Bgde. HQ Suffolks, Middlesex, H.L.I.	
"	3.9.18		Visited 26. M.V.S No2. Coy. Train, 14 Div. Signals.	
"	4.9.18		Visited 44 Field Ambulance now running II Corps rest station in back area. Arranged for putting up of model stabling for them	
"	5.9.18		Visited 42 & 43 Inf Bgdes with A.D.V.S. II Corps	
"	6.9.18		Visited 42 & 43 Field Ambulances. & No 3. Coy. Train. A.F. 2000 sent.	
"	7.9.18		Visited Div. M.M.P & Div HQ	
"	8.9.18		Office Routine. Visited 26. M.V.S.	

D. D. & L., London, E.C. (A8004) Wt. W1771/M2 31 750,000 5/17 Sch. 52 Forms/C2118/14

Instructions regarding War Diaries and Intelligence Summaries are contained in F. S. Regs., Part II. and the Staff Manual respectively. Title pages will be prepared in manuscript.

WAR DIARY
or
INTELLIGENCE SUMMARY.
(Erase heading not required.)

D.A.D.V.S., 14th DIVISION.
No. ....
Date. – 9 . 18

Army Form C. 2118.

Place	Date	Hour	Summary of Events and Information	Remarks and references to Appendices
Chateau Courthove	9.9.18		Visited S.A.A Section No 2. Coy Train 26. M.V.S. Called at A.D.V.S II Corps Office 1/1 Yorkshire Dragoons join Division on 10th Sept.	
" "	10.9.18		Visited No 3. Coy Train. Attended conference at A.D.V.S. Office II Corps.	
" "	11.9.18		Inspected Div. H.Q. Div. M.M.P No 4 Coy Train. Acted on Board to Examine 4 men as shoeing smiths	
" "	12.9.18		Inspected 43 Brigade H.Q 20 Middlesex, 12 Suffolks, 10 H.L.I 6th R.F. H.Q. 42. Brigade, 6 Wilts, 16 Manchesters, 14 Arg. & Suther. Detachment of 42 Field A. Loyal N. Lancs. "A" "B" "C" & "D" Coys 14 Machine Gun Battalion.	
" "	13.9.18.		Inspected 26. M.V.S. & also S.A.A section – Sent away 10 cases of debility from latter. AF 2000 Sent	
" "	14.9.18		Inspected 43 Field Ambulance and 42nd Field Ambulance.	
" "	15.9.18		Inspected H.Q. 41 Brigade, 18 Yorks & Lancs. 33 London, 29th Durhams.	
" "	16.9.18		Inspected H.Q 43. Brigade, 20 Middlesex, 12 Suffolks, & 10 H.L.I also 26. M.V.S.	

D. D. & L., London, E.C.
(A8004) Wt. W1771/M2 31 750,000 5/17 Sch. 52 Forms/C2118/14

Instructions regarding War Diaries and Intelligence Summaries are contained in F. S. Regs., Part II. and the Staff Manual respectively. Title pages will be prepared in manuscript.

WAR DIARY
or
INTELLIGENCE SUMMARY.
(Erase heading not required.)

D.A.D.V.S., 14th DIVISION.
No. ....
Date – .9.18

Army Form C. 2118.

Place	Date	Hour	Summary of Events and Information	Remarks and references to Appendices
Chateau Coutlers.	17.9.18		Inspected S.A.A. Section + No 4 Coy. Train. Visited A.D.V.S II Corps.	
			Inspected No 2. Coy. Train and 14 Div. Signal Squadron.	
" "	18.9.18			
" "	19.9.18		Inspected 42 Field Ambulance + 15 Loyal North Lancs. Also 89. Field Coy R.E.	
ABEELE	20.9.18		Moved to ABEELE.	
" "	21.9.18		Inspected 41 Bgde H.Q. and No I Coy. Train. The latter has the best lot of animals I have seen in France.	
			Visited A.D.V.S 19th Corps, under whose administration we now come.	
" "	22.9.18		Visited 42 Field Ambulance and 44 Field Ambulance	
" "	23.9.18		Visited H.Q. 46 Bgde R.F.A. + "A" "C" + "B" Batteries also "B" + "C" 47 Bgde R.F.A.	
" "	24.9.18		Visited "D" Battery 46 Bgde R.F.A, 41 Bgde H.Q. 18 Yorks + Lancs, 33 Londons, 12 Suffolks, 29 Durhams, + No 2 Coy. Train	
" "	25.9.18		Visited H.Q. Machine Gun Coy + "D" Coy Machine Gun. D.V.S. France visited 26. M.V.S. – very pleased.	

D. D. & L., London, E.C. (A8004) Wt. W1771/M2 31 750,000 5/17 Sch. 52 Forms/C2118/14

Army Form C. 2118.

D.A.D.V.S.,
14th DIVISION.
No. ....
Date. -.9.18

Instructions regarding War Diaries and Intelligence Summaries are contained in F. S. Regs., Part II. and the Staff Manual respectively. Title pages will be prepared in manuscript.

WAR DIARY
or
INTELLIGENCE SUMMARY.
(Erase heading not required.)

Place	Date	Hour	Summary of Events and Information	Remarks and references to Appendices
ABEELE	26.9.18		Visited H.Q. 47 Bgde R.F.A. and "A" & "D" Batteries also Div H.Q.	
" "	27.9.18		Office Routine.	
" "	28.9.18		Leave Starts - Capt Beal A.V.C. acts for me while I am away. Moved to Orwell Camp. 28 G 19 d.	
28 G 19d	29.9.18		Advanced M.V.S. post at Dickebush commences to function	
" "	30.9.18		Moved to 27 K 24 c 5.8.	

D.A.D.V.S.,
14th DIVISION.
No. ....
Date 30.9.18

J. Blakeway Major.
D.A.D.V.S. 14 Division

D. D. & L., London, E.C.
(A5004) Wt. W1771/M2 31 750,000 5/17 Sch. 52 Forms/C2118/14

Confidential

War Diary

of

D.A.D.V.S. 14th Division

1st to 31st October 1918

Army Form C. 2118.

Instructions regarding War Diaries and Intelligence Summaries are contained in F. S. Regs., Part II. and the Staff Manual respectively. Title pages will be prepared in manuscript.

WAR DIARY
or
INTELLIGENCE SUMMARY.
(Erase heading not required.)

Place	Date	Hour	Summary of Events and Information	Remarks and references to Appendices
WARATAH CAMP	1.10.18		From 1–12 I was on leave, and my duties were carried out by Capt Beal. A.V.C. O.C. 26. M.V.S.	
CAESTRE.	7.10.18		Divisional H.Q. moved to CAESTRE	

D. D. & L., London, E.C.
(A8004) Wt. W1771/M2 31 750,000 5/17 Sch. 52 Forms/C2118/14

Army Form C. 2118.

WAR DIARY
or
INTELLIGENCE SUMMARY.
(Erase heading not required.)

Instructions regarding War Diaries and Intelligence Summaries are contained in F. S. Regs., Part II. and the Staff Manual respectively. Title pages will be prepared in manuscript.

Place	Date	Hour	Summary of Events and Information	Remarks and references to Appendices
CAESTRE	12.10.18		Returned from leave to 14th Division. Rear H.Q. at Caestre.	
" "	13.10.18		Visited Div. H.Q. (advanced) at KANDAHAR FARM – office routine.	
" "	14.10.18		Visited A.D.V.S. office, 15 Corps at HAZEBRUCH.	
" "	15.10.18		Visited 26. M.V.S.	
" "	16.10.18		Visited No 1 & No 2. Sections D.A.C.	
			Inspection by Col. Miller, D.S.O. the horsemaster, who reported that the system of horse management, & the condition of the animals in the Division the best he had seen in France	
			Moved from CAESTRE to NEUVE EGLISE	
NEUVE EGLISE	17.10.18		Visited 15 Loyal N Lancs. 41 Bgde H.Q. 33 Londons, 18 York & Lancs, 29th Durham 43 Field Ambulance, Div. H.Q. & No 2. Coy. Train.	
KANDAHAR CAMP	18.10.18		Moved to KANDAHAR CAMP.	
BLANC FOUR	19.10.18		Moved to BLANC FOUR	

D. D. & L., London, E.C.
(A8004) Wt. W1771/M2 31 750,000 5/17 Sch. 52 Forms/C2118/14

Army Form C. 2118.

Instructions regarding War Diaries and Intelligence Summaries are contained in F. S. Regs., Part II. and the Staff Manual respectively. Title pages will be prepared in manuscript.

WAR DIARY
or
INTELLIGENCE SUMMARY.
(Erase heading not required.)

Place	Date	Hour	Summary of Events and Information	Remarks and references to Appendices
BLANC FOUR	20.10.18		Visited 26 MVS.	
MOUSCRON	21.10.18		Attended reception at TOURCQUING on the occasion of visit of French President to that town, after its liberation from the Germans. Moved to Mouscron, just over the Belgian Border.	
" "	22.10.18		Visited 26.MVS	
" "	23.10.18		Visited 29th Durhams, 'D' Battery 47th Brigade, 33 Londons, H.Q. 41 Bgde 43rd & 44th Field Ambulances and 14th Divisional Signal Squadron.	
" "	24.10.18		Visited 'C' Battery 46th Bgde, 'A' Battery, 'D' & 'B' batteries all of same brigade Also H.Q. 14th Divisional Machine Gun Batt, & 'B' Battery 47th Bgde R.F.A.	
" "	25.10.18		Visited 'A' & 'C' batteries 47th Brigade R.F.A.	
" "	26.10.18		Visited 'A' 'C' & 'B' Coy's 14th Divisional Machine Gun Batt	
" "	27.10.18		Visited 26.MVS.	

D. D. & L., London, E.C. (A8094) Wt. W1771/M2 31 750,000 5/17 Sch. 52 Forms/C2118/14

Army Form C. 2118.

Instructions regarding War Diaries and Intelligence Summaries are contained in F. S. Regs., Part II. and the Staff Manual respectively. Title pages will be prepared in manuscript.

WAR DIARY
or
INTELLIGENCE SUMMARY.
(Erase heading not required.)

Place	Date	Hour	Summary of Events and Information	Remarks and references to Appendices
MOUSCRON	28.10.18		Visit by A.D.V.S 15th Corps. Arranged with him for transfer ~~to the base~~ for inefficiency of No. 14109, S/Sergt McLachlan A.V.C. attached to 'D' Battery, 47 Bgde R.F.A.	
" "	29.10.18		Visited 89 Field Coy R.E. 20 Middlesex, 10 H.L.I. 16 Manchesters, 12 Suffolks, 43 Field Ambulance & 44 Field Ambulance. 18 Yorks & Lancs 33 Londons, 29 Durhams, 41 Bgde H.Q.	
" "	30.10.18		Visited H.Q. D.A.C. 14th Division, & Nos 1 & 2 Sections. Also visited S.A.A. Section.	
" "	31.10.18		Visited 14 Div. Signal Squadron, & H.Q. 14 Division	

D.A.D.V.S.
14TH DIVISION.
No. ....
Date 31.10.18.

J. Blakeway
Major
D.A.D.V.S. 14 Division

D. D. & L., London, E.C.
(A8004) Wt. W1771/M2 31 750,000 5/17 Sch. 52 Forms/C2118/14

Confidential

War Diary

of

D.A.D.V.S. 14 Div.

for

November 1918

Instructions regarding War Diaries and Intelligence Summaries are contained in F. S. Regs., Part II. and the Staff Manual respectively. Title pages will be prepared in manuscript.

WAR DIARY
or
INTELLIGENCE SUMMARY.
(Erase heading not required.)

Army Form C. 2118.

D.A.D.V.S., 14th DIVISION.
No. ....
Date ....

Place	Date	Hour	Summary of Events and Information	Remarks and references to Appendices
Mouscron	1/11/18		Routine as usual. Visited C/47 R.F.A. & found all correct also visited & inspected D/47 R.F.A. found them in the open field cast several blind horses for M.V.S. In after-noon visited 6th Wilts this transport has improved considerably since I last saw them.	
	2.11.18		Conference at A.D.V.S. XV Corps.	
	3:11:18		Routine as usual Shoeing Board.	
Turcoing	4:11:18		Moved to Turcoing & M.V.S. moved to Wattrelos. 1 H.D. of Div Hdq fell through skylight & evacuated him to 15. V.E.S.	
	5.11.18		Routine as usual visited 14th Div. Signals, 44 F.A & 43 F.A units all smart & animals in good condition.	
	6.11.18.		Visited B/46 R.F.A. animals well stabled & look well cared for. D/46 R.F.A also good new O.C. Major Tyler R.F.A.	
	7.11.18		Visited 14th Div Train animals all in excellent condition this is an exceedingly fine unit, does credit to the Division.	
	8:11:18		Routine as usual Visited 61 Field Coy RE, 10th H.L.I, 12th Suffolk Regt, 29th D.L.I, 33rd London Regiment all in satisfactory condition & I found nothing to complain of.	
	9:11:18		Visited 18 Yk Lancs, Argyle & Sutherland, 16th Manchesters these last two units can be said to be fair, they are certainly the worst transport of the Division.	
	10.11.18		Routine as usual one day at office work visited D/47 R.F.A.	
	11.11.18		Armistice Day. Visited 41st Inf Bde HQ.	
	12:11:18		Visited Office of ADVS XV Corps.	
	13:11:18		Visited 26 M.V.S all satisfactory, passed on to B/46 R.F.A. & finally on to No 3 Coy 14th Div Train.	

J P D Beal Capt RAVC
actg DADVS

D. D. & L., London, E.C. (A8094) Wt. W1771/M2 31 750,000 5/17 Sch. 52 Forms/C2118/14

Instructions regarding War Diaries and Intelligence Summaries are contained in F. S. Regs., Part II. and the Staff Manual respectively. Title pages will be prepared in manuscript.

WAR DIARY
or
INTELLIGENCE SUMMARY.
(Erase heading not required.)

Army Form C. 2118.

D.A.D.V.S. 14th DIVISION. No. ...... Date ......

Place	Date	Hour	Summary of Events and Information	Remarks and references to Appendices
Turcoing	14/11/18		Routine as usual. Visited DADOS re Hay Nets & Nose Bags for units.	
	15/11/18		Visited HQ 46th Bde R.F.A. A/46, B/46, C/46, D/46 R.F.A. spent one whole day with 46th Bde R.F.A. Evacuated several blind cases & animals of a bad stamp so as to improve unit in case of General Inspection which can be expected frequently now that we are on a sort of Peace Standing.	
	16/11/18		Routine as usual day at Office work.	
	17/11/18		Visited Loyal N. Lancs. No 4 Coy Div Train, 44th F. A & found things satisfactory.	
	18/11/18		Visited 42nd Inf Bde H.Q. also 6th Wilts, Argyle & Sutherland, & 16th Manchester Rgt. am not quite satisfied with conditions in the latter 2 units. D.A.D.V.S. Major Blakeney went on leave	
	19/11/18		Visited 89th & 61st Field Coys R.E. Capt Beal. W.R.D. O.C. 26 M.V.S. takes over duties as Actg D.A.D.V.S. from this date. Visited Nos 1 & 2 Coys 14th Div Train	
	20/11/18		Visited No 3 Sect 14 D.A.C. this unit is not up to standard required. Visited No 3 Coy 14th Div Train.	
	21/11/18		Routine as usual. Spent a day between Office of D.A.D.V.S. & 26 M.V.S	
	22/11/18		Visited A/47 & B/47 R.F.A. issued 1 sack of Bran for each unit for Lidebow cases.	
	23/11/18		Visited & Inspected 14th Div Signals animals well housed & well cared for prior to Corp Commander's inspection.	
	24/11/18		Routine as usual visited No 1 Sect 14 DAC.	
	25/11/18		Visited 6th Wilts in stables, visited 16th Manchester in stables & 14 Argyle & Sutherland Highlanders the latter two units not up too much. Mange in Argyle & Suth	

D P B Beal

D. D. & L., London, E.C. (A8004) Wt. W1771/M2 31 730,000 5/17 Sch 52 Forms/C2118/14

Army Form C. 2118.

Instructions regarding War Diaries and Intelligence Summaries are contained in F. S. Regs., Part II. and the Staff Manual respectively. Title pages will be prepared in manuscript.

WAR DIARY
or
INTELLIGENCE SUMMARY.
(Erase heading not required.)

D.A.D.V.S., 14th DIVISION. No. .... Date. ....

Place	Date	Hour	Summary of Events and Information	Remarks and references to Appendices
Turcoing	25/11/18		Highlander amongst Officer Chargers 2 evacuated & 2 in contacts isolated, Stables & Saddlery Equipment thoroughly disinfected it should now cease.	
	26/11/18		Routine as usual visited 42nd F. A.	
	27/11/18		——— ——— returns.	
	28/11/18		I started inspecting the Brood Mares of Division B/46 R.F.A.	
	29/11/18		D/46, & No. 1 Sect. DAC, inspected for Brood Mares.	
	30/11/18		No 1 Coy 14 Div Train & 26 M.V.S. Routine as usual.	

[signature] Capt R.A.V.C.
Actg D.A.D.V.S.
14th Div.

D. D. & L., London, E.C. (A8004) Wt. W1771/M2 31 750,000 5/17 Sch 52 Forms/C2118/14

Confidential

War Diary

of

DAD.V.S. 14 Div.

(1st to 31st December 1918.)

Instructions regarding War Diaries and Intelligence Summaries are contained in F. S. Regs., Part II. and the Staff Manual respectively. Title pages will be prepared in manuscript.

WAR DIARY
or
INTELLIGENCE SUMMARY.
(Erase heading not required.)

Page I

D.A.D.V.S., 14TH DIVISION.

Army Form C. 2118.

Place	Date	Hour	Summary of Events and Information	Remarks and references to Appendices
Rue Chanzy Turcoing.	1/12/18		Office routine.	
	2/12/18		Visit outside units A/47 & B/47 find 2 of the old Brood mares in A/47 & 5 in B/47 rest are casualties. Both units housed in stables & animals looking well.	
	3/12/18		Spent day at 26 M.V.S. in improvements for mens comfort.	
	4/12/18		Visit Loyal N. Lancs found a suspect Mange case otherwise unit housed well, & animals looking well. Visit No 2 Coy 14 Div Train well housed & animals in excellent condition & are a credit to Capt De Pass the O.C. No 2 Coy. Visit 30th Middlex animals well housed & looking well, a vast improvement in this transport since I last saw them. Office routine as usual. Received report of Major Blakeway D.A.D.V.S. 14th Div's death.	
	5/12/18		Visit 89 Field Coy R.E. animals well housed & looking well. Visit 44 Field Ambulance animals well housed & looking well. Received official notification of Major Blakeway's death.	
	6/12/18		Visit No 4 Coy 14 Div Train find 31 poor animals belonging to Town Major housed in same building. Animals of No 4 Coy well housed & look well. Visit to Town Major Tourcoing & represented matter re above 31 animals & received instructions from Area Comdt Tourcoing that they would be moved forthwith which was done.	
	7/12/18		Shoeing Board 22 men came up for shoeing of which 11 wished to be tested as shoeing smiths of this number 10 passed, Pte Fullwood of 18th Y & Lancs failing. The other 11 were examined as Cold Shoers & passed. Report re S/S forwarded on A.F. A.2. to respective C.O's.	
	8/12/18		Visited A.D.V.S. XV Corp Office. RE Major Blakeway's Death. Office routine as usual.	
	9/12/18		Visited 14th Div Signals animals well housed & animals looking well.	

[signature] Capt R.A.V.C.

Instructions regarding War Diaries and Intelligence Summaries are contained in F. S. Regs., Part II. and the Staff Manual respectively. Title pages will be prepared in manuscript.

WAR DIARY
or
INTELLIGENCE SUMMARY.
(Erase heading not required.)

Page 2.

D.A.D.V.S., 14TH DIVISION.

Army Form C. 2118.

Place	Date	Hour	Summary of Events and Information	Remarks and references to Appendices
Rue Chazzy	10/12/18		Routine as usual. Office routine at DADVS Office & 26 M.V.S.	
Tuncoing	11/12/18		Sent out notification to all units that Brood Mares parade 13th inst. Routine as usual	
	12/12/18		Capt G. S. Monewell reports sick in bed with Influenza. Office routine as usual	
	13/12/18		Col Perry ADVS XV Corps. Col Miller DDR V Army & Major Horner D.A.D.V.S. 36 Div	
			inspect 114 Brood Mares submitted, they take 18 mares & brand same.	
			Col Miller DDR 5th Army congratulates Division on having such beautiful	
			animals.	
	14/12/18		Office Routine as usual.	
	15/12/18		A.D.V.S. XV Corps informs me a new O.C. M.V.S. is on his way up from base & that I have	
			been appointed DADVS to the Division.	
	16/12/18		Capt J. R. TURNER R.A.V.C. Special Reserve reports his arrival. I take him over to	
			26 M.V.S. Capt G.S. Monewell reports he is out of bed but very weak & is on light	
			duty.	
	17/12/18		Lt-Col Perry A.D.V.S. XV Corp visits 26 M.V.S & instructs me to proceed to Divisional	
			Hdqrs & hand command of 26 M.V.S over to Capt J R Turner. DADVS Office routine as	
			usual.	
	18/12/18		Capt W. P. B BEAL R.A.V.C. reports to Q 14 Div that he has been appointed DADVS 14th Div	
			Office routine as usual. Took over the late Major Blakeway's billet, servants &	
			horses. Took an inventory of his kit. Capt G.S. Monewell much better & about again.	
	19/12/18		Routine as usual. Brigade Major of D.A. visits me re Veterinary	
	20/12/18		Visit 14th Div Signals & evacuate 3 horses to 26 M.V.S. Office routine as usual	
			Lectures to Officers of 14th Division Riding School.	
	21/12/18		Visit C/47 R.F.A. all animals in good condition, well housed. Proceed to draft-	
			Vet Lectures for instructional of members of Riding School. Office routine as usual.	W P B Beal Capt RAVC

D. D. & L., London, E.C. (A8004) Wt. W1771/M2 31 750,000 5/17 Sch. 52 Forms/C2118/14

Instructions regarding War Diaries and Intelligence Summaries are contained in F. S. Regs., Part II. and the Staff Manual respectively. Title pages will be prepared in manuscript.

WAR DIARY
or
INTELLIGENCE SUMMARY.
(Erase heading not required.)

Page 8

D.A.D.V.S.. 14TH DIVISION.

Army Form C. 2118.

Place	Date	Hour	Summary of Events and Information	Remarks and references to Appendices
Rue Chanzy Turcoing Hdq 14 Div	22/12/18		Visit 26 M.V.S. & found new site for M.V.S.. Saw a case of Mange from 14 Argyll & Sutherlands which is inclined towards over dressing for mange. Forwarded Xmas Cards to 26 M.V.S. Capt Turner forwards A.F. Z.15. No Sergt Thelkeld RAVC Vet Sergt to No 1. DAC demobilized as a coal miner report same to ADVS XV Corps & RAVC Base Records.	
	23/12/18		Lecture to 14th Divisional Riding School on Veterinary Subjects. Visit Units Loyal N. Lancs & 10th H.L.I. Office routine as usual.	
	24/12/18		Lecture to 14th Div Riding School. Visit No 4 Coy 14th Div Train & 43rd Field Ambulance also 20th Middlesex. After-noon visited 89th Field Coy R.E. in evening. Menu attached.	I.
	25/12/18		Xmas Day. Visit 26 M.V.S & had dinner with men	
	26.12.18		Office closed. Attended ½ day.	
	27.12.18		Routine at Office as usual. Lecture to officers at Riding School. Visit Loyal N. Lancs.	
	28.12.18		Visit to A D V S XV Corps Office re Demobilization Scheme on Horses. Visit H.Q. 14th Division. Lecture to Riding School	
			Inspection of horses 14 Div Signals & Argyll & Sutherland Highlanders. Lecture to Riding School	
	30.12.18		Office routine as usual. Visit 14th Argyll & Sutherland Highlanders. Lecture to Riding School	
	31.12.18		Office routine as usual. Lecture to Riding School.	

G P Heal
Capt RAVC
A/D.A.D.V.S.
14th Div

D. D. & L., London, E.C.
(A8004) Wt. W1771/M2 31 750,000 5/17 Sch. 52 Forms/C2118/14

Confidential

War Diary

of

D.A.D.V.S. 14 Div.

(January 1st to 31st 1919).

Instructions regarding War Diaries and Intelligence Summaries are contained in F. S. Regs., Part II. and the Staff Manual respectively. Title pages will be prepared in manuscript.

WAR DIARY
or
INTELLIGENCE SUMMARY.
(Erase heading not required.)

D.A.D.V.S.
14TH DIVISION.
No. ....
Date ....

Army Form C. 2118.

Place	Date	Hour	Summary of Events and Information	Remarks and references to Appendices
Turcoing 14 Div HQ. Rue Chanzy	1/1/19		New Years Day. Office closed mid-day.	
	2/1/19		Visited 26 M.V.S. Office routine as usual. Papers received re Categories of animals for Demobilization.	
	3/1/19		Commence work of Board on Categories of Animals 15 Loyal N. Lancs. A.F. A 2000 for Division forwarded to A.D.V.S. XV Corps.	
	4/1/19		Major Peters R.A.S.C. reports as Remount Officer on Demobilization of Horses states he wishes to class 800 horses a day, impossible for it to be done, later on he finds he cannot do 800 animals a day, the average works out at about 400 per day. 14 Machine Gun Battallion 233 animals categorised.	
	5/1/19		Office routine as usual. A/47 & B/47 animals categorised. Find I cannot get on without assistance of Motor Car.	
	6/1/19		C/47 & D/47 R.F.A. animals categorised.	
	7/1/19		No 2 Coy & No 4 Coy 14 Divisional Train also 44 Field Ambulance animals categorised. Q 14 cannot give me a car, a 30 cwt lorry detailed to me in lieu of car.	
	8/1/19		29 Durham Light Infantry, 33rd London Regiment, & 18 York & Lancashire Regt animals categorised, also 41st Inf Bde H.Q.	
	9/1/19		42nd Inf Bde H.Q. 14 Argyle & Sutherland Highlanders & 16th Manchester Rgt animals categorised, also 42nd Field Ambulance.	
	10/1/19		46th Bde R.F.A. animals categorised.	

[signature] Major R.A.V.C.

D. D. & L., London, E.C. (A8004) Wt. W1771/M2 31 750,000 5/17 Sch. 52 Forms/C2118/14

Instructions regarding War Diaries and Intelligence Summaries are contained in F. S. Regs., Part II. and the Staff Manual respectively. Title pages will be prepared in manuscript.

WAR DIARY
or
INTELLIGENCE SUMMARY.
(*Erase heading not required.*)

D.A.D.V.S.
14TH DIVISION.
No.............
Date...........

Army Form C. 2118.

Place	Date	Hour	Summary of Events and Information	Remarks and references to Appendices
Turcoing 14 Div H.Q.	11/1/19		Office Routine as usual. 43rd Inf Bde H.Q. 20th Middlesex Regt, 12 Suffolk Regt & 10th Highland Light Infantry animals categorised, also 43rd Field Ambulance. Lunch with General Perriera C.M.G. D.S.O. at Bde H.Q. a very tiring day.	
Rue Chanzy	12/1/19		H.Q. 14 Div, 14 M.M.P, CRA, C.R.E, & 89 Field Coy R.E. animals categorised	
	13/1/19		H.Q of 96 A.F.A. 407 & 410 batteries of 96 A.F.A. animals categorised.	
	14/1/19		408, & 410 batteries of 96 A.F.A. animals categorised.	
	15/1/19		14 Div Signal Section, & 96 B.A.C. animals categorised.	
	16/1/19		To-day a journey to Scheldt River to do 61st Field Coy R.E. & then on to Lille to do 62nd Field Coy R.E. A very tiring day to categorise about 130 animals	
	17/1/19		6th Wilts Regt, NO 1 Coy 14 Div Train & NO 3 Coy 14 Div Train animals categorised.	
	18/1/19		Parade at Place Thiers joint with Remount Board to categorise & class Miscellaneous Units.	
	19/1/19		14 D.A.C. animals categorised. Commenced Malleining all animals of Division.	
	20/1/19		Animal Demobilizing commenced. 100 C.Z. cases moved from Division on transfer to Linselles Animal Collecting Camp.	

J. W. Mead
Maj. A.V.C.

D. D. & L., London, E.C.
(A8004) Wt. W1771/M2 31 750,000 5/17 Sch. 52 Forms/C2118/14

Instructions regarding War Diaries and Intelligence Summaries are contained in F. S. Regs., Part II. and the Staff Manual respectively. Title pages will be prepared in manuscript.

WAR DIARY
or
INTELLIGENCE SUMMARY.
(Erase heading not required.)

D.A.D.V.S.,
14TH DIVISION.
No.............
Date...........

Army Form C. 2118.

Place	Date	Hour	Summary of Events and Information	Remarks and references to Appendices
Turcoing 14 Div H.Q. Rue Clamsy	21/1/19		Routine as usual. Everything connected with animal demobilizing seems to be rushed through. Continuation of Malleining.	
	22/1/19		Telegram received to commence the sale of D animals for slaughter & fit for human consumption. Continuation of Malleining.	
	23/1/19		100 C Z animals dispatched to Linselles Collecting Camp. Continuation of Malleining. All horses from Linselles returned to units no A.F.0.1640 accompanied animals. Units state they know nothing of form. Several copies of old forms in this office, so 100 are run off by my clerk on Q duplicator for units to go on with. My experience is that units want a lot of fathering, pay no attention to the administrative instructions & trust the Veterinary Officers & department to get them out of a whole if anything goes wrong.	
	24/1/19		Only Returns from units of Veterinary Categories & Remount Classes come in. Only six returns right in the Division, remainder returned to units for correction. Continuation of Malleining.	
	25/1/19		Routine as usual. A long day with figures in office. Visit 26 M.V.S	
	26/1/19		To-day B Z animals moved off 50 in number to Turcoing Collecting Camp.	
			W P McNeal Maj. AVC	

D. D. & L., London, E.C.
(A8004) Wt. W1771/M2 31 750,000 5/17 Sch. 52 Forms/C2118/14

Instructions regarding War Diaries and Intelligence Summaries are contained in F. S. Regs., Part II. and the Staff Manual respectively. Title pages will be prepared in manuscript.

WAR DIARY
or
INTELLIGENCE SUMMARY.
(Erase heading not required.)

D.A.D.V.S., 14TH DIVISION.
No.
Date.

Army Form C. 2118.

Place	Date	Hour	Summary of Events and Information	Remarks and references to Appendices
Tourcoing 14 Div H.Q.	27/1/19		Visit to D.A.D.V.S. XV Corps Conference. Mallein continuation.	
	28/1/19		Routine as usual. Correct returns of classification come in.	
Rue Chanzy	29/1/19		Routine as usual. Visit 26 M.V.S. & 62nd Field Coy R.E.	
	30/1/19.		Routine as usual, reclassify 2 D animals to C.Z.	
	31/1/19		" " "	

J P O'Neal
Major R.A.V.C.
D.A.D.V.S. 14 Div

D. D. & L., London, E.C. (A8004) Wt. W1771/M2 31 750,000 5/17 Sch. 52 Forms/C2118/14

Confidential

War Diary

of

D.A.D.V.S. 14 Div.

(1st to 28th February 1918).

Instructions regarding War Diaries and Intelligence Summaries are contained in F. S. Regs., Part II. and the Staff Manual respectively. Title pages will be prepared in manuscript.

WAR DIARY
or
INTELLIGENCE SUMMARY.
(Erase heading not required.)

Page I.

D.A.D.V.S. 14TH DIVISION.

Army Form C. 2118.

No.............. Date..............

Place	Date	Hour	Summary of Events and Information	Remarks and references to Appendices
Hdq. 14th Division	1/2/19		Office Routine as usual. 50 Y animals leave division on demobilization. Malleining animals nearly completed for division.	
Turcoing	2/2/19		Very cold a fall of snow. Visited Turcoing Animal Camp. Visited Linselles Animal Camp with Capt. Renwick + reclassified a lot of Y animals to X + Z. Picked out several M mares for repatriation to England. Sent 34 D animals to 8 V.E.S. La Madeline Lille for Butcher.	
	3/2/19.		Hard frost during night. Stopped several animals from working in streets, as not shod with frost cogs, animals were slipping about + expending all energy + doing nothing against the slippery road except falling down.	
	4.2.19.		Hard frost continues, with a fall of snow roads very bad. Malleining Animals finished to-day. Sent 6 D animals to 8 V.E.S. Office routine as usual, owing to Q detailing me to demobilize animals, I am kept very busy. This means to say I am doing D.A.D.V.S work, + also am demobilising animals at the same time. Q give me extra clerk.	
	5/2/19		Two clerks report for duty. A very hard frost during night, roads very bad. Visit Turcoing Animal Collecting Camp. Made out Mallein reports on A.F.	
	6/2/19		Forwarded all Mallein reports in triplicate to ADVS XV Corps. Capt Thornewill RAVC. Veterinary Officer 46 Bde sent to Michelham Home Cap Martin Mentone for 3 weeks convalescent rest, debility following after Influenza, departed on 5th inst. Office routine as usual. As no animals are likely to move on leave during spell of frost, sent in application for leave to A.D.V.S XV Corps.	

W.P. Bell
Major R.A.V.C.

D. D. & L., London, E.C.
(A8004) Wt. W1771/M2 31 750,000 5/17 Sch. 52 Forms/C2118/14

Instructions regarding War Diaries and Intelligence Summaries are contained in F. S. Regs., Part II. and the Staff Manual respectively. Title pages will be prepared in manuscript.

WAR DIARY
or
INTELLIGENCE SUMMARY. Page 2.

(*Erase heading not required.*)

Army Form C. 2118.

D.A.D.V.S. 14TH DIVISION.

Place	Date	Hour	Summary of Events and Information	Remarks and references to Appendices
ADQ 14 Divn: Turcoing	7/2/19		Office routine as usual. One clerk returned. 240 animals left Turcoing Collecting Camp for rail head Muscron en route for ENGLAND. Leave sanctioned by ADVS XV Corps & forwarded to Q14 for warrant. Frost continues. Capt Turner T.R Special Reserve takes over Office. Leave granted 9th to 20th	
	8/2/19		Left by civilian train 18.30 for Calais arrive Calais 23.00 hours. Cold journey. On board 08.30 hours left Calais 09.00 hours arrive London 11.00 hours a very quick journey. Crossing terribly cold.	
	9/2/19		D. animals butcher cases arranged for Municipality Turcoing & Wattrelos to accept at 1.25 per kilo live weight to feed civil population. Frost still continues. Office routine as usual.	
	10.2.19.		50 Z animals move to Linselles Camp on demobilization.	
	11.2.19		Capt Turner receives instruction to move his M.V.S to Muscron & to help O.C. 15th V.E.S in the sales of Z animals to French & Belgians. Routine as usual.	
	12:2:19		26 M.V.S move & join up pro tem with 15 V.E.S at Rouge Croix Muscron–Turcoing Road.	
	13:2:19		50 Z animals transferred to Linselles Animal Camp on demobilization.	
	14:2:19		3 D animals sent to Maire of Turcoing for slaughter. Office routine as usual.	
	15:2:19		Capt Turner attends sales at Warcoing.	
	16:2:19		Capt Turner examines 65 Y animals at Place Theirs prior to transfer to Turcoing animal collecting Camp for repatriation to England.	

D. D. & L., London, E.C. (A8004) Wt. W1771/M2 31 750,000 5/17 Sch. 52 Forms/C2118/14

Instructions regarding War Diaries and Intelligence Summaries are contained in F. S. Regs., Part II. and the Staff Manual respectively. Title pages will be prepared in manuscript.

WAR DIARY
or
INTELLIGENCE SUMMARY.
(Erase heading not required.)

Page 3

Army Form C. 2118.

D.A.D.V.S. 14TH DIVISION.

No. .... Date........

Place	Date	Hour	Summary of Events and Information	Remarks and references to Appendices
Hdq	17/2/19		Office routine as usual. 50 Z animals transferred to Linselles Animal Collecting	
14 Division			Camp. Break up of frost. Thaw precautions on	
Turcoing	18/2/19		Letter from Maire of Wattrelos requiring animals for slaughter to feed civilians. 2 D	
			animals sent him. Office routine as usual.	
	19:2:19		Conference at Q. office re posting of X animals in Division for Cadre B.	
			Office routine as usual.	
	20:2:19		Major W.B.D. BEAL RAVC DADVS 14 Div: returns from leave to U.K. Return reported ADVS XV Corps	
	21.2.19		Office Routine as usual. Capt Bennett Remount Officer 15 Corps visits Office requires	
	22.2.19		50 Infantry chargers & troopers for cavalry. Inspection arranged for 25th with Col: Miller	
			DDR 5th Army. DRO drafted for Q14 all Y riders parade 25th.	
			nil to report. No 8143 Sergt H Mason Vet Corps 42nd Inf Bde demobilized.	
	23.2.19		100 Z animals left for Linselles Animal Collecting Camp.	
	24/2/19		31 Y riders left for Turcoing animal Camp. These animals picked by Col: Miller DDR	
	25/2/19		5th Army. Linselles Animal Collecting Camp. Office routine as usual	
	26/2/19		100 Z animals left for Linselles animal collecting Camp. No Z animals left in Division	
	27/2/19		8 Z animals left for Linselles Office routine as usual.	
			except 4 Z with M.M.P.	
	28/2/19		100 X L D's left Division for Turcoing animal Camp to go to Army Occupation	
			Rhine. During month all Veterinary Officers have worked at very high	
			pressure. The services of Capt. Thornewell away on convalescent leave, & Lt Mc	
			Manus with Turcoing & Linselles Animal Collecting	
			Camp have not been available.	
			W.B.D. Beal Major RAVC DADVS 14 Div	

D. D. & L., London, E.C.
(A8004) Wt. W1771/M2 31 750,000 5/17 Sch. 52 Forms/C2118/14

www.ingramcontent.com/pod-product-compliance
Lightning Source LLC
Chambersburg PA
CBHW080922230426
43668CB00014B/2179
* 9 7 8 1 4 7 4 5 0 8 6 6 7 *